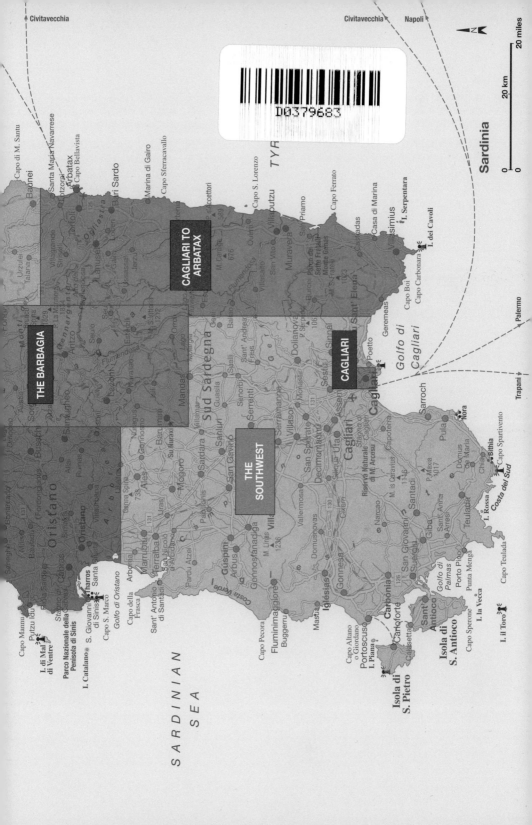

INSIGHT ⊙ GUIDES

SARDINIA

◉ Walking Eye App

YOUR FREE DESTINATION CONTENT AND EBOOK AVAILABLE THROUGH THE WALKING EYE APP

Your guide now includes a free eBook and destination content for your chosen destination, all for the same great price as before. Simply download the Walking Eye App from the App Store or Google Play to access your free eBook and destination content.

HOW THE WALKING EYE APP WORKS

Through the Walking Eye App, you can purchase a range of eBooks and destination content. However, when you buy this book, you can download the corresponding eBook and destination content for free. Just see below in the grey panels where to find your free content and then scan the QR code at the bottom of this page.

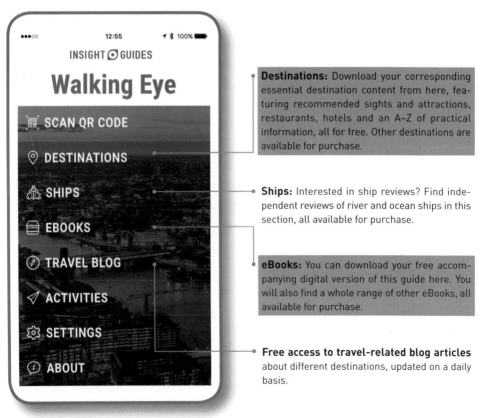

Destinations: Download your corresponding essential destination content from here, featuring recommended sights and attractions, restaurants, hotels and an A–Z of practical information, all for free. Other destinations are available for purchase.

Ships: Interested in ship reviews? Find independent reviews of river and ocean ships in this section, all available for purchase.

eBooks: You can download your free accompanying digital version of this guide here. You will also find a whole range of other eBooks, all available for purchase.

Free access to travel-related blog articles about different destinations, updated on a daily basis.

HOW THE DESTINATION CONTENT WORKS

Each destination includes a short introduction, an A–Z of practical information and recommended points of interest, split into 4 different categories:

• Highlights
• Accommodation
• Eating out
• What to do

You can view the location of every point of interest and save it by adding it to your Favourites. In the 'Around Me' section you can view all the points of interest within 5km.

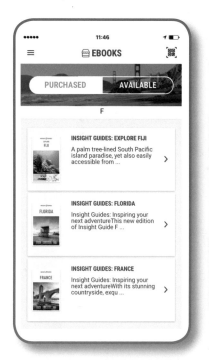

HOW THE EBOOKS WORK

The eBooks are provided in EPUB file format. Please note that you will need an eBook reader installed on your device to open the file. Many devices come with this as standard, but you may still need to install one manually from Google Play.

The eBook content is identical to the content in the printed guide.

HOW TO DOWNLOAD THE WALKING EYE APP

1. Download the Walking Eye App from the App Store or Google Play.
2. Open the app and select the scanning function from the main menu.
3. Scan the QR code on this page – you will then be asked a security question to verify ownership of the book.
4. Once this has been verified, you will see your eBook and destination content in the purchased ebook and destination sections, where you will be able to download them.

Other destination apps and eBooks are available for purchase separately or are free with the purchase of the Insight Guide book.

CONTENTS

LEGEND
  🔎 Insight on
  📷 Photo story

THE BEST OF SARDINIA: TOP ATTRACTIONS

△ **Costa Verde.** Miles and miles of unspoilt golden beaches backed by rolling sand dunes and lush *màcchia* vegetation make the southwestern Green Coast a playground for sunbathers, beachcombers and horse riders. See page 192.

△ **Cagliari.** The citadel district of Castello reeks of history and power, and is dominated by the Pisan-Romanesque cathedral. Set on a hill with spectacular views over the city, Castello is also home to aristocratic mansions, ancient defensive walls and excellent museums. See page 101.

▽ **Nuragic relics.** More than 7,000 Bronze Age towers called nuraghi pepper the Sardinian landscape, each providing intriguing glimpses of a mysterious civilisation.

△ **Grotta di Nettuno.** Set sail to Capo Caccia for a journey into the otherworldly wonders of this marine cave, including eerie chambers filled with ancient stalactites, stalagmites and simmering pools. See page 163.

△ **Bosa.** Up and down medieval alleyways to the castle of Malaspina, there are captivating glimpses of Bosa's Pisan and Catalan-ruled past through its crafts, architecture and food. See page 179.

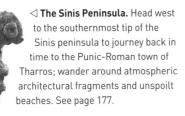

◁ **The Sinis Peninsula.** Head west to the southernmost tip of the Sinis peninsula to journey back in time to the Punic-Roman town of Tharros; wander around atmospheric architectural fragments and unspoilt beaches. See page 177.

▷ **Trenino Verde.** The "little green train" rattles over a narrow-gauge railway (dating from 1888) which penetrates deep inside Sardinia's wild interior; this is the way to see the lush gorges and rocky peaks of the Gennargentu national park. See page 120.

△ **Trekking in the Sopramonte and Ogliastra.** Get kitted out in your best outdoor gear for trekking adventures in Sardinia's wild mountains, which include Europe's deepest gorge, Gola di Gorroppu, and one of its most challenging routes, Il Selvaggio Blu. See page 217.

▽ **Alghero.** Catalan Culture, cuisine and Alguerès dialect still reign supreme amid the cobbled lanes, fortifications and bustling eateries of this beguiling seaside town. See page 159.

△ **Golfo di Orosei.** Charter a speedboat and explore 40km (25 miles) of wild coastline, where dizzying limestone cliffs tower over marine grottoes, isolated pebble beaches and enchanting bays in ever-changing blue-green hues. See page 123.

THE BEST OF SARDINIA: EDITOR'S CHOICE

MOST MEMORABLE BOAT TRIPS

Capo Caccia. Frolic with dolphins on the Andrea Jensen sailing boat while cutting through the azure waters around Capo Caccia and Grotta di Nettuno. A bountiful lunch is served and there are plenty of stops for snorkelling. See page 163.

Isola di San Pietro. Explore the volcanic rocky coastline of this island in the southwest where you can spot Eleonora's falcon, and sample Carloforte's curious Tunisian-Ligurian culture and cuisine. See page 188.

Golfo di Orosei. Hop on a speedboat from Arbatax or Cala Gonone and let the Golfo di Orosei's limestone wonders – marine caves, hidden coves and towering cliffs – unfold. See page 123.

Isola Tavolara and Isola Molara. Head to stunning beaches below

Isola Tavolara's dramatic 6km (4 mile) limestone ridge and the granite sculptural folds of Isola Molara, off the Gallura coast. See page 131.

Arcipelago della Maddalena. Escape Costa Smeralda's uber-rich crowd by taking a boat from Palau to navigate pristine waters around the national park of the Maddalena archipelago. Here you'll spot abundant birdlife, including cormorants and peregrine falcons, and absorb the untouched beauty. See page 141.

Pescaturismo at Teulada. Fishermen take groups and families around their favourite bays; after helping haul in the nets, and splashing about in limpid waters, there's the freshest *pescato del giorno* (catch of the day) for lunch. Tel: 340-603 6978.

For the best views, take a boat trip.

Su Nuraxi, one of the finest examples of Nuragic civilisation.

BEST MUSEUMS AND GALLERIES

Cittadella dei Musei. Cagliari's citadel and former arsenal is home to a 1960s-built museum complex which contains mesmerising archae-ological finds, artworks and Siamese treasures. See page 101.

Galleria Comunale d'Arte, Cagliari. Stunning 20th-century art including haunting sculptures by Francesco Ciusa housed within a gunpowder store turned neoclassical palazzo. See page 107.

MAN, Nuoro. The Museo d'Arte di Nuoro has works by Sardinia's brooding artistic luminaries Biasi, Ciusa and Nivola alongside

temporary shows. See page 215.

Museo Nazionale G.A. Sanna, Sassari. Dig deep into the island's prehistoric and ancient civilisations, disco-vering 3,000-year-old *bronzetti* as well as Etruscan, Greek and Roman artefacts. See page 153.

Su Nuraxi. One of Sardinia's most famous museums and a Unesco World Heritage site, Su Nuraxi consists of an impressive Nuragic fortress dating from the 13th to the 6th century BC, surrounding a 15th-century BC defensive tower with a well. See page 193.

FRESHEST SEAFOOD

Fresh lobster.

Lillicu, Cagliari. Amid the marble tables and open kitchen of this long-time favourite, enjoy the ebb and flow of lively banter, delicious seafood and good wine. Tel: 070-652 970.
Rifugio dei Peccatori, La Maddalena. This rural osteria is a perfect place to try simply prepared authentic Sardinian specialities. www.rifugiodeipecca tori.com.
Da Ugo, Castelsardo. Pick your *pesce* before tasting the fishy delights at Castelsardo's best eatery. www.ristorantedaugo.eu.
Nicolo, Carloforte. The Pomata family mix Carloforte's Sardinian, Ligurian and Arabic influences at this renowned *ristorante*. Luigi Pomata in Cagliari echoes these sublime culinary creations. Tel: 0781 854048.
Peschiera San Giovanni, Tortolí. Run by a fishermen's cooperative, this no-frills place serves excellent sea bass, bream, red mullet, shellfish and *bottarga* (cured fish roe). Tel: 0782 664415.

BEST SPORTS AND OUTDOOR ACTIVITIES

Treks in the Supramonte di Baunei. Scramble around the limestone pinnacles and caves above the Golfo di Orosei then plunge down to the isolated beach of Goloritzè. See page 122.
Canyoning in the Barbagia. Get acquainted with nature's power by following the course of a river, clambering over sculpted rocks and dangling over dizzying chasms. www.barbagia nolimits.it.

Canoeing and kayaking. Glide and paddle along the river Coghinas, in the far north near Castel sardo, exploring banks covered in *màcchia*, lakes and canyons rich in birdlife. www.newkayak sardinia.com.
Diving, windsurfing and kitesurfing near Palau. Set off for the Maddalena archipelago's fabulous dive sites off the northeast coast (www. oystersub.com), or tackle the wind-whipped waves at L'Isuledda Porto Pollo.

Kitesurfing at San Giovanni de Sinis, Oristano.

STUNNING BEACHES

La Pelosa. Fine white sand and transparent waters give this sheltered beach at Capo del Falcone a tropical feel. See page 146.
Chia. The long golden sands of Spiaggia Campana and Spiaggia Su Giudeu have a wild backdrop of sand dunes and broom-covered granite outcrops. See page 185.
Cala Goloritzè. Plunge into the azure waters that lap some of the smoothest white limestone pebbles on the Golfo di Orosei. See page 123.
Spiaggia di Tavolara. A curvy promontory of dunes and pebbles makes for a spectacular bathing spot below Tavolara's awe-inspiring cliffs. See page 131.
Spiaggia Rosa, Maddalena Isola. Budelli's famous pink beach with its sparkly, rosy complexion is due to the pebbly remains of protozoan organisms. See page 142.
Is Arutas and Sa Mesa Longa. The Sinis peninsula has stunning beaches and surging surf – Is Arutas has sparkling quartz sand, while Sa Mesa Longa has a long table-like rocky platform that forms a marine pool – perfect for families. See page 177.

The sculpted granite silhouette of Isola di Tavolara.

Cala Goloritzè, a secluded cove in the Golfo di Orosei.

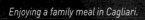
Enjoying a family meal in Cagliari.

Country track leading to the simple church of San Pietro di Golgo in the Altopiano del Golgo.

Nuraghe Losa at Abbasanta.

THE RUGGED JEWEL

With its rich history, rugged coastline and fabulous beaches – some of the best in the Mediterranean – the island of Sardinia has universal appeal.

Alfresco lunch on Piazza Costituzione in Cagliari.

Sardinia is the second-largest island in the Mediterranean after Sicily. Its geographic position prompted D.H. Lawrence to write that the island was "lost between Europe and Africa and belonging to nowhere". This isolation has worked both for and against the island, producing the unique character of its people and flora and fauna but also attracting a succession of foreign rulers eager to exploit its strategic position and fertile land.

Phoenicians and Romans, Arabs and Spaniards, Savoyards and Italians have all left their mark on the cultural, artistic and architectural life of the island. Historically mingling these influences with their own has produced a rich and varied Sardinian identity, which is difficult to grasp at first. Although Sardinia has been part of Italy since 1861, even today many islanders wish it were not.

There remain striking differences between the island and the mainland. Sardinia's individual regions are completely different from one another, and villages which may lie only a few kilometres from each other will often seem worlds apart, so much so that the island can appear to be a miniature continent.

Sardinia's beaches have attracted many visitors and some unfortunate overdevelopment. The expansion of the tourist industry has seen the growth of watersports facilities, and dive

Fonni, Barbagia.

centres have been set up to explore the island's thriving marine life. Birds of prey can be found swooping over the mountains of the interior and flamingos rest during their winter migration in the coastal marshes and lagoons. The Barbagia region in the interior offers opportunities for hiking, rock climbing and speleology. Horse trekking has also become very popular with the development of *agriturismo* (farm holidays) in the provinces of Oristano and Sassari. The cities of Cagliari and Sassari have renewed vibrancy through their student and artistic populations, while recent civic plans are aimed at improving facilities and enhancing cultural life.

A local barista, Sassari.

THE SARDINIAN CHARACTER

Loyal but wary of outsiders, witty, stoical and brave, this diverse group of islanders has evolved a tough and independent spirit shaped as much by geography as by the successive waves of invaders.

To some Italians on the mainland, the jokey view of a Sardinian is a proud, sturdy shepherd who lives a rustic, old-fashioned existence. A similar stereotype was even transposed onto Willie, the feisty Scots groundskeeper, who gets a Sardinian accent in the Italian version of *The Simpsons*. The reality is somewhat more complicated of course, although independence, stoical strength, bravery, loyalty, warmth and occasional bouts of dour mien laced with sardonic wit are descriptions you could ascribe to Sardinians.

The Sardi are proudly attached to their own piece of terra sarda, expressed through festivals, crafts and hearty cuisine, all of which vary from village to village.

Sardità, or Sardinian-ness, has been shaped firstly by environment – the sea and mountains that have contributed to intermittent invasion and isolation. Its diverse dialects and the character of its people reflect a mixed-up and compelling history characterised by foreign domination and cultural assimilation. A succession of foreign interlopers has left its mark, leaving deep impressions on *Sardità*. Periods of relative peace and natural barriers have allowed for its myriad close-knit communities to grow independently. Every Sardinian town and village has a different story to tell. *L'isola delle storie*, the "island of stories", they call it, and a literary festival in Gavoi, in the once impenetrable mountains of the Barbagia, celebrates this storytelling tradition.

Sardinian nonna and grandchild.

BREAKING AWAY

Around 60 million years ago some colossal rocks which would become Sardinia and Corsica were chipped off the European landmass and drifted southwards as an archipelago. After much upheaval, sea incursion and erosion they ended up marooned halfway between the Italian mainland and North Africa. Although part of Italy, Sardinia is something apart from the mainland peninsula. *Quasi un continente*: almost a continent, as a saying-turned-slogan to lure visitors across the Tyrrhenian Sea would have it.

Neolithic peoples were the first to inhabit Sardinia 8,000 years ago. It wouldn't be too fanciful to suggest that Sardinian traits of self-reliance, togetherness and ingenuity derive from these prehistoric Sardi. Natural resources including obsidian – volcanic glass used to make arrowheads and tools – made them some of the wealthiest people on the planet back in the Stone Age. Trade flourished in this black gold, and Sardinian Neolithic culture peaked with the Ozieri civilisation (3500–2700 BC), who built the curious *domus de janas* tombs ("fairy houses") to honour their dead.

A SUCCESSION OF INVADERS

One of the island's best-known maxims is *"Furat chi benit dae su mare"* (Whoever comes by sea

methods. A happy coexistence between the Punic settlers and the tribes lasted until the 7th century BC. Carthaginians took over, enslaving the locals and stripping away the Nuragic past.

Sardinia's strategic location meant it was fought over by African, Middle Eastern and European powers, and each trading partner, invader and ally left its mark on the inhabitants.

The Sardinians are understandably proud of their cheeses.

The island of San Pietro.

comes to rob us). Sardinians are said to be wary of outsiders (unsurprising when you consider their history) and are generally less animated than other Italians. Foreigners who come here often comment that it is hard to strike easy friendships, but once in a circle of friends they warm up and are very loyal. So where did this social conservatism come from? *Sardità* is an island mentality like no other. Sardinia's strategic position meant that it became a pawn in the battle for western Mediterranean supremacy, fought over by African, Middle Eastern and European powers. First it was the Phoenicians who began coastal settlements in 1000 BC and brought Greek, Etruscan and North African influences: writing, crafts and new building

Sardinians were now colonial subjects. Romans came during the Punic Wars, but the ferocious mountain people, the Barbarie (from the Barbagia) put up a fight. The Sardi Pelliti (Hairy Sardinians) wore animal skins and fought heroically to preserve their land and culture. The Romans brought infrastructure and Latin – from which Sardinia's language, Sardo, derives. In the end the Byzantines and monastic orders spread Christianity on the island, but facets of the polytheist past survived, as witnessed in today's rich and often strange folk traditions.

A RICH HERITAGE

Subsequent landlords, the naval powers Pisa and Genoa, then Aragonese Spain, the

Savoyards and a unified Italian state divvied up the island and its people, introducing new blood and culture. Present-day Alghero, Iglesias and Oristano all have evidence of Catalonia in their architecture, dialect and ceremonial exuberance. Carloforte's residents speak Tabarkino, an 18th-century Genoese dialect, and blend Tunisian and Ligurian cuisines, eating couscous and tuna. In the north, the purest form of Sardo – Lugodorese – is spoken, while down south Campidanese is coloured by Pisan traits. In the Barbagia mountains the people survived off the

and Eleonora fought for independence against the Aragonese. In the 14th century Eleonora penned the Carta de Logu, a set of progressive laws that introduced new concepts like female suffrage and servant citizenship. During the Italian Risorgimento's resurgence of liberal ideas, Sardinia hosted inspirational leader Giuseppe Garibaldi on Caprera – debates over the benefits of being part of Italy still rage on, though. After World War I, the Sardinian unit Brigata Sassari were hailed as fearless heroes renowned for their united spirit. Their wartime

Local man from Abbasanta with his horse.

land and largely turned their backs on the sea, which generally brought nothing but trouble. Their struggle against poverty and wariness of outsiders is embodied in strange, solemn processions that combine pagan fertility rites and exorcism of evil spirits with Catholic iconography. Those strange masked and fur-clad carnival dresses of *Sos Mamuthones* and *Issohadores* conjure images of pagan festivities.

INDEPENDENT SPIRIT

Sardinians may have assimilated a hotchpotch of overseas cultural and linguistic influences, but many possess an innate independent spirit, stoical determination and moral fibre. Historical figures like Arborea's Mariano IV

⊘ SARDITÀ VERSUS ITALIA

Sardinia is the only region of Italy whose native peoples are recognised as an ethnically distinct group, related to the island's original inhabitants. Even though the island has been part of Italy since 1861, not all Sardinians are happy with the alliance. There is a feeling that the Italian state uses the island's space and resources to the detriment of Sardinians.

NATO has numerous Sardinian bases, and it's easy to find examples of natural resources plundered, profits siphoned off and indigenous culture tainted. The Aga Khan's Costa Smeralda has brought tourism to the island, but at what cost?

experiences and interaction with mainland Italians led to the establishment of the Partidu Sardu (Partito Sardo d'Azione), which aimed

A few villages in central Sardinia have some of the world's highest concentration of male centenarians. Ten times as many men celebrate their 100th birthday here than the world's average.

administration reversed taxes on super yachts and curbs to coastline development. Modifying Soru's landscape plan, it also scrapped the futuristic museum building project in Cagliari. In 2014, Cappellacci was succeeded by centre-left Francesco Pigliaru.

Disillusioned with both Sardinian and Italian politics, a group of activists called Canton Marittimo are calling for Sardinia to become the 27th canton of Switzerland. They argue that this is the way for landlocked Switzerland to get miles of amazing coastline, and for Sardinia to ben-

Vibrant, colourful youth.

at furthering Sardinian independence. Italian Fascism largely absorbed and contained these political tendencies.

DISILLUSIONED SARDINIA

Despite misgivings towards Italy's use of the island, the movement for more autonomy is splintered, mired in the nepotism of Italian politics and short-term alliances. However, in recent years there has been renewed vigour to protect the islanders' interests. Entrepreneur Renato Soru's Progetto Sardegna Party introduced measures to limit development near coastlines and encouraged local industry in the interior. In 2009 Soru was replaced by Berlusconi-backed Ugo Cappellacci. The new

efit from administrative efficiency and economic wealth. "The madness does not lie in putting forward this kind of suggestion," Andrea Caruso, co-founder of the Canton Marittimo said. "The madness lies in how things are now."

As Italy continues to struggle with recession, one of the more serious suggestions put forward to boost the island's economy has been to turn Sardinia into a tax haven. Indeed since 2013 Porto Scuso has been the island's first free-trade zone Although it's unlikely that this scheme will expand to include the whole island, one cannot underestimate the exceptional Sardinian instinct for survival and indomitable spirit, which may turn this dream into a reality.

THE SARDINIAN LANGUAGE

Sardinian, made up of several dialects, has never been standardised. Many fear that, unless this happens, it will be overwhelmed by Italian.

Sardinian is an old Romance language with a highly original and, in some cases, extremely archaic vocabulary. It is linked to Italian and all other Romance languages by the Latin of Roman times. During the Roman conquest of the island, Latin took over all the existing languages introduced by the Phoenicians and the Carthaginians. In addition to its Latin skeleton, the vocabulary of Sardinian reflects the entire history of the island.

Place names, in particular, retain roots from the Phoenician, Etruscan and Byzantine periods. By the 14th century, Sardinian had developed from vulgar Latin. For the next 400 years, first Catalan and then Castilian were the official languages; in Alghero, people speak a variation of Spanish Catalan introduced in the 14th century, and there are traces of Spanish in all the island's dialects infused from Spain's 300-year colonisation of the island.

A RICH MIX

During the 13th and 14th centuries a quasi-official Sardinian language also established itself through the promulgation of laws in Sardinian by the ruler-kings of Arborea. The dialects spoken in Sassari and Gallura to the north reveal close links with the languages of Tuscany and Corsica due to waves of migration during the 17th century. On the isle of San Pietro, off the southeast coast of Sardinia, a strong Piedmontese dialect is spoken, mixed with an ancient Genoan dialect dating back to the 18th century.

Today, the rich and complex language is an amalgam of the island's many dialects: Logudoro in the northern central region, Campidano in the south, and a number of ancient dialects in the mountainous region around Nuoro.

LINGUA SARDA

All the regions are bilingual, and it is only recently that Sardinian has taken second place to "standard Italian". In general, people use their dialect in informal situations only. The issue of standardising the Sardinian dialect remains unresolved, although there were attempts made during the 1970s to identify the main body of the language and to intro-

Proud Sardinian, Oristano.

duce it to the media and literature. This fragmentation of Sardinian is a major problem for the island's writers and poets. All the great Sardinian writers, including Sebastiano Satta, Grazia Deledda, Giuseppe Dessì and Gavino Ledda, have felt obliged to write in Italian. During the 1970s the Partito Sardo d'Azione launched campaigns to persuade the regional authorities to put Sardinian on an equal footing with Italian. Today, the main threat to the survival of the Sardinian language is undoubtedly posed by the Italian media. More than a million Sardinians (about 80 percent of the population) speak a form of Sardinian, which makes it the largest linguistic minority in Italy. In 1996 a law was passed to encourage the study of Sardo.

DECISIVE DATES

350,000 BC
First traces of human presence found.

6000 BC
Trade in obsidian with Corsica and south of France.

4000–2700 BC
Archaeological finds at Bonu Ighinu and Ozieri.

1800–500 BC
Period of the nuraghe, squat, cone-shaped stone buildings used as forts and citadels.

1000 BC
The earliest Phoenician traders arrive in Sardinia.

500 BC
Carthage controls the Sardinian economy.

264–238 BC
The First Punic War between Rome and Carthage. Rome annexes Sardinia but unrest continues in the island.

1st century BC–5th century AD
Period of Roman rule in Sardinia.

5th–8th centuries AD
Roman empire collapses as barbarian tribes invade Western Europe.

AD 711
Arab raids on Sardinia.

815–27
Arab conquest of Sicily cuts off Sardinia's links with Christian powers, affecting the economy.

1015–16
Victory by combined Genoese and Pisan navies over an Arab fleet from Mallorca. Rivalry between Genoa and Pisa for control of Sardinia. Island divided into four *giudicati*.

1130
Comita d'Arborea, *giudice* of Oristano, tries to seize control of the island with Genoese backing.

12th century
Supported by Emperor Frederick Barbarossa, Barisone d'Arborea is crowned King of Sardinia. Monastic

orders improve Sardinia's agriculture.

1190–1200
Pisa in firm control of Sardinia.

1284
Genoa becomes the dominant power in the north-western Mediterranean.

1297
Pope Boniface VIII names James II of Aragon as regent of Sardinia, in an effort to end the Pisan-Genoese rivalry.

1323
Defeated at Santa Gilla, Pisa renounces its claims to Sardinia, which becomes part of the Kingdom of Aragon.

14th century
Sardinia is subdivided into 376 fiefs, many awarded to Spanish noblemen, after an Aragonese viceroy.

1392
Eleonora Doria publishes the *Carta de Logu*, a constitution of common law written in the Sardinian language.

1417
The *giudicato* system ends: direct rule by Aragon.

15th century
Plague and famine reduce Sardinia's population from 340,000 to 150,000. Catalan immigrants and Jewish settlers arrive.

1469
King Ferdinand of Aragon marries Isabella, Queen of

Palaeochristian fresco in Sant'Andrea Priu.

Castille, creating the Kingdom of Spain.

1708
During the War of the Spanish Succession English and Austrian forces seize Sardinia from King Philip V of Spain.

1718
Briefly reassigned to Spain, Sardinia is then given to the Dukes of Savoy by terms of the Treaty of London.

1730
The Duke of Savoy, Charles Emmanuel III, becomes King of Piedmont and Sardinia, and remains king until his death in 1773.

1793
French troops attempt to invade Sardinia but fail.

1839
Abolition of the Sardinian feudal system.

1861
Victor Emmanuel II proclaims himself King of Italy.

Nuragic sacred well.

1870–1904
Banditry increases as nomadic sheep-farming revives. Growth of mining and tragedy at Buggerru.

1915–18
13,000 Sardinians die in World War I.

1924
Fascist "Law of the Milliard" against Sardinian unrest.

1926
Grazia Deledda (1871–1936) wins the Nobel Prize for Literature.

1940
Italy enters World War II.

1946
Italy becomes a republic.

1948
Sardinia established as autonomous region.

1962
Heavy industry and business sectors are stimulated. The Aga Khan creates the Costa Smeralda syndicate and tourism opens up.

1995
Mining industry in crisis.

2001
An ancient fleet of Roman cargo ships is unearthed in the Bay of Olbia.

2004
Renato Soru, the owner of Tiscali, is elected president of Sardinia; encourages foreign investment and limits coastal developments.

2009
Soru replaced by Berlusconi-backed Ugo Cappellacci, who

Giuseppe Garibaldi (1807–82).

reverses curbs on coastline construction and taxes on super yachts.

2013
Cyclone Cleopatra hits the island; 18 people perish and 3,000 are made homeless.

2014
Francesco Pigliaru of the centre-left Democratic Party becomes president of Sardinia.

2016
Matteo Renzi resigns as Italy's prime minister and is succeeded by Paolo Gentiloni.

2018
The March Italian general election gives no clear majority to any political party. In April, the two parties with the most votes, Northern League and Five Star Movement, hold talks on forming a new government.

Embroidered bench cover from Santa Giusta, now in the Museo Nazionale G.A. Sanna.

FROM PREHISTORY TO THE 12TH CENTURY

From the earliest times, Sardinia's island status has protected its distinct culture. Yet its natural wealth and strategic location were coveted by successive imperial powers.

The first Sardinians probably came from the European mainland, but who they were and when the island was first settled is less certain. Fairly precise dating has attributed human and animal bones found in the Grotta Corbeddu – a cave near Oliena – to the late Palaeolithic era, 13,000 years ago. During glacial periods the sea level dropped and Sardinia and Corsica formed one large island, separated from the coast of Tuscany by a relatively narrow strip of water. After this, though, Sardinia remained cut off from the continent for thousands of years. It was not until the beginning of the Neolithic era that a completely different race of men appeared on the island.

Hard, black obsidian was ideal for the manufacture of tools and weapons, and trade in this prized raw material helped establish a high level of civilisation in Sardinia during the Neolithic era.

These new inhabitants had clearly reached a more advanced stage of civilisation than their predecessors. To them, Sardinia must have been like the proverbial happy land, with its dense forests filled with game, broad lagoons with an inexhaustible supply of fish and shellfish, fertile plains and rolling hills for arable farming, excellent conditions for cattle raising, and – above all – obsidian, their "black gold". By the 4th millennium BC, they had achieved a considerable degree of cultural independence. Their customs and conventions were further developed and refined over the centuries, in two principal periods which archaeologists have named after the sites at which signs of life were first discovered:

Nuragic sacred well at Santa Cristina, Paulilatino.

the Bonu Ighinu culture (c.4000–3500 BC) and the Ozieri culture (3500–2700 BC).

ARTISTIC ARTEFACTS

The discoveries from these cultures include relatively sophisticated pottery, frequently decorated with pictorial and geometric forms, engraved or scratched before firing and sometimes filled out in colour. Limestone was used to make perfectly formed stone vessels and female cult statues.

The most noteworthy relics left, however, are over 1,000 burial chambers, hewn from solid rock with stone chisels. The simplest of these, dating to the Bonu Ighinu period, consist of a hidden vertical entrance shaft and a small chamber usually large enough for only one body. These were known as *forredus* ("ovens") because of their spherical shape. In later years several such chambers were linked together to form underground burial apartments with a common antechamber and an entry

---

*Domus de janas means "house of the fairies".
More than 1,000 of these tombs can be found in
Sardinia, often carved into rocks and mountains,
with reliefs decorating the walls.*

---

corridor. The Sardinians called the tombs *domus de janas*. According to local superstition, the powerful but not always benevolent *janas* (fairies) are tiny female creatures who live in these houses (*domus*). There are particularly impressive examples in Sant'Andrea Priu near Bonorva, and Montessu near Santadi, where several dozen linked tombs form a town of the dead.

The Neolithic era was followed by a transitional period of approximately 1,000 years, often known as the Copper Stone Age. Then new influences brought Western Megalithic culture to the

Horn reliefs in a burial niche at Montessu.

island: dolmens, obelisks, stone circles, rows of menhirs and even well-developed menhir statues hitherto only found in northern Italy and southern France. This cultural heritage gave birth to Sardinia's great Bronze Age civilisation.

THE NURAGIC CIVILISATION

The Nuragic civilisation lasted from around 1800 BC to 500 BC. Sometime during the first half of the 2nd millennium BC the first nuraghi appeared, circular towers dotted across the Sardinian countryside like giant upturned buckets. The largest and technically most perfect Megalithic buildings in Europe, they are found only in Sardinia, in awe-inspiring profusion – today some 7,000 are registered as historic monuments.

The basic form of a nuraghe is a blunt-topped cone. An entrance corridor at ground level leads to the interior, a more or less concentric circular room with a domed vaulted roof. This classic design is similar to the famous "Treasury of Atreus" near Mycenae in the Peloponnese. Both the Mycenaeans and the Nuragic built these structures from about the 16th century BC, although the basic principles differed. In addition to the solitary towers, there are hundreds of nuraghi settlements of all sizes, some full-size fortresses. The largest and most interesting are the Nuraghe Santu Antine

the nuraghi, they have no parallel on the mainland. They were built from well-matched stones and usually covered by a more carelessly constructed burial mound that, from the outside, resembles the hull of an upturned boat. On each side of the entrance, at right angles to the main chamber of the grave, a pair of walls was added. They demarcate a semi-circular forecourt 10–20 metres (32–65ft) wide. The imposing facade thus formed gave the graves an appropriately monumental and possibly mournful and private ambience.

Interior of a prehistoric tomb (domus de janas) at Sant'Andrea Priu decorated with a fresco.

near Torralba, the Nuraghe Losa near Paulilatino, the Nuraghe Su Nuraxi near Barumini and the Nuraghe Arrubiu near Orroli. The function of these strongholds was probably similar to that of medieval castles: in peacetime they may have served as the official residences of tribal chiefs and centres of a wide range of communal activities, and in war as a refuge for the inhabitants of the surrounding villages, as is evident from their numerous defensive strategic features.

GRAVES AND TEMPLES

The tombs of the men who built the nuraghi are as monumental as the towers themselves. Sardinians call these burial places *tumbas de sos zigantes* (in Italian, *tombe di giganti*). Like

The forecourt contains a fireplace and often an encircling stone platform used as a seat or table for sacrificial offerings. This was the setting for both funeral rites and commemorative ceremonies in honour of the dead. The members of a tribal group, clan or village met to pay their respects to the dead, who were buried by the community with no consideration for rank or privilege, and without funeral gifts of any value. The graves of the giants constructed by the Nuragic should be seen rather as charnel houses, in which the bones of the dead were piled up after skeletonisation was complete. Some graves contain as many as 100 to 200 skeletons.

The most elaborate structures from this era, however, are water temples, built on the site of natural springs. The heart of a water temple is the Nuragic domed vault, in which the sacred spring water was collected. A staircase linked

> Phoenician art blended styles from trading partners with its own aesthetic traditions to create highly individual works. As well as burial gifts, these include frightening masks to keep evil spirits away from the dead.

Sacred well at the Nuragic village of Santa Cristina at Paulilatino.

this pump room with the temple antechamber at ground level. The antechamber was ringed by small stone benches upon which votive gifts or cult objects were placed. There was also often a sacrificial stone with a small gully; this seems to point to blood sacrifices or specific rites involving the use of what was believed to be holy water.

Some particularly fine temple complexes, such as Predio Canopoli in Perfugas, Su Tempiesu near Orune, Santa Cristina near Paulilatino and Santa Vittoria near Serri, were thought to date from the 8th to 6th centuries BC. More recent finds, however, have led archaeologists to believe that the temples are several centuries older than this, reaching back into the time of

close contact with the late Mycenaean kingdom in Greece and Cyprus.

THE MYSTERIOUS SARDANA

Recent theories support the notion that the Nuragic of Sardinia may have been the mysterious people known as the Sardana, mentioned in 14th-century BC Egyptian texts. Certainly by this time there was a remarkable increase in Nuragic communications with eastern Mediterranean societies, especially Cyprus – even after the 12th century BC when, following the Trojan Wars and the eclipse of the royal house of Mycenae, Greece entered a dark age which was to last many centuries.

It was thanks to its trading links that Sardinia continued to flourish culturally. This is confirmed by remarkable artefacts such as the statues of warriors found in 1974 on Monte Prama. They are exact copies of Nuragic votive statuettes, but are almost 3 metres (10ft) tall and carved in stone. If, as has been suggested by archaeologists, the first large Nuragic sculptures were created in the 8th century BC, they predated even the oldest Greek sculptures. These statues are among the signs that, in some places, Nuragic life was moving towards a city-based social structure. Archaeologists have no doubt that the reason for this development was the arrival at this time of the first Phoenician settlements on the Sardinian coast.

PHOENICIANS AND CARTHAGINIANS

The first Phoenician traders probably arrived in about 1000 BC. During the 9th and 8th centuries BC, they built their first urban colonies around the principal harbours on the Sardinian coast: Karali (Cagliari), Nora and Bithia (both near Pula), Sulki (Sant'Antioco), Tharros (near Oristano), possibly Bosa and others. Scarcely 100 years after they founded the city of Sulki, the colonists had succeeded in conquering the entire fertile hinterland and the access routes to the lucrative mining areas, securing their conquests with smaller outposts and fortified towns.

In the 6th century BC the Nuragic banded together to mount a counterattack. In 540 BC Carthage sent an army of reinforcements to its Phoenician sister cities, but the expedition ended in disaster, and the army was routed. In Carthage, the shock of this defeat gave rise to a reform of political and military institutions, and well-organised armies of mercenaries were despatched to Sardinia. The island was soon so firmly under Carthaginian rule that, in 509 BC, the Romans were compelled to sign a contract recognising that all trading with Sardinia was subject to Carthaginian control.

By the 5th century BC the Carthaginians occupied two-thirds of the island. They founded towns such as Macopsisa (Macomer), built numerous forts, including those on the northern boundary of the Campidano high plains and in the northern Giara region of Gesturi. Hand in hand with a vigorous policy of deforestation, farming land was criss-crossed by an amazingly dense network of paths and farmsteads: the island was being transformed into the granary of Carthage.

Outside the museums traces of this period are not so accessible, since the Romans destroyed virtually everything, but Monte Sirai and Tharros are well worth a visit.

Monte Sirai is an excellent example of a self-sufficient garrison town complete with necropolis and its own sacrificial altar for burnt offerings. Tharros is situated on a narrow

Sign to Santa Cristina.

⊘ LITTLE BRONZE STATUES

Of the countless votive presents that visitors to the water temples would leave behind, a number of little bronze statues have survived, now housed in the archaeological museums in Sassari and Cagliari. These statues take the form of household items, farming implements, tools, weapons and boats, but also exquisitely naturalistic representations of wild and domestic animals and, above all, people. With a little imagination we can glimpse their different activities and recognise the social strata: shepherds, farmers, musicians, worshippers, the sick, mourners, priests, aristocrats and soldiers, some of whom, armed with assorted weapons, bear the terrifying countenance of demons.

It has proved impossible to date the figures with any precision, although recently support has been won for the theory that some Nuragic bronze art is much older than comparable artefacts found in the western Mediterranean – in contrast with the accepted picture of the Nuragic civilisation as one of the relatively unimportant fringe cultures of the Mediterranean. According to experts, the island's rich ore deposits, especially its lead and copper, played a key role, and the Nuragic golden age coincided with an upsurge in metalworking. It seems likely that the bronze boom and the resulting trade with the eastern Mediterranean gave the island a cultural impetus not shared by anyone else.

promontory about 2km (1.25 miles) long, with two hills: one for the town, one for the necropolis. It is a classic example of a Phoenician coastal town: it has a safe harbour, an easily defended single narrow land approach, shallow lakes with copious stocks of fish nearby and an extensive, fertile hinterland.

ALLIES AGAINST ROME

In 238 BC, three years after the First Punic War, Roman troops annexed Sardinia without encountering much resistance. In the course

Bronze Nuragic sculpture from around 800 BC.

Ⓞ CHILD SACRIFICES

A little-understood Phoenician custom was the sacrifice of children by fire to the deity Baal, or later to the Carthaginian goddess Tanit. The sacrificial altars, referred to as *tephatim* in the Bible, were erected outside towns. The first was found not in the Middle East but near Nora in Sardinia. Here, and on half a dozen other *tephatim* discovered on the island, archaeologists found thousands of clay urns filled with charcoal and human remains. Some urns contain remains of substitute animal sacrifices, and it is also evident that children who died of natural causes were cremated in the *tophet*.

of the Second Punic War (218–201 BC), the Carthaginians on Sardinia, supported by the local mountain dwellers, made several unsuccessful attempts to overthrow them. As the war dragged on, the citizens of Rome started to view the island as an unnecessary burden. In 54 BC, when Cicero took on the defence of a certain Scaurus, a man who had acquired excessive wealth during his time as governor of Sardinia, the lawyer's plea for his client echoed the popular mood: Sardinia was a Roman province but not a single town was friendly towards Rome; and the Sardinians as a race were the descendants of the nefarious Carthaginians.

As the Roman republic approached its last days, Sardinia was the only one of more than 30 Roman provinces without a single city whose inhabitants were entitled to Roman citizenship. Cicero was basically right in his depiction of Sardinians' provenance. The year of Sardinia's annexation was of purely political significance; in cultural terms, the Carthaginian influence on Sardinia remained evident for many centuries after Carthage had been destroyed by Rome.

The general situation on the island improved during the reign of the emperor Augustus. The residents of many towns were awarded the right of Roman citizenship, and a dramatic upsurge in the amount of building testifies to increasing prosperity. By now even the mountain folk had accepted Roman rule and the occupiers could restrict their supervisory activities to mediating in the feuds between sheep-farming tribes and Sardinian peasants on Roman estates. But to the Romans the island was doomed to remain a much-hated imperial doormat, not least because the dreaded malaria was found to be prevalent there.

THE ARABS

Arabs first ventured ashore on Sardinia in AD 711, capturing the town of Cagliari and occupying various regions along the coast. Their visit was short-lived, and they perished in a storm during the journey home. This mishap did little to discourage the Arabs, who resumed their raids, terrorising the Sardinian coast, stealing food and kidnapping the natives. The initial, ill-fated raid on Sardinia was followed by others in 722, 735–6 and 752–3. Despite some unexpected naval victories, by 815 the Sardinians were in desperate need of liberation. They sent a plea for assistance to Emperor Louis the Pious, to no avail: in 816 and again the following year, Cagliari was destroyed.

The occupation of Sicily by the Arabs in 827 cut off Sardinia's links with Byzantium and forced the island to rely on its own resources. Countless raids by a succession of new invaders followed: many of the seaside towns and villages were destroyed or left to decay. Since the Sardinians believed even then that danger

the Tyrrhenian Sea were roused from their lethargy by the fact that en route the Saracens had raided some Tuscan coastal towns. They also feared that the invaders might revive their former ambitions of empire and use Sardinia as a base from which to conquer Italy and the rest of Europe.

Pope Benedict VIII felt particularly threatened and used his influence over Pisa and Genoa to persuade them to unite in the common cause against the Arabs on Sardinia. In 1015–16 the fleets of Genoa and Pisa duly put to sea and

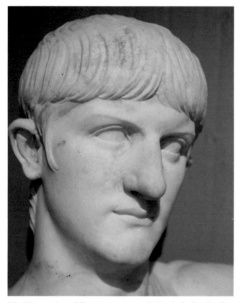

Marble carving of Roman emperor Caligula in Cagliari's archaeological museum.

Engraving showing Louis the Pious (778–840), emperor and king of the Franks from 813.

invariably came from across the sea, many left the fertile coastal regions in order to make new homes in the interior. They paid dearly for the security thus acquired: whilst life in the new settlements was marked by hardship and became progressively more depressing, large stretches of the previously fertile coastal margin regressed into malarial swampland.

The Arab prince known to the Italians as "Museto" had already conquered the Balearic Islands and Denia in Spain when he set sail from Mallorca with a fleet of 120 ships. He had recognised the strategic importance of Sardinia and now sought to subjugate the island once and for all. The states bordering

routed the Saracens, aided by the armies of the Sardinian *giudici*, with whom they then established lively trading links.

THE GENOESE AND THE PISANS

The fierce rivalry between the two maritime republics soon affected Sardinia. At the beginning, Pisa had the upper hand, not only in military success but also in its archbishop, who was the metropolitan of two Sardinian dioceses. After AD 1130 Genoa decided to support the *giudice* of Oristano, Comita d'Arborea, in his attempt to unite the entire island under the aegis of the d'Arborea family. There was vigorous opposition to this plan from the other three *giudici*; in 1146 a provisional peace treaty was concluded, but a few years later Barisone d'Arborea took up the struggle once more. The troops of the *giudicato* of Torres supported the

> *Dorgali, on the Bay of Orosei, was founded in about 900 by Saracen pirate Drugal. Its people display characteristics distinguishing them from other islanders.*

Pope Benedict VIII, pope from 1012–24.

Pisans; together, they besieged Barisone in his castle in Cabras. With Genoese help the latter broke the siege, then appealed to Emperor Frederick Barbarossa to proclaim him King of Sardinia. This was duly done and he was crowned on 10 August 1164.

Even this success was not enough to satisfy Genoa, which took the precaution of ensuring the benevolence of the Papal States and then persuaded all four *giudici* to sign a number of treaties which declared them to be virtually the vassals of Genoa. This was a severe blow for Pisa, but again Emperor Frederick intervened, dividing the island into two separate dependent territories; Lugudoro and Campidano were subject to Genoa, and Gallura to Pisa. From this time onwards, wealthy Ligurian and Tuscan families with a long tradition of seafaring and trading brought increased prosperity to the island's economy. Both Genoa and Pisa sent monks from a number of orders to convert the islanders to Catholicism, building abbeys and churches the length and breadth of the island.

At the end of 1190, following a complicated dispute over the succession, the governor's throne in Cuglieri (Cagliari) was occupied for the first time by a man from the mainland, Oberto di Massa, who adopted a policy favouring Pisa. In 1215 the death of his successor, Guglielmo di Massa, revived the power struggle between the two seafaring republics, but this time the first families of Sardinia were also involved.

⊘ GIUDICI AND GIUDICATI

Sardinia was divided into four provinces, called *giudicati* – Torres, Gallura, Oristano and Cagliari – each of which had its own jurisdiction and social order. The ruler of the *giudicato* was known as the *giudice*; he lived with his family and an armed bodyguard in a castle. He was responsible for the administration of justice and the government of affairs of state. He was aided by the clergy and a secular civil service, as well as by the *curatores*, each of which governed in his name a *curatoria* consisting of a number of villages and estates. The individual communities were run by the *majori*, men who enjoyed the trust of the *curatores*.

The social hierarchy was divided into estates into which one was born: freemen – ranging from wealthy and powerful owners of large estates to the poor – and peasants and serfs.

The latter were further subdivided into three groups, depending on how many days per week they were required to work for one or more masters. The *integri* had to work the whole day for their master, the *laterati* owed him half a day's work and the *pedati* worked for him for a quarter of the day. On their time off the *laterati* and *pedati* could work on their own plot of land – if they possessed one – or could undertake other work.

By the middle of the 13th century, a complicated policy of arranged marriages brought virtually the entire island under Pisa's sway, although, supported by various Ligurian families, the *giudicato* Logudoro attempted to organise resistance to the Pisans. The majority of Sardinians, most of them being too involved with the everyday problems of town life, took no part in the affair.

Thus came the end of a highly promising golden age in which culture, religion, the arts and the economy had all flourished, without

Corsica. At first this change of regency had little effect on the island, but during the early years of the 14th century James II saw his opportunity to take an active part in the affairs of the

> *The monasteries attracted local labourers and farmers anxious to learn the agricultural methods that the monks had brought with them from mainland Europe.*

Holy Roman Emperor Frederick I (1123–90), known as Barbarossa or "Redbeard".

Portrait of Charles Albert, King of Sardinia, by Horace Vernet (1789–1863).

giving rise to any local political or economic power that could take overall control of the country's future.

PISA LOSES CONTROL

Between 1250 and 1260 the *giudice* Ghiano di Massa drove the Pisans from Cagliari, and towards the end of the 13th century, against the backdrop of the bitter feud between the Guelphs and the Ghibellines, the position of the factions in Pisa itself deteriorated; it was not long before the effects spread to Sardinia too. In 1297 the Papal States intervened again. Pope Boniface VIII named James II of Aragon as seigneur in perpetuity over the islands of Sardinia and

land. On 28 February 1323, the armed forces of Aragon and Pisa met at the Santa Gilla Lagoon, just outside Cagliari. Pisa suffered defeat; later that same year, on 19 June, a peace treaty was signed in which the vanquished state abandoned its claim to almost all of its rights associated with towns and estates on the island. Only one section of the fortress at Cagliari and the harbour remained in their possession, and that only for one more year.

This marked the beginning of the suzerainty of the Kingdom of Aragon, which was followed over four centuries by the kings of Spain in an institution which – as if by some irony of fate – came to be known as the *Regnum Sardiniae*.

THE STRUGGLE FOR IDENTITY

Oppressed by the Spanish, misruled by Savoy and exploited under the new Kingdom of Italy, Sardinian national consciousness survived against the odds.

Once James II had appeased Sardinia, the island was placed under the regency of a viceroy from the Kingdom of Aragon. Half of the land was awarded to Spanish noblemen, whose one aim was to increase their fortunes at the expense of their Sardinian estates. The underpopulated, impoverished, malarial island was entirely at the mercy of foreign interests; its fate was decided in faraway Zaragoza, over the heads of the local citizens.

> On his 1535 visit, Charles V lifted the ruling whereby all Sardinians had to leave the Castello quarter of Cagliari by sunset. Previously, anyone disobeying the cry "Foras los Sards" ("Sardinians out!") was thrown over the wall.

Peter IV, King of Aragon and Sardinia, being visited by Guillaume-Raymond Moncada.

Of Sardinia's former masters, only the rulers of Arborea had been able to maintain their previous position. In order to destroy their power the Spanish encouraged discord between the two sons of the *giudice* Hugo II by favouring the younger son, Giovanni, rather than his elder brother Mariano. However, Mariano came to power and decided to fight with the Genoese Doria clan against the Spanish. He received valuable assistance from one of the Dorias, named Brancaleone, "The Lion-Catcher". In order to confirm the latter's allegiance, Mariano agreed in 1367 that Brancaleone should marry his daughter Eleonora. Subsequently known as the Giudicessa, Eleonora is still remembered by Sardinians today as a symbol of the island's independence.

Mariano was succeeded not by Eleonora but by her brother, Hugo III. He ruled harshly and strictly, imposing a high tax burden and rigid military conscription, for he was obsessed with the aim of freeing his country from the hated Aragonese. His approach, however, was too dictatorial; on 6 March 1383 he and his daughter were assassinated during an uprising in Oristano. Three days later Brancaleone appeared at the court of the King of Aragon in Zaragoza and proposed that his son Frederick should succeed Hugo, with his wife Eleonora as regent.

Eleonora brought the country under control within a few months. Her popularity increased when, in 1392, she published the *Carta de Logu*, a written constitution of common law on which her predecessors and their legal advisers had worked for half a century, and which was to remain in operation until the beginning of the 19th century. Though this legal code contained no innovations, it was written in the Sardinian

> During the 400 years of Spanish colonial rule strict censorship was imposed, even in the cultural sphere. Catalan Gothic and Spanish Baroque styles were permitted, but the Italian Renaissance was banned.

some three years later. One hundred years after its first military invasion, the Kingdom of Aragon finally had the entire island under its control.

IMMIGRATION

Epidemics of plague, failed harvests and famine followed, and the population declined drastically; at the beginning of the 14th century there were 340,000 inhabitants; by 1483 this figure was reduced to 150,000. To provide compensation for this decline and to increase the Spanish element on the island, settlers from the Iberian peninsula

Statue of Giudicessa Eleonora di Arborea in the square of the same name, Oristano.

language and thus became one of the cornerstones of Sardinian national consciousness.

Eleonora died in 1404, followed by her son in 1407 and Brancaleone soon afterwards. Margrave William III of Narbonne, a distant cousin of Eleonora, took over the post of ruler in the *giudicato* of Arborea. He found himself having to face Aragon in battle shortly after arriving on the island. He and an army of 20,000 Sardinians were defeated by the King of Sicily, Martin of Aragon, whose force was smaller but possessed better strategy and weapons. William fled from Sardinia; King Martin died of malaria shortly afterwards, whereupon William III returned, leaving the island for the last time in 1417 and abdicating his rights in return for adequate compensation

were transported to Sardinia. During the 14th century the town of Alghero was resettled with Catalan immigrants, after the native population had been driven away in retaliation for an attempted coup against the Aragonese rulers.

Jewish immigrants also reached Sardinia at about the same time as the Catalan settlers. They established themselves in Alghero and Cagliari as money-changers, traders and doctors; however, in spite of their contribution to the otherwise stagnant local cultural life, they were driven out towards the end of the 15th century. The few who preferred conversion to Christianity were forced to face the Spanish Inquisition. Suspects were expropriated and sentenced to large fines – if they escaped being burnt at the stake.

FORGOTTEN ISLAND

Ferdinand and Isabella now ruled over an expanded united kingdom. In 1492, following the discovery of America, their interest was diverted towards the more promising territories in the New World, and Sardinia slipped into oblivion. Nor could the Sardinians expect a greater share of the attention of Charles V, the grandson of Ferdinand and Isabella and heir of the Habsburg Emperor Maximilian; he was fully occupied by his wars against King François I of France and problems caused by the spread of the Reforma-

rulers supplied the Sardinians with weapons. Since the latter were required to pay for the arquebuses and lances they received, the cost to the Spanish crown was actually nil. An equally neat solution was found in the case of the coastal watchtowers, which Philip II, who had succeeded Charles V, had constructed towards the end of the 16th century. A survey indicated that to provide real protection against enemy attack, Sardinia would have needed 132 "Saracen towers", standing at 15km (9-mile) intervals along the coast. In fact, only 66 were built,

A Spanish fort (no longer standing) in Sassari.

tion. Sardinia was no more than a pebble on the beach of his world empire.

Yet in 1535 and 1541, Charles V passed through Sardinia with Andrea Doria, a Genoese mercenary leader, on a joint expedition against the buccaneers of Algiers. On the second visit, during his brief stay in Alghero, the emperor described the local inhabitants as *todos caballeros* – "all gentlemen" – in a speech thanking the citizens for supplying food for the mercenary forces while their ships lay in the bay.

In the turbulent years of the 16th century, Sardinia's totally inadequate system of coastal defences lay in the hands of 86 men, who stood watch over the island from hilltops near the coast. Instead of sending troops, the colonial

☉ THE INQUISITION

In 1469, with the marriage of King Ferdinand of Aragon and Isabella of Castile, the linking of the two crowns created a unified Spanish kingdom. In order to be able to deal "appropriately" with the large numbers of Arabs and Jews in their land, the two monarchs – who were highly praised for their Christian virtues – asked the Pope to reintroduce the Inquisition, requesting the right to appoint the Inquisitors themselves. The long arm of the Inquisition reached as far as Sardinia. Here, however, influential people were able to avoid its grasp thanks to their powerful protectors; those who landed in its net were "small fry".

financed by the barons or the town councils on whose property they stood.

A detailed map of Sardinia entitled *Description de la Isla y Reyno de Sardena*, printed during the 17th century under Philip II, shows illustrations of these coastal towers. The map also depicts the coat of arms of the Kingdom of Sardinia: a shield with a red cross and four Moors' heads bearing a headband as a sign of their royal status. Across the centuries, the band slipped down, representing their complete defeat. Since the 19th century the Moors' heads with

Portrait of Charles V, c. 1520, by Bernaert van Orley.

⊘ BAD REPORT

The regular reports sent from Sardinia to the capital, Turin, by the Baron de Saint-Rémy – the first Viceroy of the Piedmont – did not sound encouraging: "The nobles are poor, the country itself miserable and depopulated, its citizens idle and without any sort of trade – and the air is most unhealthy." Further on, he claimed: "The vices to which these people are most inclined are theft, murder and cheating." Nor do the 400 years of Spanish indifference seem to have been good for the clergy: the priests showed so little respect in their personal appearance "that they wear a peasant's cap and greatcoat in public, even at church during celebration of the Mass".

the blindfolded eyes have remained symbols of the Sardinian claim to the self-determination denied them for so long.

DECLINE AND FALL

To keep close tabs on the better-educated classes, in the middle of the 16th century Jesuits were sent to the island, founding colleges in Cagliari and Sassari. They were also responsible for imposing Castilian (i.e. Spanish) as the official language. The country people, though, spoke exclusively Sardinian: in these times, in which they had been robbed of almost all they possessed, it represented their only wealth. The towns demanded their grain at cut-throat prices, the Church demanded its tithes, the nobles and merchants would only lend them money at exorbitant rates of interest, and the Spanish monarchy commandeered soldiers, horses, grain and vegetables.

This blatant injustice sowed the seeds of Sardinian banditry. Lacking protection, the poor resorted to self-defence. A particular problem was posed between 1610 and 1612 by the 20-strong band of robbers under Manuzio Flore from Bono. He incited the populace to refuse to pay its taxes, and, like a Sardinian Robin Hood, directed his attacks against all officials who were "poor when they assumed office and rich when they retired".

Towards the end of the century, the attention of the major powers in Europe was directed towards the declining Iberian monarchy. Charles II, the last Spanish Habsburg king, had no male heir. In 1708 the Spanish were forced to surrender to the English and the Austrians on Sardinia. In 1714 the island was ceded to Austria, and in 1718, as part of the Treaty of London, Sardinia was passed to the Dukes of Savoy in exchange for Sicily. Victor Amadeus II therefore became king of Sardinia until 1730.

THE SAVOY MISMATCH

Sardinia was not a country to which Savoy had aspired. They could muster little interest in the island, nor could they make themselves understood there. The natives spoke Sardinian and the educated classes Castilian and Catalan; the rulers of Savoy-Piedmont, however, spoke French. During the first years of their rule the Piedmontese observed and detailed weekly reports to Turin. Their aim was to get to know this new, unknown

European country and to assist it towards more order and discipline by means of administrative reform. Unfortunately, in doing so they tried to make the Sardinians fit a Piedmontese mould.

Apart from their concern at the poverty of the island, the Piedmontese were troubled by the unrest and lawlessness. In some regions the bandits had formed armies. Signore de Rivarolo, a former governor of the Savoy prisons who served as Viceroy of Sardinia from 1735 to 1738, tried to eradicate banditry with military expeditions, accelerated trials and harsh punishments. Dur-

of the king, whereupon the mob reverently doffed their hats and fell down on their knees, calling out *Viva il re!* (Long live the king!).

During the last years of the 18th century the riots increased in frequency due to the presumptuousness of the feudal lords. When French troops invaded Sardinia in 1793, believing they had discovered a "revolutionary" land, they were defeated by a 4,000-man Sardinian regiment. As a reward for their courageous defence of their native land, the Sardinians requested the king in Turin to appoint Sardinian natives to all public

Victor Amadeus II, king of Sardinia 1718–30.

Count Giovanni Battista Bogino.

ing his three years in office he had 432 people executed and over 3,000 condemned to severe punishments. His deterrents brought few results.

REFORM, RIOT AND REVOLUTION

Count Giovanni Battista Bogino, who was appointed Minister of State of the Piedmont in 1759, began to introduce a reform programme, concentrating on encouraging agriculture by the distribution of seed and loans for farmers. Not all reforms met with success, but the Piedmontese were unable or unwilling to grasp the situation. In April 1780, the starving peasants in Sassari rioted, plundering the granaries and storming the town hall. The revolt was quelled not by force of arms, but by holding up a portrait

positions, and to grant them direct involvement in all governmental affairs. Their wishes were denied; in response, on 7 May 1794 the Sardinians arrested 541 Piedmontese officials and shipped them back to the mainland. For the first time in 500 years, Sardinia was under Sardinian rule – but the royal standard still fluttered from all public buildings, and protestations of loyalty to the monarchy could be heard from all quarters.

PROPERTY PROBLEMS

The Piedmontese had still not succeeded in giving the necessary impetus to Sardinian agriculture. All their attempts in this direction failed because there was no private ownership of land: one year a field would be available to the peasants for agricultural purposes, and the next to the shepherds as pasture. With the "Olive Tree Enactment" of 1806, a peasant who planted olive trees was granted the right to enclose his land; planting more than 4,000 trees gained him a title. In 1829 an Enclosures Act was introduced to put an end to the perpetual conflict between peasants and shepherds by providing a clear distinction between agricultural land and pasture. Once again, however, it was the wealthy who gained the upper hand: with more labour at their disposal and more skill at cutting through

Giuseppe Garibaldi (1807–82), Italian military and nationalist leader, c.1870, by Vincenzo Cabianca.

In 1848 Frederico Fenu stated: "The attempt to transfer mainland laws to Sardinia... can be compared to an attempt to make adult clothes fit a child or to dress a man in a woman's skirt."

the bureaucratic jungle, they were able to lay claim to larger areas of land.

Once again, riots broke out. In the first instance the Piedmontese were ruthless in quashing the unrest; in 1833, however, they were forced to repeal the edict. Six years were to pass before the enclosure of land was permitted

again, as part of a large-scale reorganisation of property laws following the abolition of the feudal system. Sardinia thus took an important and irreversible step forward into the modern world. But the traditional equilibrium within island society had been destroyed for ever.

"FUSION WITH THE MOTHERLAND"

The islanders could see only one way out of this economic catastrophe: the incorporation of Sardinia into Piedmont, in order to guarantee the same treatment as the much wealthier mainland state. In November 1847, a delegation of Sardinia's leading citizens made the journey to Turin, where they requested the island's "perfect fusion with the Motherland". Unification with Piedmont was proclaimed on 30 November.

Thus with trusting enthusiasm Sardinia became part of the embryonic state of Italy, which was being formed by a Piedmontese politician, Count Camillo Cavour (1810–61), fought for by the leader of a volunteer army, Giuseppe Garibaldi (1807–82), and ruled over by the House of Savoy. The islanders had high hopes that the Italian Risorgimento would pave the way for a second resurgence in their own neglected homeland. However, instead of the hoped-for improvements, the Sardinians found themselves faced with still more disadvantages: nomadic sheep farming was banned, entire forests were felled, and the mines were exploited by foreign companies.

Conditions on Sardinia were deplorable. Despite the exorbitant taxes levied, communities received nothing in return. In addition, there was enmity between the north and south of the island, especially between Sassari and Cagliari. The Piedmontese, expelled from Cagliari by the local citizens in 1794, would have been pleased to transfer the capital to Sassari, where most inhabitants were immigrants from the mainland. Carlo Baudi di Vesme, a Piedmontese nobleman, proposed a solution: in administrative and religious affairs (except in sermons), the Sardinian dialect should be banned and the use of Italian obligatory. "Unity of language would lead to a closer unity of spirit... thus overcoming the deep-rooted differences between the inhabitants of the various regions." In other words, since no one really knew what to do with the island as it was at the time, the plan was to destroy its national identity.

However, in 1860 a rumour began to circulate on the island that Piedmont was hatching plans to cede Sardinia to France. Giuseppe Garibaldi, who had settled on the nearby island of Caprera, intervened, and Sardinia remained a part of Piedmont. On 17 March 1861 it became part of the new unified Italian state. Victor Emmanuel II proclaimed himself King of Italy, and Sardinia ceased to be the kingdom in its own right which it had been for the previous 650 years.

men were killed during violent clashes with the army. But repression didn't change anything. The entire working population of Sardinia was

The poems of Sebastiano Satta, like the novels of Grazia Deledda, attracted the attention of Italian intellectuals to Sardinia's archaic language and folklore, which retain many traces of pagan influence.

Workers pose for a photograph during construction of the railroad from Tirso to Chilivani via Ozieri.

EXPLOITATION

Despite high property taxes, a rising cost of living, starvation and revolt, Italy started to improve conditions on Sardinia. The road network was completed in 1862 and the first railway in 1880. But the antiquated methods of production in agriculture and the management of pastureland defied all attempts at progress.

Sardinia's mines could have brought the island prosperity, but too small a percentage of the profits was reinvested. The miners began to voice demands for better conditions, and in 1900 went on strike, following in the footsteps of the ferry crews of Carloforte and the printers of Sassari. The wave of strikes reached a tragic climax in 1904 in Buggerru, when three

in a state of unrest, and a new political awareness was dawning.

During World War I, thousands of Sardinians laid down their lives for their country. The dauntless men of the Brigata Sassari were mentioned in four military dispatches, and more than 13,000 of them died brutal deaths on the battlefield. Disenchantment with the government, which again failed to keep its promises, embittered the ranks of returning troops. Within the next few years they united to form the Partito Sardo d'Azione, the Action Party of Sardinia. At long last, after centuries of inaction, Sardinians were once more sufficiently conscious of their national identity to take their fate into their own hands.

MARZO
APRILE
1914

THE SHAPING OF SARDINIA TODAY

The shift from sheep rearing to tourism in the last century has had profound effects on the island's economic structure and population.

The events of World War I were to provide the main impetus for Sardinia to abandon its insular existence and enter the modern world. This transition was marked by success and failure in equal measure.

> In World War I, Sardinians met people whose culture and history were different from their own. These encounters were to leave a lasting impression on the islanders.

The number of Sardinians who took part in the war was unusually high. So, too, was the number of casualties. Almost one-eighth of the entire population, approximately 100,000 soldiers, saw active service; 13,602 of these never returned. Following the war, many Sardinians realised for the first time that Italy and Sardinia shared a common heritage; and that they must also accept joint responsibility for the fate of Italy as a whole. They fought for a country which they hoped would not forget their valour once the war was over, and which would help them end the reign of misery on their native shores. Italy certainly acknowledged Sardinia's soldiers, in particular the legendary Brigata Sassari. Qualities of bravery and mutual cooperation between officers and men made the Brigata a symbol of the indomitable spirit of the Sardinians.

POST-WAR CONFIDENCE

Sardinian feelings of ethnic unity intensified during the post-war years. The encounter with other people who had already profited from economic progress and whose standard of living

Putting food in the oven, Tratalias, c.1925.

was much better than their own was bound to make the demobilised Sardinian soldiers ponder their lot and draw unfavourable comparisons. Many ex-soldiers joined together to form a *Movimento Combattentistico*, a movement of front-line fighters. They held their first congress in May 1919 in Nuoro. A few months later, three members of the party were elected to the Italian Parliament. Many cherished the secret hope that they would finally be allowed to carry the island's economy and society forward into the 20th century on an independent footing.

THE SARDINIAN ACTION PARTY

For Antonio Gramsci from Cagliari (1891–1937), the movement was "the first people's country party, above all in central and south-ern Italy". Although Gramsci was about to turn his back on the socialists in order to found the Italian Communist Party, in 1921 the Sardin-ian front-line fighters, foremost among them Camillo Bellieni and Emilio Lussu, decided at their congress in Oristano to form the Sardin-ian Action Party, the Partito Sardo d'Azione. The central elements of the party programme were a varied array of demands directed towards Rome, plus the concept of self-deter-mination for Sardinia.

IN THE WAKE OF FASCISM

In 1923 Paolo Pili, the leader of the wing with Fas-cist sympathies, brought about a split in the party when he and fellow-sympathisers left to join the PNF, the Partito Nazionale Fascista, the Fascist Party. Pili was skilful in taking advantage of Fas-cist policies as well as part of the cooperative programme of the Sardinian Independence Move-ment in order to further his own cause, until he fell from favour and was expelled from the PNF.

The declared political aim, that of "providing a new framework for some aspects of the Partito

Rural workers at the end of the 19th century.

⊙ FROM RURAL TO POLITICAL

One of the prime achievements of the Movimento and later of the Partito Sardo d'Azione was their encour-agement of an active political awareness in large numbers of young people and peasants who had lost patience with the old liberal democratic order.

As the population became more politically active, so their representatives put into practice with greater fervour the views acquired in the trenches, that a unified Sardinia was a powerful regional entity. And so, for the first time, Sardinia possessed a strong people's party. Even the rural population gathered together, lured out of their exile from polit-ical and social life.

Sardo d'Azione within the Fascist Party", was never achieved. In the 1924 elections the Sardin-ian Action Party did less well than the Fascist uni-fied list of candidates, but it was still represented – much to the chagrin of the Fascists. Thanks to the influence of Emilio Lussu and Camillo Bellieni, the Sardinian Independence Movement became more popular and more anti-Fascist in tone.

After the assassination of the socialist Giac-omo Matteotti, Lussu withdrew from the govern-ment and hardened his anti-Fascist stance, one of the most radical in Italy.

WATER SHORTAGES AND DAMS

From 1924 the Fascist Party laid great empha-sis on including in their own programme some of the characteristic demands of the Sardinian Independence Movement, such as the abolition of unemployment and an increase in productivity. The state of the island at the time was in many respects truly wretched. In two-thirds of the communities there was no running water; only seven communities had their own sewage system. In 1925, the Inspectorate of Public Works was established to give priority to the Sardinian "renaissance". Several swamps were reclaimed around the island and agrarian communities founded, mainly in the area of Oristano, where the village of Mussolinia (now called Arborea) was located, and in the Nurra, where the town of Fertilia sprang up.

Efforts were made to overcome the island's chronic water shortage: in 1923 the king officially commissioned the Tirso Dam, while in 1926 the Coghinas Dam was put into operation and construction work began on the hydraulic station on the Flumendosa.

MUSSOLINI'S SARDINIAN POLICY

Following Mussolini's declaration of absolute rule, exploitation of the metal and coal mines on the island was intensified, especially in the Sulcis Basin, where the town of Carbónia was founded in 1938. From here coal was exported via the port of Sant'Antioco. The settlement grew rapidly, acting as a magnet for Sardinia's unemployed as well as for workers, peasants and shepherds from all over the island. The development naturally led to the rapid formation of a working class – the first in the country.

Nuoro became the provincial capital in 1926, but failed to develop to meet expectations and requirements. In the interior of the island things remained as they had always been: the inhabitants eked out a meagre existence as labourers and shepherds, while many of the more august leading citizens discovered an unexpected taste for Fascism, using their position as head of the district council or as mayor to promote their own interests. Corruption was rife.

The Fascists failed utterly in the most remote country areas, where the population continued to adhere to traditional working methods and social norms. However, in the most densely populated towns they attracted more active support. Between 1921 and 1931 the population of Cagliari almost doubled, reaching a total of almost 100,000. During the same period Sassari topped the 50,000 mark, and smaller towns – Olbia, Alghero, Oristano, Tempio, Iglesias and Carbonia – also gained in significance.

WAR AGAINST BANDITS

The inhabitants of the interior devoted themselves exclusively to their own problems rather than to national politics. Orgosolo was the scene of a bloody feud; between 1925 and 1935 there was further unrest. This was the heyday of the legendary bandits, who were soon translated by folk tales and popular song into resolute, phil-

19th-century photo of children playing cards.

In the 1930s Sardinia was dominated by the Fascists, who took the wind out of the sails of independence movements such as the Sardinian Action Party, which had arisen after World War I.

anthropic heroes. The best-known of these Sardinian Robin Hoods were undoubtedly Samuelo Stocchino from Arzana and the Pintore brothers from Bitti. Mussolini's representatives fought with particular determination against the *banditismo*. All suspects were utterly at the mercy of the prefect, commander of the *carabinieri* or chief of the militia. Even a hint of suspicion was sufficient to put someone behind bars; informers flourished and old feuds were revived – but went unreported by the heavily censored press.

LAND REFORMS OF THE 1930S

Italy exhibited a diminished concern for the island's problems for a number of years, but showed a revived interest during the years leading up to World War II. The 1933 Land Reform Ordinance for the whole of Sardinia had the ambitious aim of developing one-quarter of the entire island. This was intended to bring about improved crop produc-

SARDINIAN AUTONOMY

At the end of World War II, the worst effects of which the island was largely spared, Sardinia felt itself more isolated than ever from the political and economic situation of mainland Italy, so hopes became concentrated on autonomy, universally considered to be the only way of tackling the province's numerous unresolved problems.

In 1944, the government in Rome appointed a High Commissioner to supervise the running of the island. A regional assembly was created to advise him, with two main aims: to produce a

Coal boats on Iglesiente beach, 19th century.

tion and an increase in the population, which had stagnated. New crops were introduced, such as the cultivation of rice near Arborea. By 1938 only about 10 percent of the target had been developed.

SHORTAGE OF LABOUR

During the years leading up to World War II, the Ethiopia Campaign and the Spanish Civil War led large numbers of Sardinians to join the armed forces for a second time. There was a shortage of male labour in all areas of industry; many projects begun by the Fascists were never completed, and the lack of men to work on the land made farming even less productive than it had been. Furthermore, a fresh malaria epidemic on Sardinia took a heavy toll of victims.

draft statute of autonomy, and to submit plans to improve the island's economy and the health of its people. The Sardinian Statute, which became law in 1948, stated that Sardinia and its islands were an autonomous region, which could lay claim to their own legal responsibility within the framework of the Republic of Italy.

This autonomy has contributed to the remarkable economic progress Sardinia has made since World War II. In the 1950s the Rockefeller Foundation supplied the DDT needed to drain the coastal marshes and finally eradicate malaria, freeing more land for agricultural development. Investment from mainland Italy also transformed the production of Sardinia's famous pecorino cheese, opening up export markets and increasing profits.

In the 1960s the Cassa per il Mezzogiorno (Southern Italy Development Fund) bankrolled the building of huge industrial concerns run by state-run organisations such as ITALSIDER (steel), ENI (chemicals) and EGAM (mining). The oil crisis of the 1970s hit Sardinia's oil refineries particularly badly, and migration from rural provinces to the bigger cities and mainland Italy peaked between 1955 and 1975. During this period, Italy was a battleground of Cold War politics which, combined with Sardinia's tradition of banditry, produced kidnappings and Red Brigade terrorist bombings.

blossomed, enthusiastically transforming previously uninhabited or uninhabitable regions to attract foreign investment.

Booming tourism, industrialisation and the rapid transition from agriculture to the service industries, combined with the introduction of universal education and new transport systems, have altered Sardinia's countenance more profoundly during the past 50 years than the previous two centuries had done.

However, these developments appeared to benefit non-Sardinians and spurred the re-

The matanza, when hundreds of tuna are caught.

In the years leading up to World War II Sardinia acquired strategic importance, both as a military base and supplier of raw materials, which fuelled Mussolini's dreams of an all-powerful Italy.

POST-WAR TRENDS

In the early 1960s the tourism industry kicked off when the Aga Khan invested huge amounts of money in the Costa Smeralda, the Emerald Coast, creating an exclusive resort for close friends. Copy-cat resorts sprung up in the following decades. Businessmen were attracted to the island, and a full-scale tourist industry

emergence of the Sardinian separatist movement: the Sardinian Action Party (Partito Sardo d'Azione) re-entered the political fray and grew more vociferous in the 1990s. This, combined with a revival of kidnapping, posed a threat to the burgeoning tourist industry. On occasions, extra police have been drafted in to protect holiday homes on the Costa Smeralda belonging to such high-profile people as the clothing magnate Luciano Benetton and former Prime Minister Silvio Berlusconi. Angelo Caria, who was the leader of the Partito Sardo d'Azione, accused such "colonialists" from the mainland of illegally installing barriers on footpaths and public land next to the beaches, preventing access to the land by local people.

CONTROVERSIES IN THE 21ST CENTURY

The entrepreneur Renato Soru, owner of Sardinia's successful internet provider Tiscali, was elected president of the Sardinia region in 2004, and many applauded his left-wing measures – such as banning development within 2km (1.25 miles) of the shoreline and taxing super yachts and second homes. The grip of the economic crisis and disarray within the centre-left coalition favoured a shift in politics and the centre-right candidate Ugo Cappellacci won the 2009 election. One of Cappellacci's first acts was to repeal the tax on luxury yachts. In 2014, Francesco Pigliaru of the Democratic Party became the new president of Sardinia.

PROFOUND CHANGES

There seems little doubt that the lifestyle and character of the Sardinian population have undergone profound changes – unfortunately not always for the better. Particularly in the remote regions of the interior, they have precipitated a crisis in the native culture and behaviour patterns based on traditions reaching back over

Mussolini inspects a model of the city of Carbónia.

⊘ THE SARDINIAN STATUTE

The Sardinian statute lists areas which the region is entitled to administer independently from central government:

the organisation of offices and administrative bodies within the region, including the legal position and pecuniary situation of its employees;

the local districts;

the local community or town police force and the regional police force;

agriculture and forestry, small development measures and projects aimed at increased yields or soil quality improvement;

public works affecting only the region;

building construction and town planning;

public transport by bus or tram;

thermal springs and medicinal spas;

hunting and fishing;

the right of administration of public waterways as if they were public property;

the right of administration of mines, quarries and salt works as if they were public property;

customs and morals;

crafts;

tourism and gastronomy;

local-authority libraries and museums.

thousands of years. The adjustment to new ways of life will take time and will not be a smooth ride. The fortunes of many of the island's industries seem increasingly precarious. While there has been some growth in Sardinia's service and technology sectors – including the success of the internet service provider Tiscali and the Sardegna Ricerche science and technology centre – many industries have gone into meltdown. One sector to buck the economic trend is tourism.

Gripped by the economic downturn, Sardinia faces new socio-economic problems, experienc-

it's unlikely to happen, in 2013 a free trade zone was established in the town of Porto Scuso. Still, Sardinians will have to wait for the fulfilment of their long-cherished dream of independence and self-reliance.

Sardinian separatist spirit assumes a new shape as Sardinians want Italy to sell their island to the Swiss. This "proposal" was put forward in 2014 by the Canton Marittimo.

Porto Cervo's harbour on the Costa Smeralda, a resort designed exclusively for the very rich.

ing industrial-relations unrest and spiralling poverty in some parts of the country. To make things worse, in 2013 torrential rains and a cyclone hit the island causing floods which took 18 lives and made thousands homeless.

Continued instability and *clientalismo* in Italian politics, combined with a fragile economy, have triggered the emergence of the small-scale Canton Marittimo movement, which in the run-up to the regional elections in 2014 provocatively suggested that Sardinia should be sold to Switzerland.

Sardinia has also become a power base of the anti-establishment Five Star Movement – one of the winners of the Italian general election in 2018. Sardinians would also like the whole island free of custom duties, including VAT and fuel excise. Although

⊘ FACTS ABOUT SARDINIA

Since 1945 Sardinia's population has risen from 1.27 million to almost 1.7 million.

Nearly 70 percent of Sardinia's visitors arrive from June–August. In recent years the tourism industry has tried to encourage tourists to visit at other times of the year. Eco-tourism and cultural tourism are attracting more visitors outside the peak months. Still, 1,850km (1,150 miles) of coastline remain the biggest draw.

Sardinia has 24 NATO bases – that is more per square kilometre than anywhere else on earth. It also has a heavy Italian military presence.

In 1999 the Sardinian language was given the same official status as Italian.

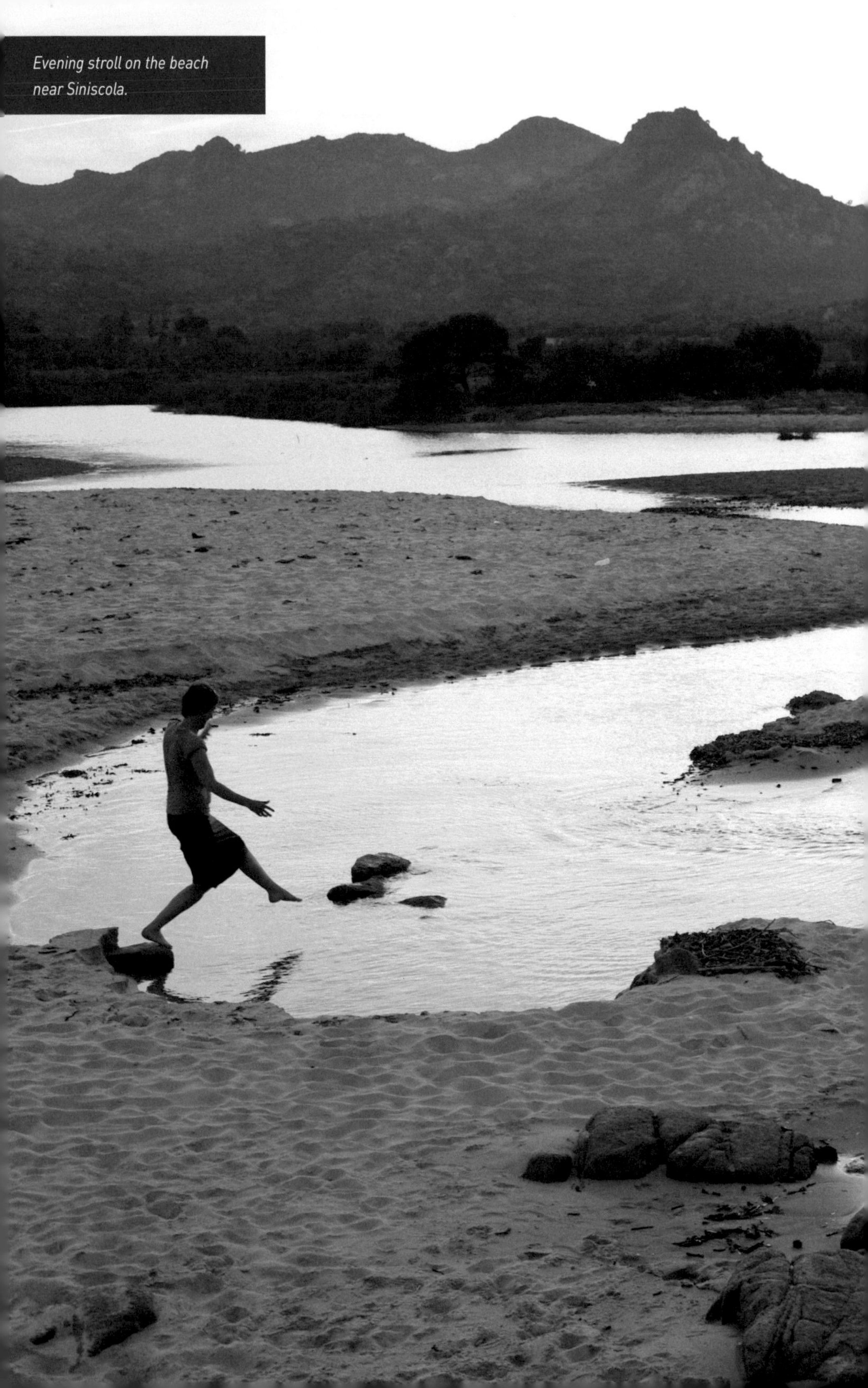

Evening stroll on the beach near Siniscola.

The wild coast at Is Arutas.

A WILD LANDSCAPE

Sardinia's diverse array of striking geological features, natural wonders and indigenous wildlife is the main attraction of the island to many visitors.

Sardinia's wildlife and vegetation are genuinely unique – the island's detached location in the middle of the Mediterranean has presented something of a natural barrier to migration and cross-pollination. The land and climate help to provide the ideal habitat for species found only in Sardinia, some parts of the neighbouring island of Corsica and certain regions in North Africa.

Two main factors have contributed to Sardinia's diverse wildlife; its isolation and its variety of terrains, ranging from rugged mountains to wind-eroded plains.

Travel west from the millionaires' paradise known as the Costa Smeralda, with its secluded beaches, cliffs and caves, and you will find forests and vineyards surrounding the city of Sassari. The forests here are dominated by cork oak, for years a source of income. Head into the central hinterland and you will probably get lost in the infamously wild and hostile hills, mountains and plateaux of the Barbagia. Descend southwards from the Barbagia and you enter the fertile plain of the Campidano, at either end of which are lagoons and reservoirs. The plains are bordered by the geologically fascinating high inland cliffs and table-like plateaux.

The island's habitat can be broken down into the following categories: coastal lagoons and wetlands, including some of the island's, and indeed Europe's, most important wildlife parks; *màcchia* (scrubland); plains and plateaux; coasts and beaches; mountains and woodland/forest; and finally, caves.

A purple gallinule, one of many species that attract birdwatchers to Sardinia.

COASTAL LAGOONS AND WETLANDS

Sardinia enjoys a reputation for having some of the most sublime beaches in Europe, typically featuring powdery white sands and limpid waters framed by dramatic rock formations. At key points the coastline also features lagoons, reservoirs and marshes, some of them spread over vast expanses. The most notable of these are the *stagni* (lagoons) of Cagliari.

It was the Phoenicians who initiated the industry of drawing salt from the marshes east of Cagliari about 10,000 years ago. The name of these marshes originates from *sumolenti* ("little donkey"), the reference being to the donkeys on whose backs the sacks of salt were carried.

Cagliari (and its sister town Quartu Sant'Elena) expanded around the waterlands.

The largest of the lagoons is Santa Gilla, west of Cagliari. This stretches over 4,000 hectares (9,800 acres) and incorporates the salt flats of Macchiareddu – the only area of active salt production remaining today. The land that at one time supported salt flats has been transformed into nature reserves.

These reserves are inhabited by an incredible 200 species of birds, that is, one-third of the number of species found in Europe. The bird population of Cagliari's reserves is estimated to be in excess of 100,000. This figure can be attributed to the fact that the sea-feeding bird population is attracted to the *stagni* by the abundance of shrimps *(Artemia salina)* that thrive in these waters. Some of the most noteworthy species are: avocets, black-winged stilts, cormorants, pintail ducks, teals and purple gallinule *(Porphyrio porphyrio)*. Purple gallinule are also often seen around freshwater irrigation canals rich in vegetation near the towns of Oristano and Cabras.

Flamingos can now be observed year-round in Sardinia.

⊘ IL FENICOTTERO ROSA – THE PINK FLAMINGO

Pink flamingos *(Phoenicopterus ruber roseus)* are one of a number of once-migratory birds that have settled permanently in Sardinia, and can be observed all year round, nesting and breeding in the lagoons. In a fascinating evolutionary development, they are no longer instinctively drawn to continue their seasonal passage between North Africa and Southern Europe.

The flamingo population, which now totals more than 4,000, sprung from an original colony of 1,000. The first arrivals nested in the Molentargius marshes of Cagliari in the spring of 1993, having flown from the winter-feeding grounds of the Camargue in France. These birds are a delight to observe, especially as they are easily accessible at relatively close quarters, and have become an attraction which draws birdwatchers from all over the world.

Of the other lagoons, the Stagno di Sale Porcus in the centre of the Sinis peninsula (in Oristano province) was so named because in the past the lagoon incorporated a small salt flat from which salt was extracted to conserve pork meat. Now a wildlife area protected by the Italian League for the Protection of Birds (LIPU), it is home to 10,000 pink flamingos, thousands of cranes, wild geese, cormorants and mallards. There is even a small museum dedicated to the pink flamingo: the Museo del Fenicottero.

SCRUBLAND AND *MÀCCHIA*

Rising inland beyond the beaches and cliffs of Sardinia's coastline, the terrain consists of rocky slopes overrun by coarse scrub, that is, species of bushes resistant to strong sunlight and able to survive with little rainfall and poor soil. This scrubland, or *màcchia mediterranea* (Mediterranean maquis), flourishes in Sardinia where once there were forests. Centuries ago Sardinia was renowned for the wood gleaned from its extensive forests. But invaders and colonists, not least the ancient Romans, ransacked the forests to the point of depletion.

The denuded land gave way to erosion and a terrain insufficiently fertile for natural reforestation. In place of the once abundant trees the maquis flourished. Still today, when fires ravage the remaining forests – a regular occurrence every year – the maquis springs up. The maquis is itself vulnerable to wildfires, thus presenting the authorities with a constant hazard.

Typically the *màcchia* consists of a tangled, heavily scented and richly colourful array of plants including juniper, lentisk, myrtle and the strawberry tree *(arbutus)*, or *corbezzolo* in Italian. Rosemary, heather, yellow-flowering broom and gorse, and both the pink- and white-flowered varieties of the cistus are all common.

From the SS 125 main road, also known as the *Orientale sarda*, a three-hour walk down the Codula di Luna, from Teletotem near the Supramonte to the sea, takes you to Cala Luna. This is one of the island's most beautiful and secluded beaches. The path describes a deep valley that follows the river bed, passing through aromatic maquis scrub. The surrounding land is dotted with shepherds' huts and entrances to caves.

The vegetation in the Codula di Luna valley, one of the island's wildest canyons, is quite beautiful; the oleander amid the thick Mediterranean maquis is particularly colourful. In summer, the song of the "gru-gru" bee-eaters can be heard throughout the day and the night. In the Sinis peninsula, on the coast between San Giovanni di Sinis and Punta Is Arutas, are more than 100 hectares (250 acres) of sandy coast with dunes covered by vegetation punctuated by cliffs and caves.

Behind the sandy dunes grows a thick Mediterranean scrub with rosemary, dwarf palm and even an Aleppo pine wood. Declared a nature reserve in 1981, this parkland is inhabited by numerous species of birds, such as the peregrine falcon and kestrel, that nest in the cliffs, and the rare Sardinian partridge.

> *The purple gallinule (swamp hen) was once hunted to the verge of extinction until it became legally protected. It is now fairly common in Sardinia.*

Pedra Mennalza, a volcanic outcrop in the province of Sassari.

THE PLATEAUX

The steeply inclining areas known as the *giare* comprise large, dark basalt plateaux formed by the lava that flowed from violent volcanic eruptions. The *giare* now appear as unique tablelands, utterly flat and supported by sheer walls of dark basalt.

The *giare* of Siddi, Serri, and especially the *giara* of Gesturi, are particularly noteworthy. They are 16km (10 miles) long and up to 6km (4 miles) wide. A stretch of cork forest, where the trees are all blown by the ever-present mistral wind, covers the plateau, with the exception of a few depressions called *pauli*. These *giare* are home to pony-sized horses called *achettas* that graze in fenced-off pastures.

COASTS AND BEACHES

Sardinia's coastline and beaches are among the Mediterranean's most beautiful. Clear waves lap shorelines whose small coves alternate with rocky ravines in which the sea changes colour from emerald green through light turquoise to a sparkling azure. The beaches are of fine golden sand; the cliffs have been smoothed and transformed into huge sculptures by the wind. The island's various coasts all have their own particular beauty. On the western corner of the province of Sassari, the Alghero features

The Roman town of Nora sits on a peninsula in the southwest of the island.

beaches and the limestone reef of Capo Caccia. La Pelosa beach, 2km (1 mile) from Stintino, the island's northwestern point, is one of Sardinia's loveliest beaches. White sand gradually descends into the sea, its colour giving the water some magnificent turquoise hues.

From here you can join an excursion to the Asinara island, once a prison and now a national park. Following some 100 years of isolation, Asinara remains a mysterious island that is home to 500 mouflons (wild sheep), wild boars, hares, weasels and white (albini) donkeys. Of the bird populations, there are coarse seagulls, crested cormorants, magpies and the Sardinian partridge. In the migrating season the royal seagull

stops here, too. The western coasts have long rocky tracts that lead north towards Bosa and Cuglieri. In the south, near the Sinis peninsula, Is Arutas beach features white quartz crystals that give the water its turquoise colour. The quartz at the nearby Mari Ermi beach is pink.

Further south, in the vicinity of Cagliari, there is the Costa Verde, and in particular Piscinas, a beach of high dunes perfumed by junipers. Here, where the mistral can be quite severe, the sand gives on to an immediately deep sea. Continuing south, Cala Domestica is a narrow fjord of transparent waters set between steeply rising rocks covered in thick Mediterranean maquis.

> With its high limestone cliff, its grottoes and isolated beaches, the Golfo di Orosei combines sheer beauty with drama. Clear waters in various shades of blue and green make it a favourite for boat trips.

Of the two sister islands you will find here, Sant'Antioco has a beautiful beach that is 18km (11 miles) long and 8km (5 miles) wide; San Pietro is the home of the falcon (*Falco eleonorae*) that nests among the rocks every summer. Today there are more than 100 of these magnificent predatory birds, named after Queen Eleonora d'Arborea who, in 1400, declared the island's falcons to be a protected species.

The southwestern coast has an uninterrupted series of beaches. Here natural shade is provided by the pine trees of Santa Margherita di Pula. These culminate in the stunning Chia beach, near the location of the Punic city of Bithia. The city of Bithia was founded around 720 BC at the foot of the Torre di Chia promontory. The ruins of the temple of Bes and the remains of the necropolis can be found here. Baia Chia is known as "the Pearl of the South", and features emerald-coloured water and pink granite sand, courtesy of dunes that reach heights of 65 metres (213ft) where the ancient gnarled junipers grow.

The eastern coast has its own beautiful and uncontaminated beaches: San Teodoro e Budoni, then Posada and Siniscola e Orosei, where the wildest terrain starts. The Gulf of Orosei at Cala

Gonone-Dorgali is interesting because one of Europe's last coastal forests grows here, right on the seafront.

Further south, the stretch of coastline between Muravera and Villasimius offers a number of delightful spots. These include the promontory of Capo Ferrato, the wild beach of Costa Rei and the fascinating inlet of Cala Sinzias. At Villasimius a very extensive and wide beach, Porto Giunco, almost gives the impression of being an African desert. The sandy shore of Capo Carbonara is so wide that one can relish the feeling of being absolutely alone. The whole region is characterised by a wild and weird natural environment. Small rocky islands here, such as Isola dei Cavoli and Isola di Serpentara, are populated by rabbits and seagulls.

Finally we reach Cagliari. The Poetto beach starts in the capital, and it is easy to reach from the city centre. The beach continues for 13km (8 miles) to Quartu St Elena, the island's third-biggest city. It is one of Sardinia's liveliest seaside stretches, from morning when families and young people meet for an hour's sun and swimming, to the evenings when the bars along the beach organise concerts, cabaret and cinema.

MOUNTAINS AND WOODLAND

Sardinia's 24,000 sq km (9,250 sq miles) are, the plain of the Campidano notwithstanding, made up largely of massifs. These were formed in the Palaeozoic age, and thus predate the Alps and the Apennines. The predominant rock is granite which, as a result of wind and other forms of erosion, has often come to resemble all sorts of things in people's imagination. Locals and tourists alike have spotted the bear, the tortoise, the elephant, the mushroom and the dinosaur among the rocks.

The deep, green woodlands, one of the most enchanting Sardinian features, form a heritage of great environmental value. The Gennargentu National Park (including a 25 sq km/10 sq mile forest that is one of the island's most beautiful), eight regional parks and several oases of flora and fauna form a network of protected areas measuring more than 59,102 hectares (146,000 acres). The mountainous landscape dominates the central part of the island. The highest point is Punta La Marmora on the Gennargentu massif, at 1,830 metres (6,000ft).

Serious trekkers can enjoy walks from the Supramonte di Oliena to the dense oak and chestnut forests along the old railway line near Belvi. The rough and inhospitable Supramonte is riddled with precipices and caves, many of them unexplored. It is covered by maquis, and springs gush from a myriad of underground watercourses. The Supramonte, which is really the heart of Sardinia, features one of the most spectacular gorges in Italy – Su Gorroppu, with walls 400 metres (1,300ft) high and the famous source of the Cologone.

Sand dunes on the Costa Verde, west coast.

⦿ PONIES AND PRICKLY PEARS

The mystery that shrouds the origins of Sardinia's wild ponies is obscured further by the isolation of the plateaux where they are found. It is widely believed that they are descendants of Arabian and Barb horses, with some Spanish equine blood thrown in.

The wild plateau is also home to the prickly-pear fig *(sa figu morisca)*. This cactus, probably introduced by Arabs, has for centuries marked the rural landscape, often demarcating the borders of landowners' territory while enriching the farms of the poor with lush fruit. The thorns mean it's best to buy the fruit rather than pick it.

The name Gennargentu derives from the Latin *janua argenti* (silver door), which refers to snow-capped peaks or the legend of silver in these mountains, according to whom you believe. This inaccessible area is well preserved and contains a 25 sq km (10 sq mile) ancient holm oak forest. Near Sassari the well-kept Foresta di Burgos features oak, cedar and chestnut trees.

The Natural Reserve of Monte Arcosu– Monte Latias is a World Wildlife Fund area that climbs 1,000 metres (3,200ft) from the sea. It includes an ancient, 3,600-hectare (8,900-acre) forest of

Rare peonies such as this one grow in the Montarbu forest.

holm oak and cork oak that is the largest green forest in the Mediterranean. Here live wildcats, Sardinian deer, hawks, kestrels, buzzards and golden eagles. Horse-riding tours, excursions and summer camps take place here.

The dark-coated Sardinian deer is the island's biggest wild mammal, though it is smaller than the mainland deer. Another difference from its larger cousin is that its mating season arrives a month earlier, around the middle of August. The Sardinian deer's favourite habitat is the thick maquis near the forest. It became almost extinct in the 1960s, when its numbers were reduced to 50 animals, but it survived with the help of WWF protection.

MOUNTAIN FOREST

The Sette Fratelli Mountain, named after the seven peaks that can be seen from Cagliari, is a gigantic granite massif with wild gorges, high cliffs and fast streams shaped over the centuries by the wind. The multifarious forms of terrain found here play a contributory role in the mountain's sense of mystery.

The mountain forest covers an area of 4,000 hectares (nearly 10,000 acres), making it one of the largest as well as one of the best-preserved sclerophyll (woody plants characterised by small, leathery, evergreen leaves) forests of the Mediterranean Basin. Replanted with pine, eucalyptus and cypress trees, the forest reaches an altitude of over 1,000 metres (3,300ft). It is one of the few remaining areas inhabited by the now almost extinct Sardinian deer.

Along the streams there is much interesting vegetation, including wild oleander, ferns, willows and alder trees. This used to be the location of royal eagle hunts and the habitat of the goshawk. The area also features the wood of Tuviois, near the Serpeddi Mount. In the torrents lives the amphibious urodele the tritone sardo *(Euproetus platycephalus)*. Among the reptiles there is the rare lizard of Bedriaga, present only in the north of Sardinia, and the del Cetti snake. The real symbol of the area is the Sardinian deer, of which there are at least 700. Another distinctive animal, now protected against the threat of extinction to the extent that it thrives all over the island, is the mouflon.

The Montarbu forest in the middle of the island is particularly rich in plant species: in addition to the holm oak, you can find yews, holly, strawberry trees, phyllireas, hawthorns, alders and the rare peony, which is also known as the "rose of Gennargentu".

CAVES

Hidden in the mountainous landscape above the town of Ulassai, amid rocky outcrops and deep ravines, is the cave of Su Marmuri, one of the most impressive caves in Europe. It has huge 50-metre (165ft) high ceilings and imposing, natural limestone towers whose white peaks stand out among the dark green vegetation.

To the south of Dorgali, the Grotta del Bue Marino is named after the now-vanished monk seal, which has lost all but a few of its Western Mediterranean habitats, where it dives to depths of almost 20 metres (65ft) in its quest for fish and octopus. Also in the Dorgali area is the impressive cave of Ispinigoli. Here one can admire a 38-metre (125ft) high stalagmite and, at the rear, the Abyss of the Virgin chasm, where human sacrifices were made in prehistoric times. Along the Codula di Luna river is the entrance to one of the island's biggest and most extensive caves, the Su Palu, which was discovered in 1980.

In the Capo Caccia area the caves include the Grotta di Nettuno, which has 2km (1 mile) of chambers and small lakes and can be reached by hired boat. Other caves in the area that are worth exploring are the Grotta Verde and the Grotta dei Ricami. The former is so called due to the moss which covers its stalactites and stalagmites. There is a small lake where examples of ancient "graffiti" have been discovered.

Fonni, one of the highest towns in Sardinia, nestles on a wintry Mount Spada in the Barbagia.

⦿ GORGEOUS BEACHES AND RED ROCKS

Among the many delightful spots on the Golfo di Orosei is the stunning beach of Cala Luna, with six enormous caves and an oleander wood, especially impressive in summer and early autumn when the trees are in bloom.

The combination of amazing rocky landscapes and the clear transparency of the Tyrrhenian Sea is compelling: sheer cliffs rise from the sea, wooded slopes are inhabited by an interesting array of wildlife, and enchanting beaches can be found in such spectacular bays as Cala Sisine, Cala Biriola, Cala Marioulu and Cala Coloritzè. The entire gulf is part of the Gennargentu national park, which was created in order to safeguard the flora and fauna of this part of Sardinia. One of the region's most picturesque stretches is around Arbatax, which is dominated by the maquis-covered Capo Bellavista.

Much of the island's coast is formed by dark granite or limestone, but the rocks of Arbatax (whose name exemplifies the Arabic influence in Sardinia) are an exception. Composed of red granite porphyry, the rocks' astonishing rosy colours flare up when reflecting the slanting rays of the sun. From this point the topography changes somewhat. The terrain is dotted with wild oleaster, the *oleastru* after which the Ogliastra region is named.

📷 SARDINIAN WILDLIFE

Sardinia's island ecology has given rise to some unique species of wildlife, which are now protected in popular reserves and national parks.

In recent years marine and wildlife reserves have been set up to protect Sardinia's unique habitats. Being on the migration route for birds between Africa and Europe, the island is particularly rich in birdlife. The best time to see some of the 170 species of birds identified here is between August and March, which is also when the flamingos arrive.

Flamingos and other migratory birds can also be seen at the Sale Porcus Reserve on the Sinis peninsula, while the best place to spot Eleonora's falcon is on the island of San Pietro. Other habitats for rare animals include the sand dunes at Piscinas, where loggerhead turtles come to lay their eggs. The shy and rare Sardinian deer is often glimpsed on the slopes of Arcosu in the Sulcis region and in the Gennargentu national park on the east coast.

Marine life is best observed in the clean, warm waters of one of Sardinia's marine reserves, including Tavolara. Dive trips go to the islands and to the coasts of Asinara and Gallura and the Golfo di Orosei. Dolphins can be spotted off the Maddalena archipelago and many bird species can be seen on the Golfo di Orosei.

Cinghiali (wild boar) can be found all over the island but favour woodland areas.

The Sardinian tree frog, or Tyrrhenian tree frog (Hyla sarda), is found in Corsica, Sardinia and the Tuscan Archipelago.

Fallow deer (Dama dama), seen here in Oglistra, prefer shrub areas and open woodland.

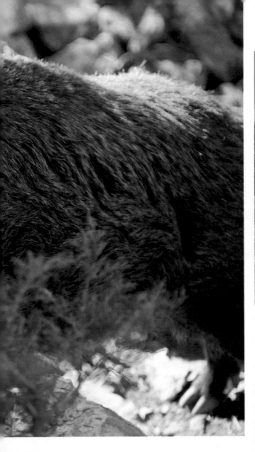

Trees growing on a mountain in the Gennargentu national park.

The Gennargentu National Park

The Gennargentu national park in the province of Nuoro covers 59,100 hectares (146,000 acres) and includes Punta La Marmora, the island's highest peak, and the prehistoric village of Tiscali. In the valleys and lower mountain slopes are holm oak forests. Further up, maple and bay oak trees can be found, with clusters of juniper, holly and yew trees towards the summit. On the mountain tops are plum trees and Corsican junipers. At springtime peonies flower, and in summer oleanders carpet even the most barren of places. Mouflon, marten, wild boar and foxes inhabit the mountains in large numbers. In the woods are wildcats, hares, partridges, sparrow hawks and goshawks, while buzzards and kestrels hunt in stretches of open space. The rare monk seal may have disappeared from the park's coastline, but you can still spot the Corsican seagull and Eleonora's falcon.

The ocellated skink (Chalcides ocellatus) inhabits coastal areas in particular.

Pink flamingos winter in the lagoons of Cagliari and Oristano during their migration to Africa. A small colony of birds now nest in Sardinia permanently.

On the island of San Pietro, colonies of the rare Eleonora's falcon can be seen.

Traditional costume: wooden mask and sheepskin of the Mamuthones of Barbagia.

FESTIVALS, FOLKLORE AND MUSIC

Sardinians are especially proud of their music, folk roots and festivals. These are celebrated and preserved island-wide by all generations.

At the end of the 18th century, Sardinia was known as an *India de por acá*, an "India in the midst of the Western World". And thus, strictly speaking, it was to remain, at least until the end of World War I, an exotic culture about which virtually nothing was known, even by the few visitors whose spirit of adventure drove them to explore the island. Sardinia fitted into no specific category except perhaps that of "living antiquity", a place in which time had stopped dead.

> *Grazia Deladda, born 1871 in Nuoro, rejected the traditional role of women in Sardinian society and wrote many books in an earthy, realist style about the island and its people.*

EARLY VISITORS

It wasn't until D.H. Lawrence visited the island in 1921 with his wife and wrote *Sea and Sardinia* that it was brought to the attention of the English-reading world. Many, including the novelist and critic Anthony Burgess, have felt that Lawrence managed in six days what others had failed to do in years: "A single week's visit was enough for him to extract the very essence of the island and its people." But Lawrence's conclusions were in part grounded in the inscrutability of the island and islanders that had confounded others. "Lost between Europe and Africa and belonging to nowhere... as if it never really had a fate. No fate. Left outside of time and history," he pronounced.

The geographic and cultural character of the island, noted by Lawrence, has not lost its poignancy some 80 years later. The interior of Sardinia, with its harsh, sun-drenched terrains reminiscent

A musician plays a launeddas, a type of flute found only in Sardinia.

of North Africa, still presents an aspect of inhospitability. The lives of its inhabitants have for centuries been marked by drudgery and privation.

In addition, a diffidence towards visitors from outside these tight-knit communities completes this picture. However, do not be mistaken: this is Europe, and a region of one of the world's richest, most industrialised nations. Yet, even so, a haunting paradox as to Sardinia's fate and destiny persists. Sardinians jealously guard the autonomous nature and character of their culture, while remaining, on the whole, committed Italians.

Sardinia is, after all, both geographically and culturally separate from mainland Italy. And Sardo is a distinct and recognised language, as opposed to one of Italy's myriad of dialects. It is not surprising, therefore, that you may still hear mainland Italy referred to by Sardinians as *il continente*.

FOLK ROOTS

Traditional folklore and culture, tied as it is in Sardinia to the land and agriculture, is under threat of disappearing, as elsewhere in the developed world. What remains will inevitably lose something of its authentic value, being a celebration of the past, rather than the rituals and festivities that express the average Sardinian's real-life activities and way of living. That said, as an expression of regional pride modern generations of Sardinians (often now part of the modern urban population) have striven to keep the historic traditions of past generations alive and to preserve distinctive characteristics of the indigenous culture.

Genuine folklore and its essential links with the island's traditions are a colourful and complex aspect of the Sardinian national heritage. They are, however, all related to each other, as well as being inextricably interwoven with both the civilisation and the legal, economic and social struc-

Mosaic depicting shepherd life in Dorgali.

⊘ INSPIRING ARTISTS

Writers such as Sebastiano Satta, Nobel Prize-winner Grazia Deledda and Giuseppe Dessì all wrote about their native land, while artists like Antonio Ballero, Giuseppe Biasi and Filippo Figari painted it. The 19th and 20th centuries were characterised by an exceptional degree of artistic creativity for the island. Alan Ross, in *Bandit on the Billiard Table – a Journey through Sardinia*, said of Deledda's novels: "They are local in the best sense, touching off on almost every page illuminating truths about the Nuorese peasantry, their customs, ideas, ways of feeling... [They] are the best substitute for Sardinian landscape painting."

tures of the country. It would thus be wrong simply to dismiss Sardinian folklore as a mere cultural phenomenon, which developed among the lower social classes of the community and is of concern only to them.

To a much greater extent than in many other societies, the roots of Sardinia's cultural heritage lie in both folk culture and the customs of the so-called upper classes. Modern research has confirmed that all strata of society proudly see the cultural heritage as their common inheritance.

This is reflected in Sardinia's writers and artists. No other folkloric tradition has been so lovingly immortalised by the literature and art of its own area, whilst at the same time exerting such a profound influence on its native artists.

THE SHEPHERD'S ROLE

All classes of society see the shepherd as a symbol of their cultural heritage. The historian Manlio Brigaglia makes an interesting observation in this respect. He reports that, shortly after World War I, the artist Mario Delitala had suggested that the Sardinian coat of arms should be changed. He proposed that the four blindfolded Moors, dating from the time when Sardinia was ruled by the house of Aragon, should be replaced by motifs representing the island's "four traditional occupations" – a shepherd, a

THE LAND OF POETRY

One typical characteristic of Sardinian folklore is its penchant for pointed remarks. It would be no exaggeration to claim that language is the second, secret master of the island. From everyday encounters to special occasions, every event is accompanied, underlined and explained by a verbal commentary. Few peoples possess such a broad palette of set phrases and such an extensive and colourful vocabulary as the Sardinians. Significantly enough, another Sardinian expression

Folkloric band in traditional costume.

farmer, a mountain-dweller and a fisherman. The idea found little support on the island and a consensus was not found for the change. So the "imported" coat of arms remained, while the figure of the shepherd is seen as being truly symbolic of Sardinia.

Intriguingly, as the figures of the Moors are blindfolded, it contrasts with one of the island's best-known local proverbs originating from the shepherd communities: *Furat chi benit dae su mare* (He who comes from across the sea is a thief). Historically there is some justification for this attitude. Through the centuries Sardinia has been occupied (at times in total, at others in part) by a series of foreign invaders who have exploited its natural resources.

⊘ THE LAMENT FOR THE DEAD

The lament for the dead, the *attitidu*, is often unmistakably aggressive in tone. Usually the chant of the *attitadoras* (the wailing women who perform a similar function to the *voceratrici* of Corsica, but who in Sardinia are usually related to the deceased) is a tribute, complimenting the virtues of the deceased and their ancestors and imagining the deeds they would have accomplished had death not snatched them away. In some villages, like Samugheo, *attitadoras* still practise "waking the dead", mourning all night beside the body, singing dirges, surrounded by the family, even tearing their own hair out and scratching their faces.

describes the island as being the *Terra di Poesia* (The Land of Poetry).

It is unsurprising, then, that folkloric poetry, existing in a wide variety of genres, is such a vital

Pier Paolo Pasolini (1922–75) to describe them as a "female" lyric form of poetry which he said "knows neither brute force nor Orgosolo".

REVENGE

In Sardinia, when someone dies and was the victim of a vendetta, the job of the *attitadoras* (wailing women) is to stir up feelings of hatred and vengeance (*attizzare*, to stir up/to fan, may well explain the origins of the word). J.W.W. Tyndale, a 19th-century traveller in Sardinia, noted how "the feelings of the relatives are

> *Respected 20th-century Sardinian artists Mario Delitala, Stanis Dessy and Carmelo Floris have all painted symbolic representations of the ballu tundu.*

Performing the ballu tundu.

part of the island's culture. A rigid metricity is particularly noticeable, even in simple incantations, curses, excommunications and *berbos* (teasing rhymes), in *ninnias* (lullabies), *attitidus* (lamentations for the dead) or *Gosos* (eulogies of the saints). It extends to elaborate forms of love poetry such as the *mutos*, the miniature variations of which are called *muttettus* or *battorinas*. The rhythmical pattern of the *mutu* resembles that of the *strambotti* and *stornelli* of Tuscany (short traditional love songs written in the 17th century). It consists of two parts: the *isterria* (exposition) and the *torrada* (response). The finest *mutos* possess "a note of fantasy"; they resound with "poetic intelligence", an expression of "a higher plane and great sensitivity" which moved Italian film director

appealed to with the utmost earnestness by the Prefiche, who enumerate the murdered members of each family, recapitulate the wrongs and injuries, appeal to God, honour, and duty, and use every argument for revenge". As long ago as the mid-19th century the government was trying to prohibit these emotional incitements to avenge the death of a loved one, but the ceremony of the *attitidu*, which forms part of the *sarja* (wake), continues to be practised, particularly in some of the more remote regions of the Barbagia. Nonetheless, persistent pressure by the Church has resulted in the reluctant abandoning of the most violent curses in favour of a "quieter, more sorrowful, almost liturgical" lamentation (Gino Bottiglioni).

Max Leopold Wagner saw the *mutu* as an expression of the Sardinian tendency to melancholy, which assumes concrete form in the "grim solemnity" of the nuraghi, the ancient towers dating from the 2nd millennium BC that are dotted all over the island. Not every visitor, however, is of the opinion that the Sardinians are a melancholy people – although it is a trait which somehow seems in keeping with the rugged desolation of much of the countryside. Some observers maintain that the islanders are fundamentally a cheerful and outgoing

it is the proverbial *ghigno Sardonico* – a sardonic, spiteful laughter which is neither amusing nor an expression of joie de vivre.

Their tragedy, some maintain, is expressed by the scary masks of the *Mamuthones* and those of their companions, the *Issocadores*, both of which can be seen in the village of Mamoiada in the Barbagia, the heart of traditional Sardinia. (In Ottana and other villages in the same region the carnival processions are mostly dominated by the presence of *Boes or Merdùles*, wearing masks based on an ox's head.)

A political mural in Nuoro.

race. Many would say both attitudes are correct, for the soul of the typical Sardinian – who celebrates with such gusto, who is so full of vitality and who organises horse shows and poetry competitions between the shrewdest *improvisatori* – is remarkably contradictory.

In a work which is in essence an essay on the nature of the Sardinian, published under the meaningful title *Miele Amaro* (Bitter Honey), the writer Salvatore Cambosu maintains that the Sardinians do indeed enjoy festivals, but only because such celebrations act as an anaesthetic, numbing the painful consciousness of their tragic existence – and not because they regard them as a means of amusement. If a Sardinian actually laughs, then more often than not

The wild, cumbersome *Mamuthones* (who also wear sheep fleeces and huge bells on their backs), according to anthropologists, are caught by the *laccio or soca* (lasso) of the nimble, mocking *Issohadores*, who are nothing less than images of the island's countless foreign conquerors. Francesco Masala, one of the principal writers of Sardinia's so-called *Ideology of the Vanquished*, believes this to be the case.

THE *BALLU TUNDU*

Another remarkable manifestation of the contradictory combination of sadness and mirth is the *ballu*, the dance – a traditional form of expression held in high esteem by the Sardinians and still popular on high days and holidays.

Though similar to the national dances of Greece and Romania, the Sardinian version is usually executed more solemnly.

Traditionally, only men and women who were betrothed or married were allowed to link fingers or touch palms – though J.W.W. Tyndale noticed that this rule was not respected in the village of Osidda in the province of Nuoro, where "whether by uniform usage, or by a peculiar dispensation from the patron saint of the day, the greater part danced with their hands round waists".

A couple marry in traditional Sardinian dress.

Although tourism has popularised Sardinia's festivals, there is no better way of gaining an insight into the character and moods of the island than by taking part in one.

Here, too, the observations of travellers and researchers are in blatant contradiction with each other. It is perhaps interesting to note that the comments of the "Interpreters" of Sardinia, to adopt the phrase coined by the cultural anthropologist Alberto M. Cirese, fall into two distinct categories: calumny or eulogy. Some writers – like Baldessare Luciano – regarded the *ballu tundu*, the

"national dance" of Sardinia, as lascivious; others, such as Pater Bresciani, insisted that it was on the contrary dignified, serious and solemn, despite the occasional interludes of frivolity. Recently the semiologist Leonardo Sole drew attention to what he called the significant "mythical silence" which still surrounds the *ballu tundu*, and which bears a certain resemblance to a "sacred chorus". Ethnographer Francesco Alziator, who has made a study of the age of the *ballu tundu*, wrote: "Two basic features of this round dance support the theory that it is very ancient: firstly the *launeddas* [flutes], which traditionally accompany the dance throughout almost a quarter of the island, and secondly the association of the dance with fire. For in the olden days there was almost always a fire in the centre of the circle of dancers." It is easy enough to imagine the scene; all one needs to do is to study the paintings by Mario Delitala, Stanis Dessy, Carmelo Floris or one of the other 20th-century Sardinian artists. All the painters mentioned have frequently found inspiration in the symbolic representation of the *ballu tundu*.

The art historian Carlo Aru has discovered what may be the earliest portrayal of the Sardinian *ballu tundu* in an interesting painting that hangs in the medieval chapel of San Pietro di Zuri, which was built in 1291 by Anselmo da Como (the ruins of the adjoining historic village are now completely submerged beneath a reservoir). Aru remarks that "On the outermost right-hand pillar, on the apse side, is a painting of people dancing: tiny figures holding hands; on their heads they are wearing the *berretta* [the traditional beret of Sardinia]".

The *launeddas*, the musical instruments which provide the accompaniment for the *ballu tundu*, are thought to be very ancient indeed, possibly dating from as long ago as the time of the Nuragi. They are a type of flute, but quite unique, occurring only on Sardinia.

MUSIC AND CULTURE

In a detailed study of the *launedda*, distinguished ethno-musicologists Giulio Fara and Gavino Gabriel speculate that this "triple-piped" instrument, which looks like a bagpipe without the sound bladder, might in fact be closely related to the shepherd's flute with pipes of varying length which is described by Virgil.

Tyndale worried that the "great exertion required to blow the *launedda* has considerable effect upon the health of the musicians, who frequently play for hours together". In his remarkable summary of the island's cultural heritage, a work which has assumed the form of an ethnographic stream of consciousness, Salvatore Cambosu attributes more sinister qualities to the sound of the *launedda* than the amiable Tyndale does, defining it as an existential metaphor for a "historic illness".

All of a sudden we see again before us the terrifying, grim expression of the Sardinian with the evil eye, whose character has supposedly left its ugly mark so irrevocably on the island's history. During the 20th century the cohesive strength of Sardinian culture – which is so introverted that it has earned the nicknames "Culture of Stone" and "Culture of Loneliness" – has suffered a damaging blow which threatens to destroy utterly an entire folkloric tradition.

This transformation has happened within the framework of changes that have taken place in Sardinia this century, and is, according to the ethnologist Giulio Angioni, the result of two "conspicuous historic turning points"

Flower-bedecked carts called traccas take pride of place in the festival of Saint Efisio in early May.

⊘ FESTIVAL HIGHLIGHTS

Carnevale in Sardinia is marked with ghoulish parades and high jinks, many of which date back to pagan times. In Mamoiada and Ottana, in the Barbagia, there are masked parades while at Oristano *(Sa Sartiglia)* and Sant Lussugiu *(Sa Carrela è Nanti)* masked horsemen pound the old lanes.

Cavalcata Sarda (penultimate Sunday of May) in Sassari involves processions, colourful costumes and spectacular horse-racing.

Ardia (6 and 7 July) in Sedilo: dynamic bareback horseriders pursue a man representing San Constantino to a dry fountain whereupon much Vernaccia wine is consumed.

Candelieri, the Festival of Candles, in Sassari in mid-August: gigantic wooden candles are carried through the town in an ornate procession, which originated in the 13th century.

Corsa degli Scalzi: a bizarre barefoot race of white tunic-wearing young men carrying an effigy of Cabras's saint through the streets to the sanctuary of San Salvatore.

Madonna dello Schiavo (15 November) in Carloforte: a procession of a carved, wooden statue of the Madonna Nera, the Black Madonna – symbol of its Genoese inhabitants' miraculous journey to San Pietro from the island of Tabarka in the Bay of Tunis, and escape from enslavement.

on Sardinia: the abolition of the feudal system at the beginning of the 19th century and the monopolisation of cheese production by the large cheese-making companies on the Italian mainland during the last century. These two events challenged the basis of island society and its foundation in the pastoral culture. In an alarming, tangible way cork and plastic – the incompatible symbols of two extremely different cultures – simultaneously determined everyday life and manufacturing techniques on the island in the 1960s.

Cow bells of the Mamuthones of Mamoiada.

⊘ FESTA DI SANT'EFISIO

The island's most famous festival, dating from 1656, is that of Sant'Efisio, the martyr and patron saint of Cagliari. On 1 May, in a grandiose procession, his statue is borne high on an ox cart from the capital to Pula, the place where he was executed. Local residents in traditional costume join his train, which is accompanied by the music of *launeddas*. The festival is an annual highlight in the lives of many of Cagliari's citizens. Sardinia's festivals are like many of the islanders themselves – frequently sombre, rarely to be taken lightly. They are fiercely Christian, but often their traditions make reference to pagan roots.

SARDINIA'S FESTIVALS

Nowadays, Sardinia's great folkloric traditions are virtually restricted to the most important religious *sagre* (folk festivals), such as the processions of the *Redentore* (Saviour) in Nuoro in August, the *Candelieri* (Festival of Candles) in Sassari in August and *Sant'Efisio* (the biggest festival on the entire island, held in Cagliari each May), or the principal feudal tournaments such as the *Sa Sartiglia*, which takes place every spring in Oristano.

These are festivals in which sacred and profane elements coexist. Tourism may have commercialised the festivals, but their effect is still powerful. Nostalgic, religious and full of contradictions, they provide an ideal starting point for an exploration of the Sardinian soul. It is remarkable how so varied a people celebrate so much within such a small area. The diverse characters of the inhabitants match the marked contrasts between the coastal region and the interior.

What the descendants of settlers on the island of Sant'Antioco, who arrived from North Africa many centuries ago, have in common with those of long-established residents in Alghero, whose first language is Catalan, is that both communities cling to their own traditions, and not only in the food they eat – from couscous to lobster Catalane.

In the Easter ceremonies, the *confraternitate*, the brotherhoods, dressed in hoods and robes, file solemnly through town streets, giving an impression of deep piety and penitence, but the accompanying torch processions and bonfires date from pre-Christian times.

MACHO FESTIVALS

Another Sardinian characteristic, the strong element of *machismo*, can be observed in the *matanza*, the catching of the tuna in early summer when shoals of the fish migrate east. The fishermen begin their elaborate preparations for the bloody massacre weeks beforehand; their mood is one of anticipation and intense excitement. And in the equestrian festival of San Costantino, which takes place in Sedilo in July, religiosity and male pride combine. Many a rider has paid with his life for taking part in the wild horseback entry into the pilgrimage church, but there has never been a shortage of volunteers.

TRADITIONAL ARTS AND CRAFTWORK

Whether found in books, on the streets or in the home, the artistry of Sardinia represents cultural traditions passed down orally through the generations.

Authentic Sardinian crafts may have developed in conditions of poverty, isolation and oppression, but they also represent ingenuity, skill, pride and dignity. On an island that has long been a world of its own, shepherds and farmers, miners and craftsmen had to develop their own creativity. Thus from necessity they learnt how to give expression to beautiful forms, depending on local raw materials.

One of the oldest Sardinian crafts is terracotta production, alive since prehistoric times. At the turn of 20th century practical *strexiaus* (craftsmen who made domestic ceramic items) started making artistic pieces, coloured by an application of the essence of fresh rockrose leaves.

WEAVERS, CARVERS, GOLDSMITHS...

The island's rushes, asphodel, reeds, willow, myrtle, lentisk, straw and raffia have all been used to create baskets, hampers and mats. At Castelsardo in Via Marconi is the Museo dell'Intreccio Mediterraneo (Museum of Basket Weaving; see page 144).

Gold and silver were the driving force behind the flourishing production of amulets, talismans and necklaces. Goldsmiths prospered in Sardinia in the 14th century, through the production of religious objects. Examples include buttons shaped like breasts, earrings, necklaces and brooches studded with gems, pearl and coral. Alghero is particularly famous for coral and jewels.

The stiff, coarse wool of the island's sheep provides the raw material in the manufacture of carpets, wall hangings and furnishings. This craft also produces refined embroideries and lace. Motifs range from ornate geometrical patterns to designs from Byzantine art to the Baroque. Embroidered shawls with long fringes, adorned with colourful flower motifs and embellished with gems, are made in Oliena and often seen on festival days.

Barbagia-style woodcarving gives us richly carved wedding chests – usually made of dark chestnut – with animal, bird, flower and abstract symbols. Leather handicrafts – harnesses and

Traditional decorations and lace in Nuoro's Ethnographic Museum.

horse saddles, belts, handbags, clothing, cushions and decorative objects – are often embroidered with linen or silk thread folk motifs.

METALWORK

Sardinian knives – including the famous leppas with their sharp blade and shaft of ram or mouflon horn – are made in Pattada. Other ironwork includes railings, sculptures, lamp and light fixtures and furniture. Sardinian wrought iron, with its magical designs, recall the arabesques of the Near East and Toledo in Spain, and primitive early history.

COSTUME AND JEWELLERY

The wearing of traditional costume and jewellery is still very much an integral part of the island's festivals and feast days.

At festival time in Sardinia the streets of the villages and towns become ablaze with men and women wearing brightly coloured traditional costumes. Sardinians are big festival-goers; in the past, high days and feast days were an opportunity to meet people from other villages and mark important occasions. In this closed island society costume and jewellery were not only indicators of where you came from but of social standing and wealth. Regional variations in costume are still apparent today, and are worn with pride by village members. In general, traditional dress for women consists of red waistcoats edged with gold filigree work, and worn over white blouses with lace cuffs and collars, decorated with an elaborate brooch. Full-length layered dresses of white, black and red are usual, and a black or white embroidered headscarf is often worn. The costumes are decorated with lots of accessories. Traditional costume for men is simpler but still very colourful, consisting of a red waistcoat, white shirt, red neckerchief and a black beret called a *berreta*. All this can be seen at Nuoro's ethnographic museum (see page 215).

The Mamuthones of Mamoida wear scary masks carved wood in a festival thought to date back to pagan times.

Many of Sardinia's traditional costumes feature fine embroidery and petit-point, as this superb tunic and headdress from Desulo illustrate.

Traditionally, Sardinian women cover their head with an elaborately embroidered shawl, the result of years of work.

Festival jewellery includes su giunchigliu necklaces and filigree sos breves (silver cases) pinned to clothing containing images, prayers and magic spells.

Traditional Jewellery

Sardinian *prendas* (jewellery) is intrinsically linked to traditional costume. Made of gold, silver or fine filigree, it is handed down through the generations and reflects life, fertility and love. The quality and amount of jewellery is an important indication of social status. Worn on a dress or waistcoat, buttons have a small cylinder inlaid with a semi-precious stone at their centre. Necklaces come in two types: *su giunchigliu*, a long gold chain wrapped several times around the neck, or *su ghettau*, which has links adorned with large filigree balls. Precious stones are worn from a dark velvet choker. *Maninfide* rings, featuring two clasped hands, are given by a fiancé to his intended. The most distinctive design for brooches is the *sinnai*, a large ruby or cameo set in a sunflower design. Typical feast-day earrings are bow-shaped with a pendant, or are butterfly-shaped and made of gold leaf. Earrings with figures of a bird and joined by two cones or pyramids are also worn, as are earrings in the shape of bunches of grapes.

arved sheep's mask and traditional costume for the
ttana festival at Santa Teresa di Gallura.

ardinia is arguably the most culturally distinct region of
aly, as shown by its folk dancing, costumes and musical
raditions.

Couple dressed in traditional regional costume.

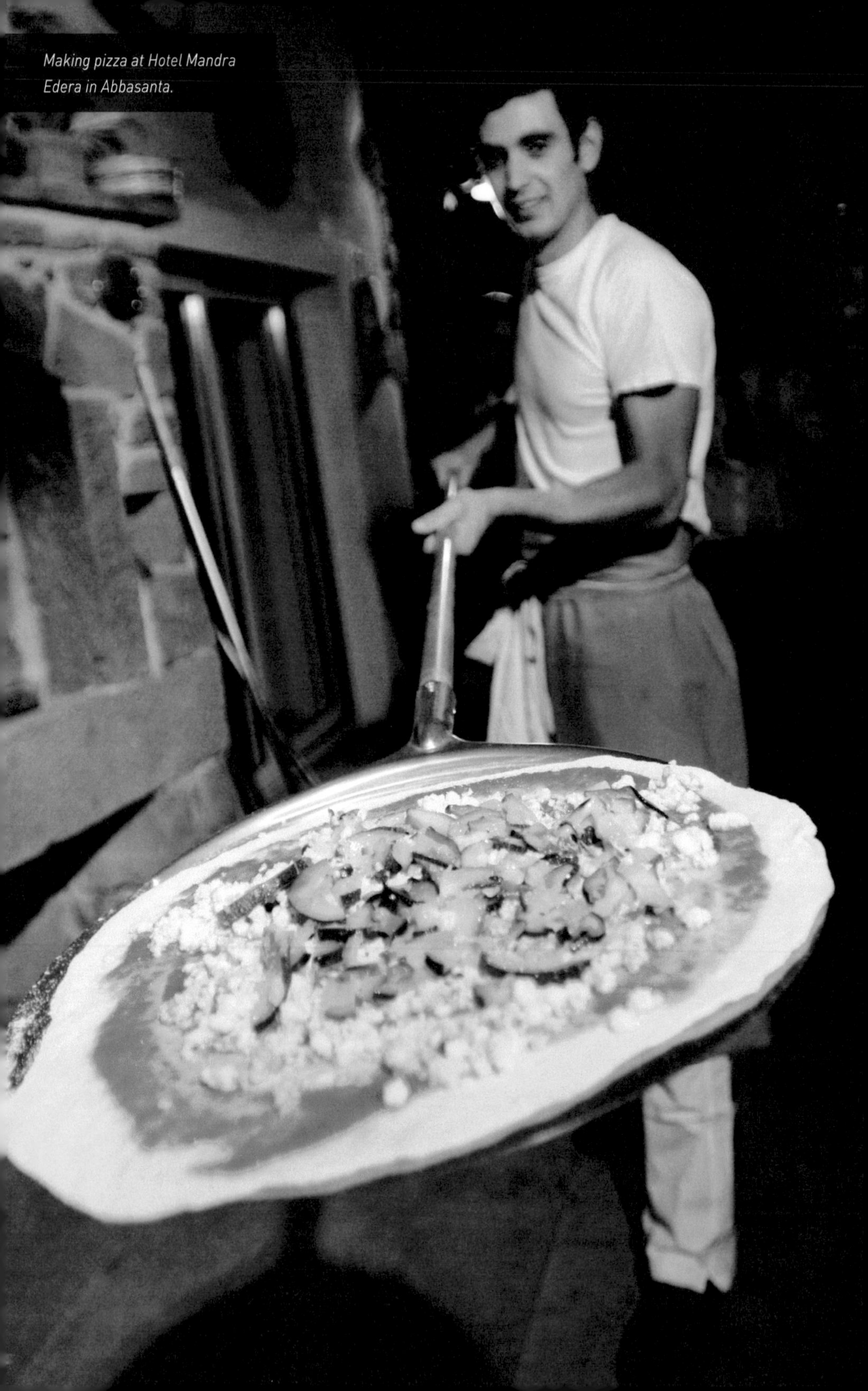

Making pizza at Hotel Mandra Edera in Abbasanta.

FOOD AND DRINK

Eating and drinking in Sardinia is a real treat. The food is simple, good value and gutsy, while the wines are some of the best produced anywhere.

Sardinian cooking comes from an agripastoral past, poor and simple. It is the cooking of shepherds and farmers who have never been rich but have made their simple dishes tastier by the use of aromatic herbs offered by the earth. An ancient inscription in the Grotta della Vipera in Cagliari mentions the use of saffron, the violet stigma of the crocus flower, in cooking. Other common aromatic herbs include myrtle, rosemary, wild thyme and mint.

> The name for sardines is thought to have come from the young pilchards caught off the coast of Sardinia, and which were one of the first fish to be packed in oil.

Sardinian cooking may be peasant in origin but it has flavour, intelligence, versatility and an exotic nature. Some recipes are still prepared in the same way as they were thousands of years ago. The native cuisine of the island has also been influenced by other Mediterranean cultures such as the Arabs. For example, in the isle of San Pietro, which has links with Tabarka in Tunisia, a popular dish is *cas-cas*, the same as North African and Arab couscous. Another, *fregula*, looks like couscous but is actually semolina pasta – it originated in ancient Rome and has a heavy Moorish influence.

In ancient times meat requirements were met by hunting or by keeping animals such as pigs, sheep, cows and goats or occasionally horses. White meat, especially poultry, was eaten only in small quantities: roast or boiled fowl was regarded as food only for invalids or pregnant

Cutting salami in Paulolatino.

women. Surprisingly for an island, fish fared no better (though the island did give the name to sardines, fished in copious numbers).

It is possible that the lack of appetite for seafood is explained by the fact that the Sardinians have never been a nation of seafarers. They have always regarded the sea as an enemy, ever bringing new waves of conquerors to their island. Even today the owners of the fishing fleets operating in Sardinian waters tend to come from Ponza, Naples, Genoa or Carloforte. The annual *matanza*, the tuna harvest, an event dating from Roman times, is these days mainly to supply the export market and is by and large backed by Japanese funds. Recent trends have led to a greater emphasis on fish in restaurants on the coast; around Cagliari, in particular, you will find excellent lobster, red and grey mullet, and in the Oristano-Cabras region, eel.

BREADS

With regard to Sardinian bread, a variety of kneading techniques, handed down by women from generation to generation, and differing forms of leavening explain the remarkable range available on the island.

Bread is art in Sardinia, and the Baroque-like splendour of *coccoi*, the elaborately snipped

Fresh dough – good bread is one of the pleasures of Sardinian food.

> The traditional dish of *sa cordula*, found on most menus, is made of rolled lamb entrails stuck on a skewer and roasted on a spit.

and fashioned loaf of bread, is central to special occasions, such as Easter, Christmas, weddings and other *feste*. In Nuoro, *coccoi a puppia* are dolls made of bread that are given to children.

The variety of bread types across the island is staggering. The best-known is the *pane carasau* (sheet of music), a crisp, flat unleavened bread. As this type of bread keeps fresh for long periods,

shepherds have traditionally taken a few *pane carasau* with them on their long wanderings. *Su pistoccu* (similar but thicker than *carasau*) and *su cifraxiu* (with a crisp crust and a soft interior) are sold in bakeries all over the island. Most restaurants serving typical Sardinian cooking list various types of breads among their specialities.

ROAST SPECIALITIES

Arrosti, roast and grilled meat specialities, are a highlight of Sardinian gastronomy, particularly in the island's interior. Only the meat of young animals – lamb, kid, suckling pig and veal – is generally used.

There are two main methods of preparation. Firstly, there is carne a *carraxiu*. As in other Mediterranean countries (in particular Turkey), a hole is dug in the ground (stakes are laid in its base and driven round the inside to shore back the earth) and a deep trench is then dug round the hole, leaving about 15cm (6in) of soil as a "wall". The meat, usually the whole carcass, is placed inside the hole (which is liberally lined with herbs), and a fire is lit above. When this is sufficiently hot, the live ashes are raked into the trench. The heat bakes the meat evenly, with the herbs lending it a delicious aromatic flavour.

In the second method, the suckling pig, lamb, kid or veal is placed on wooden or metal spits. These are then positioned vertically or horizontally around the central fire and turned from time to time to ensure the meat cooks evenly.

In some districts the finishing touch is provided by a lump of bacon fat, which is wrapped in paper and then ignited. As it drips down onto the spit, the fat colours the meat golden brown and makes it crisp. In Sea and Sardinia D.H. Lawrence describes the roasting of a kid goat and the care that is taken in doing so, in great detail.

The most impressive *arrosti* are those served on special occasions: country festivals, saints' days or weddings. For the Sardinians, any cause for celebration naturally presents a social duty to provide good and plentiful food. You can sample an *arrosto*, usually described as a typical Sardinian speciality, in nearly every restaurant on the island.

ANTIPASTO

The most popular antipasto (hors d'oeuvre), the *antipasto di terra*, is a selection of ham, smoked sausages, olives, chicken liver, *sa cordula* (lamb tripe, served rolled up and grilled or fried with peas), mushrooms and brawn. The island has a number of notable *salumi* such as *mustela sarda* (a mature peppered sausage, hung for 50 days) and *sa suppressata*. Olives in brine are always present, succulent after a period of seasoning in salted water with wild fennel seeds. Black olives sautéed in oil and garlic, then preserved in chopped parsley and a little vinegar, are another island favourite.

A superb appetiser, *bottarga* is made from slated grey mullet roe which has been pressed and dried. *Bottarga* (often called Sardinian caviar) is served

home-made; the most popular types are *malloreddus* (in the shape of ridged shells) and *maccarrones* (shaped over a thin metal wire). These

> Main dishes are usually a roast (arrosto) of suckling pig, lamb, kid, veal or wild boar, served with a delicious spicy sauce. Vegetable side dishes include lettuce, fennel, celery, radishes and artichokes.

You'll find spit-roasted pig at most Sardinian festivals.

cut in thin slices and covered in olive oil. When grated with pasta it makes a delicious first course.

Other starters include *merca*, a dish of grey mullet simmered in salted water and wrapped in marsh grass, and *bocconi*, which consists of whelks simmered in salted water served hot. *Sa burrida* can be eaten as an appetiser or a main dish. It is made of dogfish, boiled in slices and then marinated for at least 24 hours in a sauce made of garlic, parsley, walnuts, vinegar, and the chopped dogfish livers. This grey sauce tastes considerably better than it looks.

PASTA AND SOUP DISHES

As elsewhere in Italy, in Sardinia a meal without pasta is unthinkable. Here it is almost always

⊘ HONEY

Sardinia produces excellent honey. Flavoured by its native flowers, many different varieties of honey are available. Among them are eucalyptus, orange blossom and wild lavender. There is also a bitter honey made from pollen from the strawberry tree, which is prepared in December and is thought to prevent bronchial asthma. *Millefiori* or *miele della flora mediterranea* is made from a mixture of all the honey made throughout the year and is a good choice if you're looking for a pot of honey to take home with you. Honey can be bought in supermarkets, local shops or, best of all, at festivals and local fares from the people who make it.

are served in a fresh tomato sauce and herbs, sometimes with chunks of meat or pieces of smoked sausage and accompanied with a condiment of cheese melted in a bain-marie.

Two well-known stuffed pastas are *angiulotts* (ravioli-like parcels stuffed with ricotta or fresh cheese, spinach and saffron) and *culungiones* (large ravioli stuffed with potato purée, mint and a little cheese). Both are served with tomatoes or meat sauce.

Fregula is a granular pasta, similar to couscous. It is served with steamed clams, like pasta, or in broth as a thick soup. Thick broths of vegetables, meat and herbs are common; they are substantial, often meals in themselves. You could try *pecora in cappotto*, boiled mutton with potatoes, onions, celery and dried tomatoes prepared in Barbagia, or *suppa cuatta* (Italian *zuppa gallurese*), a dish with regional variations but generally made with large slices of bread and cheese arranged in a pan, sprinkled with grated *pecorino* and finely chopped garlic, then drowned in a hot meat broth. In Moni try *favata con lardo*, a soup of broad beans with sausage, lard and wild fennel.

Cheese and ham being stored in Santu Lussurgiu, Oristano.

⊘ TRADITIONAL BREADS AND SWEETS

Saludi e trigu! (Good health and wheat!) is a traditional New Year's greeting. There are countless variations of bread, from the shepherd's long-lasting *pane carasau* to the sublime *pirichitteddu*, baked in Cagliari on 3rd February in honour of Saint Biagio. The ethnographic museum in Nuoro (see page 215) keeps over 600 varieties of traditional breads, 100 of which are on display.

Sardinian sweets are closely related to the religious festivals held throughout the year. Originally from Logudoro, *sebadas* pastries are covered with honey and filled with curd cheese flavoured with lemon rind. From the Barbagia come *sa voiardi* sponge fingers, which today are used to make tiramisu. *Biachittos*, small meringues with almond and lemon rind, and *amaretti* biscuits are popular everywhere. Campidano is famous for *pirichittus*, made from eggs, olive oil and flour, and *candelaus*, iced biscuits with almond paste and in the shape of flowers, animals, jugs, fruits and shoes. *Mustazzolous* biscuits are diamond-shaped and are eaten in honour of village patron saints. Finally, *sospiri* (sighs) are round sweets made of grated almonds, sugar, lemon and orange flower water. They are delicately wrapped in coloured tissue paper and eaten on special occasions.

SEAFOOD DISHES

Seafood cuisine is a recent addition to the menu; in fact, until recently *su pisci* was really only served in Cagliari and a few other coastal places. Today there are a lot of tasty fish dishes to choose from, starting with the famous *ziminu* or *sa cassola*, a fish stew. Among the many different types of fish available in Sardinia, grey mullet, red mullet, *ghiozzi* (the local version of a *frittura de mare:* small fish tossed in semolina flour and then fried) and eels, both barbecued and fried, deserve a special mention. All of them

fried, also from Cagliari. In Oristano expect to see roasted mullet and eel soup on the menu; in Carloforte fish casserole and *musciamme* (dried tuna fish fillet); stuffed squid in Olbia; and roast cuttlefish in Dorgali.

DESSERTS AND CHEESES

A traditional lunch *alla sarda* – Sardinian-style – will conclude with cheese and dessert. The islanders have been manufacturing dairy products for more than 5,000 years, so it is not surprising that the range of fine cheeses made

Spaghetti alle vongole is mostly served on the coast.

> The Sardinian version of Vernaccia, such as Vernaccia di Oristano, is different to the Italian varieties, being more sherry-like.

may be cooked and eaten as a main course if they have been marinated in *scabecciu*, a sautéed sauce of oil, garlic and vinegar.

Popular regional fish dishes include *l'aragosta alla catalana* (Catalan-style lobster), served with oil, vinegar and onions; *polpagliara*, small octopus simmered in a spicy sauce; *fregula cun cocciula* (baby clams), best eaten in Cagliari; and *orziadas*, sea anemones rolled in semolina and

from sheep's, goat's or cow's milk is extensive. Gourmets will delight in the discovery of *caprino, fiore sardo, semicotto, caglio, casagedu, casu marzu, pepato* and *romano*.

All types of cheese are available, from soft curd to hard, with flavours ranging from slightly acid to mild and aromatic to piquant. Some are eaten simply with bread; others are grated generously over pasta.

Desserts are another Sardinian speciality; one particular favourite, *sebadas* (or *seadas*), consists of two circles of pastry, filled with a layer of curd cheese and fried in deep fat, then drizzled with honey. Invariably, a selection of fruit is offered at the end of a meal. This varies according to season. Popular, too, are dried fruits and nuts:

almonds, hazelnuts and dried figs. A favourite confection at festival time consists of shelled almonds and orange peel dipped in honey.

The most commonly served *digestivo* has always been *aquavite*, an aromatic grappa with a high alcohol content. Another powerfully flavoured liqueur has also become popular among Sardinians in recent years: *liquore di mirto*, distilled from myrtle. It is red in colour when it is manufactured from the berries, and clear if only the leaves of the plant are used. Be warned, it packs a punch.

Local wines can be excellent.

WINES

The origins of Sardinian wine go back centuries. The old Nuragus vines (the name most probably comes from the nuraghe), together with the Vernaccia vines, are the oldest on the island. The Cannonau, Girò and Torbato vines date back to the time of the Catalans and the Aragonese, the Monica and Malvasia vines to the Byzantines, Vermentino vines to the Ligurians and Moscato and Nasco vines to the Romans.

There is a wide variety of local wines; most have a high alcohol content and are full-bodied, smooth and deeply coloured. The best-known bear the description Cannonau. Wines bottled in the cooperative cellars bear the DOC, a label guaranteeing quality; this certificate of authenticity is only awarded to wines from specific wine-growing areas. The varieties available range from heavy and lighter red wines, through rosés to whites. Most tend to be on the dry side rather than sweet or heavy; some are decidedly tangy. Cannonau wines are grown in the eastern provinces and Dorgali. A lot of vineyards produce these wines; some have outlets where you can buy and taste wines.

Three wines from the district around Cagliari – Girò, Monica and Nasco – are red and sweet. The popular Moscato di Cagliari and Malvasia are available from the Cantina Sociale di Quartu Sant'Elena. Nuragus, from the nearby Monserrato winery run by the Cantina Sociale di Monserrato, is an excellent accompaniment to pasta, rice dishes, soup, white meat, fish and seafood. Meloni wines, produced by the Meloni Vini, come from vineyards throughout the island. At Selargius, the Santa Rosa estate specialises in dessert wines.

Vernaccia, perhaps the most famous Sardinian wine, is served as a dessert wine or as an aperitif and tastes rather like a dry sherry. It comes from the Cantina Sociale della Vernaccia, founded in 1953, and is grown in the fertile lower valley of the Tirso river.

Mandrolisai (red or rosé) wine from Sorgono is traditionally drunk during the feast of San Mauro and Santu Antine. The Cantina Sociale del Mandrolisai was formed in 1952 to improve the quality and distribution of the wine. Semidano, a white wine with a fruity and intense bouquet, is excellent with shellfish and also comes from this area. Another good wine to go with shellfish is Vermentino, which can also be drunk as an aperitif. It is a light wine and has an aroma of quince with a hint of bitter almond.

From the provinces of Oristano and Nuoro comes Malvasia, a sweet dessert wine. Look out for Malvasia di Bosa, one of the most outstanding DOC Sardinian wines, which featured in the documentary film *Mondovino*. The Malvasia white grape is thought to have come from the Greek port of Monemvasia, in the Peloponnese. Returning to red wines and moving to the Sulcis peninsula in the southwest, we find Carignano, a ruby red with an excellent consistency.

In restaurants the local wine (*vino locale*) is often served from jugs. It is usually very drinkable and cheaper than buying by the bottle.

SHEPHERDS AND PECORINO

The shepherd's way of life has come to symbolise Sardinia, but changes are inevitable if this aspect of island culture is to survive.

Sardinia's history has always been closely bound to that of its shepherds, whose lifestyle is as fascinating as it is full of privations. The native Sardinian sheep is small and hardy, able to withstand the harsh conditions, and produces a high milk yield in spite of often poor pastures.

Sheep rearing developed under the Romans, in the Middle Ages and especially under Spanish rule and monastic orders like the Benedictines, as the island's inaccessible, barren land lent itself to sheep rearing rather than arable farming. Today the shepherd's lifestyle is under threat from modernity: continuing migration from the land, industrialisation of the island and the growing numbers of local inhabitants employed in the service industries. With this in mind, Unesco has been approached to protect the shepherd's unique way of life. Furthermore, it is feared that a dangerous gap could arise between an impoverished interior, where sheep and dairy farming would still be the main source of income, and the wealthy tourist and industrialised regions of the island.

PECORINO, A SUCCESS STORY

A group of enterprising businessmen from Rome established industrial cheese factories between 1885 and 1890, producing the *pecorino romano* (sheep's milk cheese), popular in Italy since Roman times (Pliny the Elder refers to it in his *Historia Naturalis*).

Even as the first dairy production cooperatives were being formed, there were still extensive areas of land where farmers clung to the old order. The shepherd was upheld as a symbol of an entire culture which was in danger of disappearing as a result of the links being forged with other countries.

Pungent and tangy, *pecorino* is eaten with bread, grated over pasta and frequently used in cooking, especially pesto. Today there are more than 50 cheese-making factories on the island, and *pecorino* is the island's main export product.

VARIATIONS ON THE *PECORINO* THEME

Apart from *pecorino romano*, which amounts to just under half of overall production, they also make a sweet white variety of cheese known as *pecorino*

Pecorino romano, a sheep's milk cheese – pecora means sheep in Italian.

tipo toscanello and *canestrato*, a delicious and strong-tasting sheep's milk cheese. The district around Gavoi is famous for its *pecorino fiore-sardo*, mostly exported to Puglia. In the Abruzzi, *pecorino fiore-sardo* is served with pears. Ricotta, an excellent curd cheese, is also made from *pecorino*. At one time ricotta and *pane carasau* formed the basis of the shepherd's diet; today it is mainly used in cooking, in the preparation of ravioli and *sebadas*, and served with a large spoonful of bitter-sweet Sardinian honey. You may also encounter a special Sardinian version of *pecorino*, namely *pecorino sardo*, which has a richer taste and is less salty than *pecorino romano*.

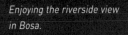
Enjoying the riverside view in Bosa.

Inside the Nuraghe di Santu Antine in the Valle dei Nuraghi.

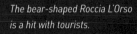

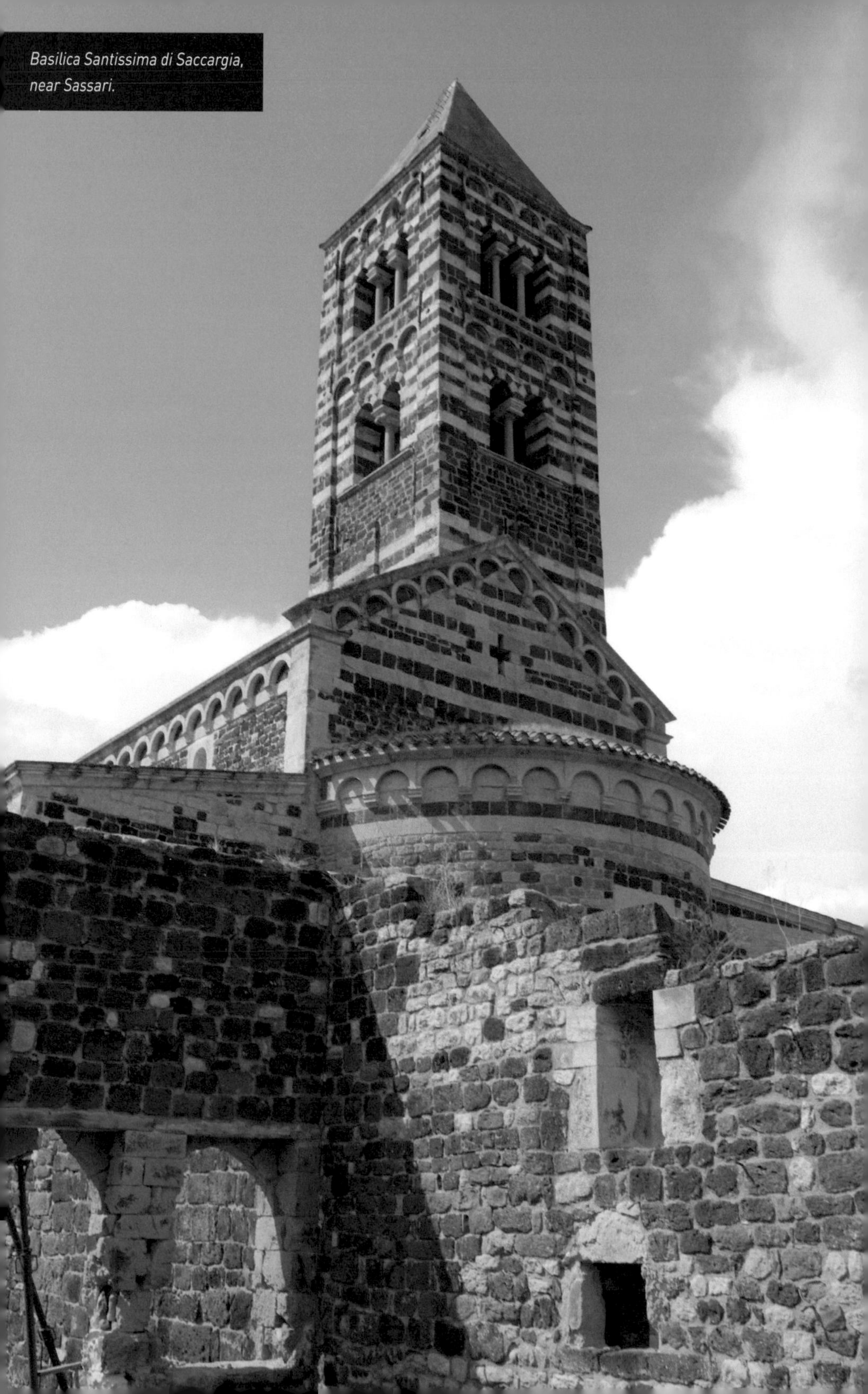

Basilica Santissima di Saccargia, near Sassari.

INTRODUCTION

A detailed guide to the entire island, with principal sights clearly cross-referenced by number to the maps.

Church detail.

One can never go by appearances alone in Sardinia. By way of example, this book's first editor cited a vivid memory from his first visit to the island, way back in 1972, when he met some village youths in Orgosolo, who showed him their pistol and insisted on arranging "safe" accommodation for him. In the end, they all finished the evening eating spaghetti, drinking rough wine and playing cards – and it didn't seem to matter that everyone else in the bar carried shotguns.

Since those days, much has changed. Mass tourism may have turned the Costa Smeralda into a jet-set haunt, but of late ecotourism and city breaks are attracting new, urbane and more adventurous visitors to Sardinia. More traditional tourists are still attracted by the pristine beaches where white sand, rose-coloured cliffs and blue-green watery hues abound.

We begin with Cagliari, one of Europe's oldest cities and capital of the island. It has a little bit of everything: the cosmopolitan character of a port city, Spanish ambience in the Old Quarter, the luxuries of an Italian shopping mecca, and beaches and pink flamingo-flecked lagoons on its doorstep.

We then travel up the east coast to Arbatax, a busy port in the province of Nuoro. Further on, past the spectacular Golfo di Orosei with its rocky coves and long sandy beaches, is Olbia, gateway to the Costa Smeralda, one of the most exclusive resorts in the Mediterranean. Then follows a tour of the dramatic countryside in the north – the Maddalena archipelago and seascapes of Gallura – before reaching

Spectacular sandy cove in the Golfo di Orosei.

Sassari. The most Italian Sardinian town has a cosmopolitan air and fine cultural attractions. Proceeding down the west coast, from Alghero to Oristano, we take in beguiling Spanish-influenced towns and then the fascinating southwest, with its colossal dunes and spectral mining landscapes. Finally we explore the Barbagia, which the Romans named after the "barbarians" they found there: this is the island's mountainous heart, where rugged Sardinian self-reliance lives on.

Such variety – wild landscapes and gorgeous beaches, the remains of an ancient culture, folk traditions and fascinating cities, make Sardinia almost a continent – *quasi un continente*, as the saying goes.

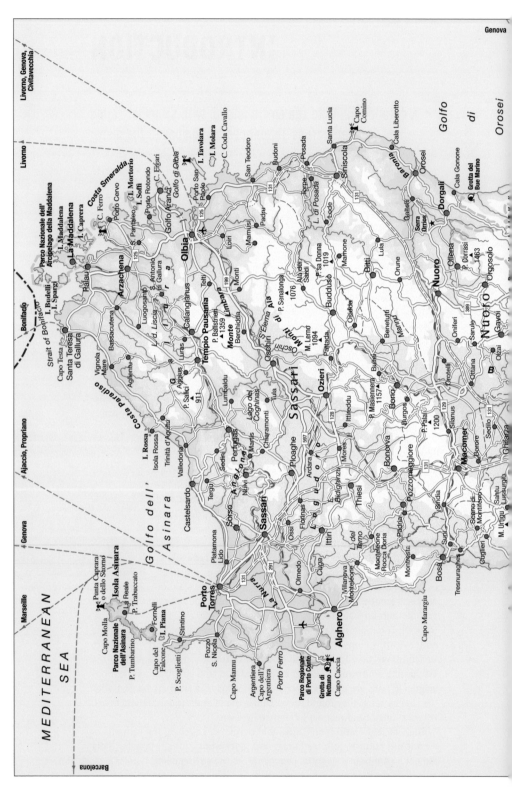

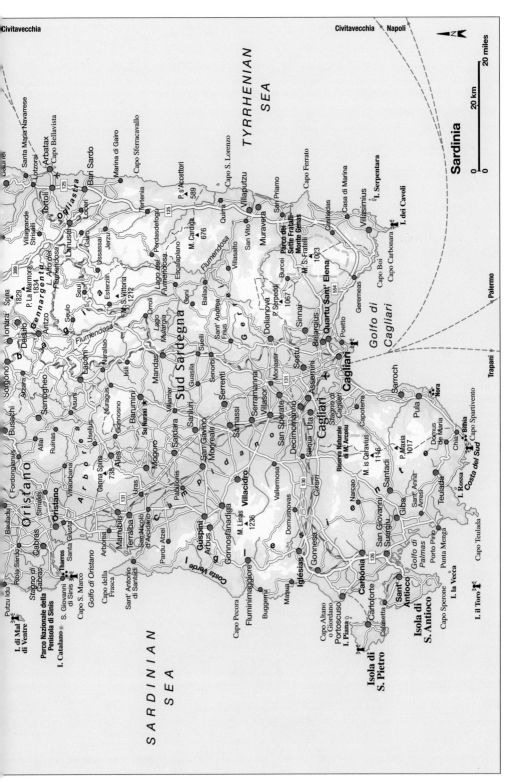

Sardinia

0   20 km
0   20 miles

N

TYRRHENIAN SEA

SARDINIAN SEA

Golfo di Cagliari

Civitavecchia

Civitavecchia   Napoli

Palermo

Trapani

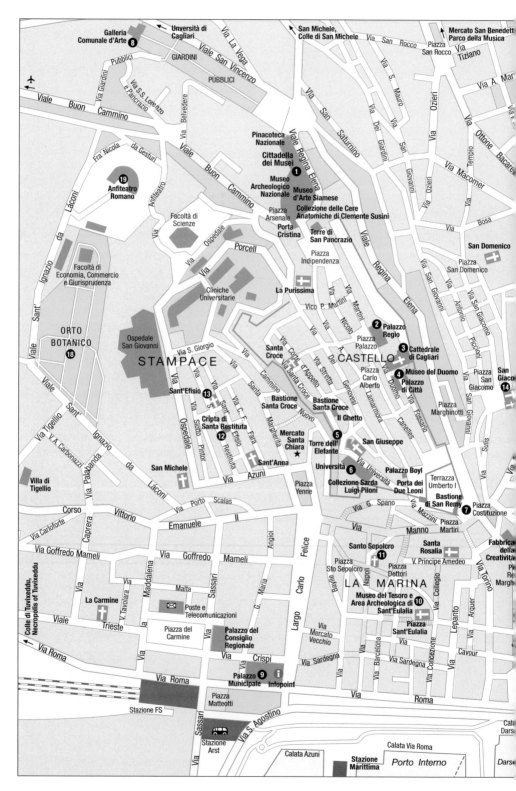

Galleria Comunale d'Arte ⑧
Unversità di Cagliari
Via La Vega
GIARDINI
San Michele, Colle di San Michele
Via San Rocco
Piazza San Rocco
Mercato San Benedett Parco della Musica
Via Tiziano
Viale San Vincenzo
Via S.S. Lorenzo e Pancrazio
Via Giardini Pubblici
PÚBBLICI
Belvedere
Via San Saturnino
Via Dei Giardini
Via S. Mauro
Via Ozieri
Via A. Mar
Viale Buon Cammino
Viale Regina Elena
Pinacoteca Nazionale
Via Macomer
Via A Ottone Bacar
Via Giardini Pubblici
Fra' Nicola da Gesturi
Cittadella dei Musei ①
Via Tempio
Anfiteatro Romano ⑲
Anfiteatro
Viale Buon Cammino
Museo Archeologico Nazionale
Museo d'Arte Siamese
Via Bosa
Facoltà di Scienze
Piazza Arsenale
Collezione delle Cere Anatomiche di Clemente Susini
San Domenico
Porcell
Porta Cristina
Torre di San Pancrazio
Via Regina Elena
Piazza San Domenico
Facoltà di Economia, Commercio e Giurisprudenza
Piazza Indipendenza
Via San Giovanni
Cliniche Universitarie
La Purissima
Vico P. Martini
Via Martini
Via Nicolo
Via Antonio
Via San Giacomo
ORTO BOTANICO ⑱
Ospedale San Giovanni
Via S. Giorgio
STAMPACE
Via Corte d'Appello
Via Stretta
Via A. Genovesi
Palazzo Regio ②
Piazza Palazzo
CASTELLO
Cattedrale di Cagliari ③
Santa Croce
Via Santa Croce
Piazza Carlo Alberto
Via Duomo
Museo del Duomo ④
Palazzo di Città
Piazza San Giacomo
San Giaco ⑭
Sant'Efisio ⑬
Bastione Santa Croce
Cammino Nuovo
Bastione Santa Croce
Via Lamarmora
Piazza Marghinotti
Piccioni
Via Sulis
Villa di Tigellio
Via Tigellio
Cripta di Santa Restituta ⑫
Via C. F. Fara
Via Santa Margherita
Il Ghetto
Via Canelles
Via Fossario
V.A. Carbonazzi
San Michele
Via Sidro Pintor
Mercato Santa Chiara
Sant'Anna
Torre dell' Elefante ⑤
San Giuseppe
Via Azuni
Piazza Yenne
Università ⑥
Via Università
Palazzo Boyl
Porta dei Due Leoni
Terrazza Umberto I
Bastione di San Remy ⑦
Piazza Costituzione
Corso Vittorio
Via Porto Scalas
Collezione Sarda Luigi Piloni
Via G. Spano
Via Mazzini
Emanuele II
Via Angioi
Via Felice
Via Manno
Piazza Martiri
Fabbrica della Creatività
Via Goffredo Mameli
Via Goffredo Mameli
Santo Sepolcro ⑪
Santa Rosalia
Via Torino
Colle di Tuvixeddu, Necropolis of Tuvixeddu
Via Maddalena
Via Malta
Via G. Maria
Via Sassari
Via Carlo
Piazza Sto Sepolcro
Via Napoli
Piazza Dettori
V. Principe Amedeo
LA MARINA
Via Collegio
La Carmine
V. Tavolara
Poste e Telecomunicazioni
Museo del Tesoro e Area Archeologica di Sant'Eulalia ⑩
Via Lepanto
Via Acquer
Viale Trieste
Piazza del Carmine
Palazzo del Consiglio Regionale
Largo
Via Mercato Vecchio
Piazza Sant'Eulalia
Via Barcellona
Via Concezione
Via Cavour
Crispi
Via Roma
Palazzo Municipale ⑨
Infopoint ℹ
Via Sardegna
Via Sardegna
Via Roma
Stazione FS
Via S. Agostino
Piazza Matteotti
Stazione Arst
Calata Azuni
Calata Via Roma
Stazione Marittima
Porto Interno
Dars
Cala Dars

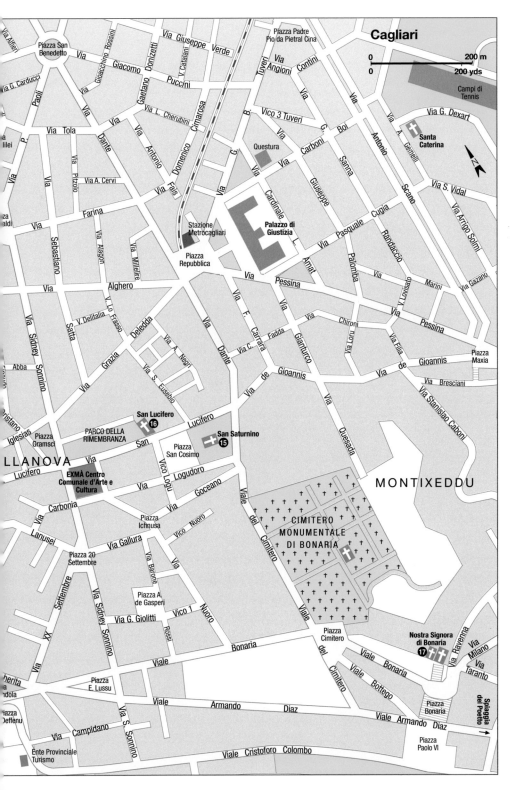

Cagliari

0 — 200 m
0 — 200 yds

Campi di Tennis

Piazza San Benedetto

Piazza Padre Pio da Pietral Cina

Via Alfieri
Via G. Carducci
Via G. Giacomo Donizetti
Via Giuseppe Verde
Via P. Paoli
Via Gioacchino Rossini
Via Gaetano Puccini
V. Catalani
Via Tuveri
Via Angioni
Via Contini
Via G. Dexart
Santa Caterina
Via P. Galilei
Via Tola
Via Dante
Via L. Cherubini
Vico 3 Tuveri
Via A. Gennell
Via Scano
Via S. Vidal
Via A. Cervi
Via Antonio
Via Domenico
Via G.
Via Carboni
Via Giuseppe
Via Sanna
Via Antonio
Via Arrigo Solmi
Via Pitzolo
Via Farina
Via Fais
Questura
Via Cardinale
Via Pasquale
Via Cugia
Via Randaccio
Via Gazano
Via Sebastiano
Via Aragon
Via Millelire
Stazione Metrocagliari
Palazzo di Giustizia
Via L.
Via Amat
Via Palomba
Via Grisorio TTA
Via Marini
Via Alghero
Piazza Repubblica
Via Pessina
Via Sidney Sonnino
V. Lo Frasso
V. Delitalia
Deledda
Via A. Negri
Via Dante
Via F. Carrara
Via C.
Fadda
Gianturco
Chironi
Via Loru
Via Filia
Via Pessina
Satta
Grazia
Via S. Eusebio
Via de Gioannis
Piazza Maxia
Abba
Iglesias
Via Gioannis
Via Bresciani
Via Stanislao Caboni
San Lucifero 16
PARCO DELLA RIMEMBRANZA
Lucifero
San Saturnino 15
MONTIXEDDU
Piazza Gramsci
San
Piazza San Cosimo
LLANOVA
Lucifero
Vico Logu
Logudoro
Quesada
EXMÀ Centro Comunale d'Arte e Cultura
Via Carbonia
Piazza Ichnusa
Goceano
CIMITERO MONUMENTALE DI BONARIA
Lanusei
Via Gallura
Vico Nuoro
Viale del Cimitero
Piazza 20 Settembre
Via Barone
Piazza A. de Gasperi
Vico 1 Nuoro
Via G. Giolitti
Rossi
Bonaria
Piazza Cimitero
Nostra Signora di Bonaria 17
Via Ravenna
Via Milano
Via Taranto
Piazza E. Lussu
Viale
Viale Bonaria
Viale Bottego
Piazza Bonaria
Spiaggia del Poetto
herita
dola
Viale Armando Diaz
Viale Armando Diaz
Piazza Deffenu
Via Campidano
Via S. Sonnino
Ente Provinciale Turismo
Viale Cristoforo Colombo
Piazza Paolo VI

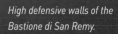
High defensive walls of the
Bastione di San Remy.

CAGLIARI

This fortress town hewn out of limestone hills is Sardinia's thriving capital of culture and commerce, honouring its historic charms while cautiously moulding a stimulating city of the future.

Cagliari is the island's capital and largest town, with a population of over 150,000 and a refreshingly down-to-earth charm. The wealth of precious objects and architecture to be found here tells of the city's complex history, which on more than one occasion has determined the fate of the entire island.

The name Cagliari is derived from the 12th-century Spanish *callaris*, meaning "a rocky place", and looking across the limestone hills and fortifications of Castello, the name certainly fits.

THE CHARM OF THE CAPITAL

Like its geography, the city and its inhabitants remain solid yet adaptable. From the buzzing Marina backstreet restaurants and Via Roma porticoes to the serene heights of Castello's historic fortifications and panoramic terraces, there is a sense of unhurried bonhomie and quiet confidence. Sardinia's capital has metropolitan verve – with traffic, port activity, tourism, shopping and smoking industrial satellites – but instead of the sense of chaos and posturing of mainland Italian cities, Cagliari has an understated allure and grace. You can explore its *quartieri* easily on foot – wandering through medieval backstreets, past Renaissance and 19th-century palazzi and the Cittadella museums, then, after a

seafood lunch in a rustic trattoria, you can sprawl out on Poetto's white sands in the late afternoon.

In recent years, creative spaces showcasing artistic talents have been added to Cagliari's historic attractions. After flirting with the idea of iconic museum architecture to spur an economic revival, the council is now focusing on enhancing the Marina and waterfront areas, encouraging imaginative conversions of old industrial buildings. In 2014, Cagliari was a candidate city for European Capital of Culture 2019, but lost its bid to

◎ Main attractions
Cittadella dei Musei
Cattedrale
Torre dell'Elefante
Università
Bastione di San Remy
Galleria Comunale d'Arte
Centro Comunale d'Arte e Cultura EXMÀ
Nostra Signora di Bonaria
Orto Botánico
Anfiteatro Romano

Map on page 96

Inside the T Hotel, one of Cagliari's trendiest hotels.

⊘ Tip

Plan sightseeing routes to suit you and your group by visiting one of the tourist offices, where they have handy free maps with themed itineraries for people interested in culture, food, crafts, art and shopping. Infopoint Palazzo Civico, Via Roma 145; www.cagliariturismo.it; Apr–Oct daily 9am–8pm, Nov–Mar Mon–Sat 10am–1pm and 2–5pm, Sun 10am–1pm.

mainland Matera. A year later, bad luck struck again when the opening events of the 2015–2016 America's Cup World Series, originally scheduled here, had to relocate to Portsmouth, England, when the Italian boat pulled out of the race.

PHOENICIANS, CARTHAGINIANS AND ROMANS

Archaeological finds from Sant'Elia, Santa Gilla, San Bartolomeo and Calamosca prove that the first inhabitants settled on this part of the island at the end of the 3rd millennium BC. Expansion came with the Phoenicians who, plying their trading routes between their native shores (the present-day Lebanon) and the Iberian peninsula, moored their ships at the Golfo degli Angeli, and colonised the area, building a series of trading ports. Carthaginians, descendants of the seafaring Phoenicians, continued the conquest by criss-crossing Sardinia with an important network of roads radiating out from Cagliari. The town developed into one of the most important trading centres on the East–West Mediterranean axis.

It is estimated that around 20,000 people lived in Cagliari in Roman times. Remains of the Roman city include the **Villa di Tigellio**, a complex of three Roman houses dating from the 1st century AD, the **Anfiteatro Romano** (Roman Amphitheatre), built directly in the rock of a natural valley, and the recently discovered archaeological area of Sant' Eulalia in the Marina quarter (www.mutseu.org; Nov–Mar Tue–Sun 9.30am–4pm, Apr–May and Sept–Oct until 6pm, June–Aug until 7pm).

CAGLIARI IN THE MIDDLE AGES

During the Byzantine era and the occupation by the Vandals the town continued to grow in importance, and the spread of Christianity rapidly elevated Cagliari to a sort of spiritual and moral capital. The year AD 704 marked the beginning of Saracen incursions along the southwest coast of Sardinia. Fear of the sea and the invaders it carried to the island wrought fundamental changes, and for almost three centuries Cagliari was to remain cut off from world history. This isolation may have been why Sardinia's

View of Cagliari.

first *giudicato*, a defensive alliance with its own jurisdiction, was formed around Cagliari. The town established contact with the French towns along the Mediterranean coast and began trading with the city states of Genoa and Pisa, which were subsequently to dominate the history of Cagliari and even Sardinia itself, first as partners and then as conquerors. Under Pisan rule, the town enjoyed a considerable demographic, artistic and economic revival.

THE SPANISH, THE HOUSE OF SAVOY AND ITALY

In 1326, following the decline of Pisa, Cagliari fell into the hands of the royal house of Aragon. Their first action was to expel all native Sardinians from the castle. In 1418 it became the official residence of the Viceroy of Sardinia, who replaced the Governor General. In 1421, in the presence of the King of Aragon, Alfonso V "The Magnanimous", the Viceroy of Sardinia, Bernardo de Centelles, inaugurated the island's first parliament. Under Aragonese rule the city's administrative system built up by Pisa was dismantled and replaced by a new arrangement resembling that of Barcelona.

Under Aragonese and Spanish rule, Cagliari's position as an important port and trading town was reinforced, and the university was founded. However, a number of unwelcome measures aggravated the local population and the Spanish were driven out, aided by a British fleet. Following the Peace of Utrecht, Duke Victor Amadeus II of Savoy became the King of Sardinia (1718). Then, in 1720, Sardinia, along with Naples, Milan and the Spanish Netherlands, was formally handed over to the Austrian Empire by the Spanish; and the island was passed on to Luigi Departes, the emissary from Savoy.

As part of the Kingdom of Savoy-Sardinia, Cagliari suddenly joined the international political arena. In the wake of the turmoil which Napoleon spread across the whole of Europe, Cagliari was to become the refuge of Charles Emmanuel IV and then Victor Emmanuel I of Savoy. In the 19th century a succession of famines and epidemics plagued the inhabitants, exacerbated by the indescribable sanitary conditions in which the population lived. The ancient regime was toppled, replaced by a new governor, namely Italy. Railways, industrialisation and new ideas brought "Fortress Cagliari" into the modern world.

CASTELLO QUARTER

A good place to start a tour is from the Castello quarter, the large ancient stronghold of the town, over which the two medieval towers of Torre di San Pancrazio and Torre dell'Elefante rise. The highlight here is the city's museum complex, the **Cittadella dei Musei ❶**, situated on Piazza Arsenale in the heart of the Old Town. Until 1966–7, when it was allocated to its present role as a documentary and cultural witness of local history, the building itself experienced a very turbulent past. The present structure rises above the remains

The EXMA building (the town's former abattoir) is decorated with cows' heads.

Laundry drying from balconies adds colour to the streets.

of the ancient Piedmontese fortress and arsenal. Standing on the highest point of Cagliari, it affords a spectacular view over the town and the bay. The two architects of the Cittadella, Gazzola and Cecchini, were successful in adapting historic elements to new uses, incorporating the Renaissance portal and splendid statue of Santa Barbara into their concrete modernist vision of curvy walkways and straight lines.

CITY MUSEUMS

The Cittadella complex houses four museums. The **Pinacoteca Nazionale** (National Art Gallery; www.pinacoteca. cagliari.beniculturali.it; Tue–Sun 9am–8pm) contains an important collection of *retabli* polyptychs. Polyptychs were introduced by the Aragonese during their conquest in the 14th century. The huge paintings were used as altarpieces, usually divided into three sections and placed behind a main altar, or they acted as the main focus of a side chapel. Intended to be instructive visual depictions of religious themes and the lives of saints, the central panel of a polyptych

Roman marble torso in the National Archaeological Museum.

often features the most important events in a saint's life. Most of the *retabli* in the collection come from the church of San Francesco in Cagliari and are attributed to painters known only by the title of Master and the village in which their work was first recognised. The *retablo della Porziuncola* by the Master of Castelsardo, painted in 1492, is probably one of the best examples of this particular period and style of painting.

Also contained in the Cittadella's complex is the **Museo d'Arte Siamese** (Siamese Art Museum; www.museici vicicagliari.it; Tue–Sun June–Aug 10am–1pm, 5–8pm, Sept–May 10am–6pm). The collection was bequeathed to the town by Stefano Cardu, a Sardinian at the court of the King of Siam in the 19th century. The collection contains Chinese and Siamese objets d'art dating back to the 11th century.

One of the most unusual museums in the complex is the **Collezione delle Cere Anatomiche di Clemente Susini** (http://pacs.unica.it/cere; Tue–Sun 9am–1pm, 4–7pm), which displays 23 disquietingly realistic anatomical wax models based on originals made by Clemente Susini in 1803. This is not recommended for the squeamish.

INSIDE THE MUSEO ARCHEOLOGICO NAZIONALE

Contained within the complex is the city's best museum: the **Museo Archeologico Nazionale** (http://museoarcheocag liari.beniculturali.it; Tue–Sun 9am–8pm). The exhibition rooms contain displays of prehistoric and early finds as well as a large number of objects illustrating the long history of the island. The first appearance of human beings in Sardinia dates to the early Palaeolithic Age (350,000 years ago), but the earliest material displayed in the museum dates back to the Neolithic period (6000–2700 BC), including pottery, obsidian tools and small fat female statuettes, which formed part of the Great Mother Goddess cult, often found in *domus de janas*.

Of particular interest are the *bronzetti* (recent and late Bronze Age bronze statues) representing people in religious contemplation, along with those depicting archers, *navicelle nuragiche* (Nuragic small boats) and votive gifts from nuraghe and Nuragic villages, grave temples and sacred springs. The majority of human figures represented are males, but among the female representations there are some extremely expressive female figures, the so-called "mothers". Seated on round stools, the figures embrace their sons on their laps. One female figure holds a naked adult in her lap instead of a male infant. This figure is interpreted as being a Nuragic Madonna with her dead son – God.

The Phoenicians' time on the island is marked by a collection of valuable objects discovered in sites scattered along the coast: imported Etruscan Bucchero vases found near Cagliari, Phoenician ceramic pots with mushroom-shaped rims and Greek cups and plates. Of great value is the fabulous Carthaginian glass paste necklace found in Olbia, which has large beads representing colourful human faces and animals. The juniper-wood statuette of a *kore* (a girl wearing festive dress) was discovered in the former Punic settlement of Olbia, as was a particularly well-preserved example of the apotropaic terracotta masks which were manufactured extensively by the Phoenicians to ward off malevolent spirits.

The Roman period in Sardinia is represented by glass vases and bottles, used to import wine from central Italy. Sigillata Italica or Arretin ware, a new type of tableware, was adopted during this time by those who could afford it. Lead ingots with the seal of the Emperor Hadrian produced in the south of the island and exported to Rome have also been found.

The last section of the museum's ground floor contains a collection of early Christian and medieval artefacts which includes metal objects such as jugs, lamps, incense burners, silver and bronze fibulae, and a number of Afro-Mediterranean clay oil lamps with varied decorations and designs. It provides a rare opportunity to appreciate the

Nuragic sculpture in Cagliari's archaeological museum.

⊙ Tip

Following Via Martini, the former Pisan blacksmiths' road, to the left is the small Piazza Martini with an open view over the eastern part of the town, the lagoon of Molentargius, the salt works and Cagliari's long beach, Il Poetto.

culture of the Byzantines and Vandals, the island's early invaders.

PALATIAL SPLENDOUR

From Piazza Arsenale outside the Cittadella and passing under the Palazzo delle Seziate, you arrive in Piazza Indipendenza. On the right is the building which housed Sardinia's mint during the 14th century and later an archaeological museum.

The **Piazza Palazzo**, created after the removal of bomb-damaged World War II buildings, has always been the centre of civil authority on the island. The **Palazzo Regio ❷** (Royal Palace or Palazzo Viceregio; summer daily 9am–7pm, winter Tue–Sun 10am–6.30pm) is the seat of the prefecture. An older building, home to the Viceroy sent to rule the island by the King of Aragon, stood here from the 14th to the 18th centuries. The present building was constructed in the 18th century on the orders of the Kings of Sardinia. Inside, it is worth taking a look at the fine staircase leading up to the *bel-étage* designed by the military engineer De Guibert, as well as at Bruschi's

Interior of the Palazzo Regio.

allegorical and realistic frescoes in the Provincial Assembly Chamber.

CAGLIARI'S CATHEDRAL

The **Cattedrale di Cagliari ❸** (www.duomodicagliari.it; Mon–Sat 8am–1pm and 4–8pm, Sun 8am–1pm and 4.30–8.30pm) was built in the 13th century, but only the belfry and the supporting beams of the main doorway remain from the original building. The cathedral has been remodelled on a number of occasions, finally receiving its Romanesque facade in 1930 in the style of Pisa and Lucca.

The Catalan Gothic-style chapel in the right transept is evidence that the building plans were changed when the invading forces of Aragon conquered the town in 1326. Inside the cathedral are two works of art of particular interest. The first is the carved reliefs of the two stone pulpits by Guglielmo da Pisa which flank the main doors. The engravings were originally commissioned in 1160 for Pisa's cathedral and later donated to Cagliari. During modernisation of the church in 1600 the original pulpit, formed by eight panels,

was split into the two we see today. The engravings show 16 scenes from the life of Christ, including the *Last Supper and the Sermon on the Mount*.

In the Gothic-Catalan chapel on the right transept is a copy of a 15th-century triptych, the *Trittico di Clemente VII*, attributed to the Flemish Rogier van der Weyden (1399–1464), the official painter of Brussels. The painting originally belonged to Pope Clement VII, but during the sack of Rome in 1527 it was stolen and ended up in Cagliari, where the original can still be seen in the **Museo del Duomo** at Via Fossario 5 (Treasury; www.museoduomodicagliari.it; Tue–Fri 4.30–7.30pm, Sat–Sun 10am–1pm and 4.30–7.30pm). Also worth seeking out here amid the silver, wooden and wax sculptures is a six-panelled polyptych, the *Retablo della Crocefissione* by Michele Cavaro (1517–84).

Under the cathedral is the crypt, carved out of the rock that forms the foundation of the cathedral; it's decorated with depictions of saints by local artists and contains the tombs of many notable people, including the wife of Louis XVIII of France. The crypt is an atmospheric space – you can often duck down here to find yourself with just an eerie silence and the cool, aged stone as company.

The **Palazzo di Città** ❹ (www.museicivicicagliari.it; Tue–Sun Sept–May 10am–6pm, June–Aug until 8pm) is the old town hall; today it has an 18th-century facade, but the original building existed during Pisan rule. For centuries it was the seat of one of the branches of Sardinia's Parliament. Some of its handsome, beautifully restored spaces host permanent collections of wooden sacred sculptures, ceramics and jewellery as well as temporary exhibitions and cultural events.

The whole of this quarter is crossed by the long Via Lamarmora, where the street-level rooms of nobiliary buildings, once used as stables and store rooms, have been transformed into quaint antique shops and artisans' workshops.

UNIVERSITY QUARTER

The quarter is delimited to the west by the imposing **Bastione Santa Croce**. The view of the gulf, of Santa Gilla lagoon and

Colourful ceramics make great souvenirs.

A wedding party outside the cathedral.

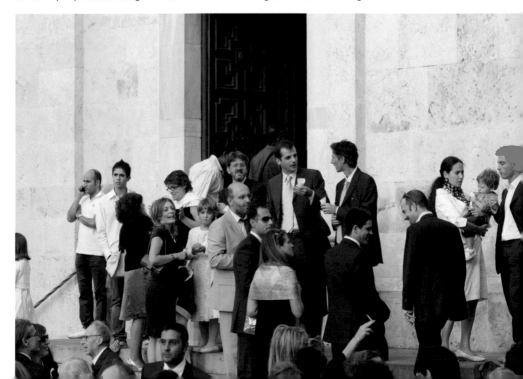

Playing inside the cathedral.

Mosaic in the Cattedrale Santa Maria del Castello.

of the Stampace quarter is breathtaking. The **Basilica di Santa Croce** (free) was built in 1661 over a synagogue abandoned after the edict of Ferdinand the Catholic in 1492, which expelled all Jews and Muslims from his land, which at the time included Sardinia.

The **Torre dell'Elefante** ❺ (www.beni culturalicagliari.it; closed for renovation at the time of writing, otherwise daily 9am–5pm), at the end of the Via Santa Croce, was built in 1307 by Giovanni Capula, a local architect, who also built the **Torre di San Pancrazio** (closed for renovation at the time of writing otherwise same hours) – the northern gate of the Castello district. The Torre dell'Elefante owes its name to the little elephant carving placed upon a plinth on its facade, under which the head of Marchese di Cea was displayed for 17 years after the tower was built. The spiked gates of the tower loom sinisterly over passers-by, which combined with a strong wind can evoke echoes of the grisly deeds that took place here.

The **Università** ❻ just to the south was established in 1606; today the rectorship, together with the library, is housed in the former Tridentine Seminary building, which dates to 1700. The noteworthy **Collezione Sarda Luigi Piloni** (tel: 070-675 2428; Mon–Fri by appointment only; free) is also kept in the same building. The collection contains 206 geographical maps of Sardinia dating from the 16th century, 54 paintings covering the same period by painters local to or related to the island, prints and drawings of 19th-century Sardinian costumes and a valuable collection of local carpets, packsaddles and chest covers.

The **Museo di Geologia e Paleontologia D. Lovisato** (Geology and Palaeontology Museum) and the Mineralogy Museum, **Museo di Mineralogia** (both museums in the Earth Sciences Department, Cagliari University, Via Trentino 51; Mon, Wed and Fri; tel: 070-675 6618 for an appointment) are devoted to the geological history of Sardinia. The displays include fossils and rocks gathered in the first half of the 19th century and a splendid collection of minerals from Sardinia's mines.

BASTIONE DI SAN REMY

At the end of Via Università, on Piazza Costituzione, is the **Bastione di San Remy ❼**, which was used to defend the castle to the south. The bastions were built upon old city ramparts in the early 18th century by the Baron di San Remy. He became the first Piedmontese Viceroy of Sardinia and made his name by enlarging the island's fortifications.

The Bastione can be reached via a magnificent staircase in yellow and white limestone built in 1902, which rises in grand stages and is framed by an imposing roofed structure with giant arches. Halfway up is the *passeggiata coperta*, a long covered arcade with bold orange walls and geometric-designed marble flooring. Its cavernous interiors are perfect for lingering, people-watching and perusing the latest exhibition.

Spectacular views of the city, surrounding landscape and sea open up from the expansive terrace of the Bastione, which is dotted with trees, benches and a few café-bars – a favourite evening hotspot and a place to see and be seen. Glass lifts are also available to the summit from a few corners and metal walkways.

Overlooking the terrace, you can't miss the peachy-hued, neo-classical **Palazzo Boyl** (1840), built over what remained of the Torre dell'Aquila (Eagle's Tower), one of the ancient Pisan towers that stood at the entrance of the city.

THE GALLERIA COMUNALE D'ARTE

Back at the foot of the Piazza Arsenale on the northern edge of Castello, walk down Viale San Vincenzo and you will come to the pleasant **Giardini Púbblici** (daily). In the middle of the gardens is the **Galleria Comunale d'Arte ❽** (www.museicivicicagliari.it; Wed–Mon Sept–May 10am–6pm, June–Aug until 9pm). The gallery has a collection of modern works by Sardinian artists and stages exhibitions of contemporary artists. Among the most notable works in the museum's

collection are paintings by Tarquinio Sini from the 1920s and Giuseppe Biasi. Early 20th-century work by Francesco Ciusa, who was honoured at the 1907 Venice Biennale, is also on show here – particularly impressive is his piece *La Madre dell'Ucciso*.

LA MARINA QUARTER

The narrow Marina quarter to the south, originally surrounded by walls, has always been tied to the ups and downs of the port's commercial activities. Its alleys are lined with a succession of welcoming little *ristoranti*. The quarter is more or less a rectangle closed on one side by Largo Carlo Felice and the elegant building of La Rinascente store, on the other by Piazza Amendola with its enormous ficus trees, palms and jacarandas. To the north the quarter ends with the pedestrian street Via Manno, under the Bastione di San Remy.

On Via Roma, parallel to the port, is the imposing, Gothic-meets-Art Nouveau **Palazzo Municipale ❾** (or Palazzo Civico; tel: 070-6771; by appointment only), the town hall, which was built in

Strolling along Via Roma.

⊘ Tip

Il Bastione di San Remy attracts collectors and the curious to its bric-a-brac and antiquarian market (June–Sept Wed–Sun 6.30pm–midnight, Oct–May Sun morning only).

the 20th century. Nearby is the **Palazzo del Consiglio Regionale** (regional government offices) in Via Sassari, built in the 1980s. This frequently criticised concrete-and-steel building contains a fine series of sculptures by the Sardinian artist Costantino Nivola (1911–88).

Via Roma enjoys a sunny position overlooking the sea. By day a multitude of little cafés under the porticoes are crowded and lively. The main harbour nearby provides a link with the Italian mainland and other Mediterranean ports, including Tunis. The **Via Manno**, the **Largo Carlo Felice** and some sections of the **Via Roma** have become popular shopping streets.

ROMAN REMAINS

Today the main historic and cultural reference point in La Marina is the 14th-century parish **church of Sant'Eulalia** in Piazza Sant' Eulalia. Under the church, recent archaeological excavations have discovered parts of the old Roman town, which can now be seen as part of the **Museo del Tesoro e Area Archeologica di** **Sant'Eulalia** ⑩ (MUTSEU, Vico del Collegio; www.mutseu.org; Tue–Sun Nov–Mar 9.30am–4pm, Apr–May and Sept–Oct until 6pm, June–Aug until 7pm). Apart from containing part of the Roman town, the museum contains wooden sculptures, silver objects, vestments and paintings.

The **church of Santo Sepolcro** ⑪ (Piazza Santo Sepolcro, off Via Dettori; www.mutseu.org; Nov–Mar Tue–Sat 9.30am–4pm, Apr–May and Sept–Oct Tue, Wed, Fri, Sat 9.30am–6pm, Thu until 4pm, Sun 2–6pm, June–Aug Tue, Wed, Fri, Sat 9.30am–6pm 9.30am–7pm, Thu until 4pm, Sun 2–6.30pm) belonged to the Templars from 1248 to 1311. It was then entrusted to the main confraternity of the Cross, which took care of the burial of the poor and those who were condemned to death. In 1538 lumps of earth brought from the Holy Sepulchre in Jerusalem were scattered here.

Nearby Via Manno, Viale Regina Margherita and Piazza Martiri were the haunts of writers and travellers such as D.H. Lawrence and Grazia Deledda.

Colourful ceramics for sale.

⊘ ART SCENE

Cagliari's thriving arts scene has been given a boost in recent years with the opening of new cultural centres. A good place to start for those interested in culture is **EXMÀ** Centro Comunale d'Arte e Cultura (San Lucifero 71; www.camuweb.it; Tue–Sun 9am–1pm and 4–8pm), housed in a former slaughterhouse building. Other exhibition and performance spaces with unusual former uses – each titled Centro Comunale d'Arte e Cultura – include **Lazzaretto** (Vecchio Borgo S. Elia; www.lazzarettodicagliari.it; Tue–Sun 9am–1pm and 4–8pm), once a hospital for plague victims, and a couple of old stone buildings that form part of Castello's fortifications: **Il Ghetto** (Via Santa Croce 18, Castello; www.camuweb.it; Tue–Sun 9am–1pm and 4–8pm) and the imposing old castle complex **San Michele**.

STAMPACE

Stampace is one of the four historical quarters of Cagliari, easily reached on foot from Piazza Yenne, under and west of the castle. In the past it was inhabited by artisans and artists, who congregated around Via Azuni and what is today the Corso Vittorio Emanuele II.

Stampace has many churches, including the Jesuit complex of the **church of San Michele** (Mon 8–11am and 7–8.30pm, Tue–Sat 8am–12.30pm and 7–8.30pm, Sun 9am–noon and 7–9pm), built at the end of the 17th century in a Spanish Baroque style. Right at the centre of Stampace, in Via Santa Restituta, is the **Cripta di Santa Restituta** ⑫ (www. beniculturalicagliari.it; daily 9am–5pm). It is a large room with traces of Punic and Roman presence later transformed into a Palaeo-Christian church. The crypt is tied to the worship of Saint Restituta, whose statue, dating from the 5th century, was found during excavations.

POPULAR FESTIVAL

The nearby **church of Sant'Efisio** ⑬ (closed for restoration at the time of writing) was built in 1700 and is the headquarters of the Gonfalone brotherhood which organises the colourful **Festa di Sant'Efisio**, a folk festival at the beginning of May each year. The festival is the biggest in Sardinia, and the whole town is involved in its preparations. Saint Efisio is credited with saving Cagliari from the Black Death, and is revered throughout the island. During the festivities the saint's statue is carried to a tiny church in Pula which stands on the spot where he was martyred. Garlanded oxen draw the statue through the town on a richly decorated cart, escorted by elegantly costumed riders and followed by a vast crowd. The sound of *launeddas*, Sardinian flutes, accompanies the party.

VILLANOVA

The **Villanova quarter** is made up of small houses originally inhabited by farmers who cultivated the fields on which the modern town has developed. Today the houses are part of a labyrinth of narrow and long alleys which give Villanova a lively and

Catching up with the news on Via Roma.

View over Cagliari to the surrounding lagoons and hills beyond.

colourful atmosphere. The 15th-century **church of San Giacomo** (Mon–Sat 7–10.30am and 5.30–7pm, Sun 7am–12.30pm and 5–7pm), on the piazza of the same name, is an important centre for the traditional and folkloristic liturgical rites that take place during the celebrations of Holy Week.

CHURCHES AND ART CENTRES

Outside the four historical quarters there are some very important churches in Cagliari: one is the **Basilica di San Saturnino** (tel: 070-662 496; Tue–Sat 10am–1pm and 3.30–7.30pm, though often closed) on the Piazza San Cosimo, just off the Via Dante. Built on the site of an early Roman necropolis, this Romanesque basilica is the oldest church on the island. Saint Saturno, the patron saint of Sardinia, was beheaded in AD 303 during a time of Christian persecution; his body was buried in a crypt over which the Basilica di San Saturnino was built.

At the corner of the same square is the **church of San Lucifero** (tel:

070-656 996; visits only by appointment). The side door of the church bears the coat of arms of Aragonese Cagliari, placed next to two dogs, symbols of the Dominicans. Excavations have revealed a Palaeo-Christian complex formed by three chapels dating from the 5th–7th centuries under the church. On Via San Lucifero is the **EXMÀ building** (see page 108).

In Piazza Bonaria is the **Basilica di Nostra Signora di Bonaria** (www. bonaria.eu; 6.30am–noon and 4.30–7.30pm), built in 1704. The basilica dominates the skyline as you approach Cagliari from the sea and is believed to give protection to sailors. A flight of steps leads up to an impressive neoclassical facade. Next to it is the less impressive but older **church of Bonaria**, built in 1326, which contains a 14th-century wooden Madonna – the centre of devotion on its main altar. This was the first church to be built in Sardinia in an Aragonese-Gothic style immediately after the arrival of Alfonso of Aragon to commemorate the conquest of Cagliari.

The steps of the Basilica di Nostra Signora di Bonaria.

In the cloister of the convent is the entrance to the interesting **Museo del Santuario di Nostra Signora di Bonaria** (tel: 070-301 747; open on request), where religious objects and ex-votos are kept, many of them in the shape of boats and ships and dating from the 18th century. The museum also contains finds from local excavations and the mummified bodies of a family who died from the plague in the 17th century.

GREEN SPACES AND A ROMAN AMPHITHEATRE

Cagliari has one of Italy's most famous botanical gardens, the **Orto Botánico**  (Viale Sant'Ignazio da Láconi; tel: 070-675 3512; Tue–Sun Apr–Oct 9am–6pm, Nov–Mar 9am–2pm; guided visits by appointment). Founded in 1858 by the town's university, it is divided into three climatic environments: Mediterranean, Tropical and Rocky-Arid. As well as the splendid variety of plants from all over the world, there is a Punic water tank, a Punic-Roman quarry and the remains of a Roman aqueduct.

To the north of the botanical gardens is the **Anfiteatro Romano**  (Roman Amphitheatre; www.benicul turalicagliari.it; daily 9am–5pm). Dating from the 1st century AD, the theatre was carved out of the rock on the hill and had a capacity of around 10,000. Today's spectators come not for bloody gladiatorial battles but for jazz and other music events. Another major complex of Roman remains is located to the south of the botanical gardens. The **Villa di Tigellio** (www.benicultura licagliari.it; daily 9am–5pm) is in fact not a single building, but a residential neighbourhood.

HILLS AND BEACHES

The hill of **Monte Urpino** rises for over 100 metres (330ft) between the modern quarters of eastern Cagliari and the Molentargius coastal marshes.

Covered by pine trees, it is, together with the **Colle di San Michele** and **Colle di Tuvixeddu**, one of the few parks in town. Colle di Tuvixeddu is home to the Phoenician-Punic necropolis opened to the public in 2014 after decades of excavation works. Dating back to 500 BC–200 BC, the **necropolis of Tuvixeddu** is one of the largest in the Mediterranean (tel: 0388-724 7420; daily Jul 5.30am–midnight, shorter hours rest of the year; park free, open from dawn till dusk). In the Parco di San Michele is the 10th-century San Michele castle bearing the same name, usually used for exhibitions (www.camuweb.it; Tue–Sun 10am–1pm, 3–6pm). A road leads to the top of the hill, where there is a stunning view over the town and the lagoons that surround it. If your itinerary can fit in a day at the beach then head for **Poetto**, one of the longest beaches in Italy, with views across to the foothills of the Sella del Diavolo. The Marina Piccola, at the southern end of the beach lined with restaurants and bars, has a lively atmosphere.

A stylish lookout for the lifesavers, Cagliari beach.

Cacti growing in the Orto Botánico.

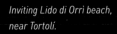
Inviting Lido di Orri beach,
near Tortolí.

CAGLIARI TO ARBATAX

This stretch of coast covers a wide range of terrain, from the Sette Frattelli peaks to the seaside resort of Villasimius and on to the wild mountains and beaches of Ogliastra.

The road from Cagliari to Olbia, the Eastern Trunk Road or SS 125, is known as the **Strada Statale Orientale Sarda**. It is one of the main traffic arteries in Sardinia, and has received much investment in recent years – with impressive tunnels and raised sections speeding the journey into this mountainous region.

Setting off from **Cagliari ❶** (see page 99) via the Viale del Poetto, you will come to **Quartu Sant'Elena ❷**, where the **Casa Museo Sa Dom'e Farra** (Via Eligiu Porcu 143; closed for renovation, tel: 070-812 340 for information), an original Campidanese farmhouse displaying traditional agricultural implements and domestic tools, is well worth stopping off for.

MOUNTAINS AND MAQUIS

A few kilometres inland, the SS 125 runs past the **Monte dei Sette Fratelli ❸** (Seven Brothers), a small range of mountains with peaks up to 1,000 metres (3,280ft) high. The Sette Fratelli regional park is characterised by a forest-maquis formed by holm oaks, cork trees and arbutus (strawberry trees). There is also a protected area for the rare *cervo sardo*, the short Sardinian stag. Following the gorge of the Rio Cannas, the SS 125 arrives at San Priamo and connects itself with the coastal road a few kilometres before Muravera.

Boats in the bay of Punta Valentis, Villasimius.

VILLASIMIUS AND ISOLA DEI CAVOLI

Sardinia's main seaside resort on the southeast coast is **Villasimius ❹**. It has enjoyed a remarkable boom in recent years and is now dotted with holiday complexes, apartment blocks, hotels and villas catering to large numbers during the summer months. Unfortunately some tourist developments have blighted the countryside in the area.

Villasimius's star-shaped 17th-century **Fortezza Vecchia** (Old Fortress) rises up above the harbour. Built for

Main attractions
Villasimius
Isola Serpentara and Isola dei Cavoli
Muravera
Villaputzu
Tertenia
Ulassai
Bari Sardo
Lanusei
Tortolí
Arbatax

Map on page 114

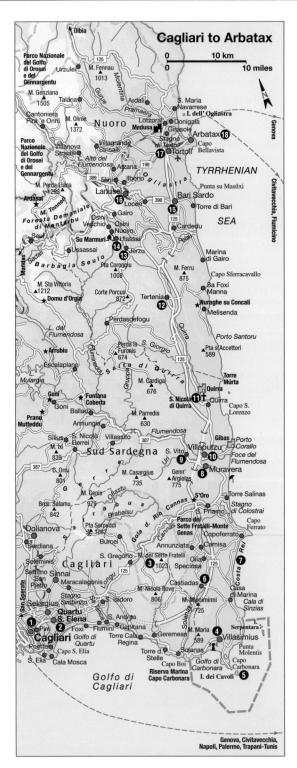

military purposes and coastal protection, it now relates the history of piracy from Byzantine times to more recent Arabic seafaring invaders. Each July Villasimius's *Sagra della Madonna del Naufrago* (Festival of Our Lady of the Shipwrecks) sees a procession of fishing boats and the scattering of flowers around the Isola dei Cavoli, to mark lives lost at sea.

Villasimius lies on the northern edge of a promontory which extends to **Capo Carbonara**; from the road there are breathtaking views of the sea and a scattering of tiny islands, the largest of which are the **Isola Serpentara** and the **Isola dei Cavoli ⑤**. Cavoli is dominated by an imposing lighthouse which houses a sea research centre. You can visit by boat as part of an excursion package. Scuba-divers will enjoy the sea around the headland, being rich in vegetation and marine life.

THE COSTA REI AND THE SARRABUS REGION

A few kilometres inland is the hamlet of **Castiadas ⑥**, surrounded by a vast agricultural area created by a penal colony that was established in 1875. At the time, open-air convict colonies were common in Europe and were founded on the assumption that hard work would aid rehabilitation. The convicts constructed all the buildings in the colony, including a hospital. The result is the small, partially restored hamlet we see today.

Back on the coast are the seemingly endless beaches of the **Costa Rei ⑦**, dotted with tourist villages, which reach right up to the foothills of **Capo Ferrato**, the lagoons of **Feraxi** and **Colostrai**, and the salt works of the **Peschiera**; the coastal marshes here attract many different species of birds, including flamingos, white egrets and herons. The flat coastal strip gradually gives way to the mountainous foothills of the Sarrabus region, through which, flanked by fields and citrus plantations, meander the **Flumendosa** and the **Picocca** rivers. Although no larger than 180 sq km (70 sq miles), the area includes a range of stunning landscapes, encompassing plains and ranges of mountains as well as lakes and superb stretches of coast.

MURAVERA

At the mouth of the Flumendosa river is **Muravera ❽**, a town swelled by summer visitors and surrounded by fragrant orange groves.

Muravera was inhabited at the time of the Nuragic civilisation; later on, under the Romans, the town must have acquired a certain importance in view of its situation on the Roman road to Olbia. The community is divided into the three districts of Castiadas, San Pietro and Costa Rei. In the vicinity, near Costa Rei, there are 22 Neolithic menhirs; six of them are still in their initial vertical positions. Comparisons with similar ancient structures on other sites in Northern Europe seem to indicate that their purpose was to mark the passage of the seasons. A

further 42 menhirs can be seen on the site of the **Nuraghe Scalas**. Of artistic interest is Muravera's 16th-century church of **San Nicola di Bari** (daily), which was built in Catalan Gothic style.

The little town itself has retained numerous folkloric customs, and every year various festivals take place. The **Sagra degli Agrumi** (Citrus Fair), which usually takes place on a Sunday in April, features processions of folk groups wearing traditional embroidered costumes and playing traditional instruments such as the prehistoric *launedda*, a flute-type instrument traditionally used by shepherds.

VILLAGES ALONG THE FLUMENDOSA RIVER

The village of **San Vito ❾**, northwest of Muravera, has around 4,000 inhabitants and a parish extending over an area of 230 sq km (90 sq miles) of mainly mountainous countryside. To the south are woods and oak groves; in the middle rise the peaks of the Monte dei Sette Fratelli; in the north lie the mountains of the Sarrabus. The entire

⊙ **Tip**

Those after adrenalin rushes should contact Ogliastra Outdoor Paradise for treks, climbs, canyoning, and hiking (www.ogliastraoutdoor paradise.com).

The lighthouse (il faro) of Capo Ferrato.

Deer inhabit the woods and oak groves of the southeast.

Porto Corallo, Villaputzu.

area is a refuge for wildlife: the Sardinian partridge, ring and turtle doves, wild boar and rabbits, the hobby and the Sardinian deer all inhabit the area in large numbers.

Mining – for silver and other minerals – was once a major industry in the area, especially on Monte Narba, and as a result the village of San Vito enjoyed a fourfold increase in its population at the turn of the 17th–18th century. Large numbers of convicts were used as forced labour in the mines. Since the completion of the **Flumendosa Barrage**, the river valley – previously subject to frequent flooding – has been exploited more intensively for agriculture.

Worth seeing in San Vito is the **parish church**; it has a fine facade, twin belfries and an interesting crucifix in one of the side chapels. The district has a rich craft tradition and produces some excellent handicrafts, such as colourful embroidery and basketwork, as well as *launeddas*. The local cuisine is also justly famous. It includes Sardinian specialities such as roast kid, *culingionis de patata* (a type of ravioli filled with cheese) and *pardulas cun meli* (pastry cases filled with a delicious mixture of honey, egg and curd cheese).

In a field near San Vito an ancient grave containing 14 skeletons and a rich store of funeral gifts has been unearthed. The collection of gold and silver earrings, bangles, fibulae and pottery dating from the 5th and 4th centuries BC can be seen in the archaeological museum in Cagliari.

SILVER MINING

Villaputzu ⑩, a small town of 5,000 inhabitants, lies just east of San Vito along the SS 125; it sits on a small plain formed by the detritus deposited by the Flumendosa river. Views extend across to the Mediterranean *màcchia* on the hills of the Sarrabus, a tangle of wild strawberries, mastic trees, phyllirea, juniper bushes and low-lying holm oaks. A closer look reveals the remains of two silver mines, **S'Acqua Arrubia** and **Gibbas**, which lie in the middle of the small coastal marshes of **Porto Corallo**. Both were in operation until the beginning of the 20th century.

At the end of the 14th century Villaputzu was the scene of the fierce quarrels between the Sardinian rulers of Arborea and the Aragonese. During the 16th century the **Fortezza Gibas** and the **Porto Corallo** were constructed to protect the town from the increasingly persistent attacks of the Turks operating off the North African coast.

CHURCHES, CASTLES AND ROCKETS

Around 20km (12 miles) north of Villaputzu just off the SS 125 stands the pretty little Romanesque church of **San Nicola di Quirra** ⑪. It was built entirely with bricks, very rare in Sardinia, by the Pisani in the 12th century and is surrounded by *cumbessias* (shelters for pilgrims). On a broad plateau demarcated by precipitous cliffs perches a grim fortress, the **Castello di Quirra**. The view is breathtaking.

Folk festivals are still important in the area, and during the *Sagra di Sant'Antonio del Fuoco* a giant bonfire is lit on the village square in accordance with an ancient pagan rite.

The SS125 climbs up to the **Salto di Quirra**, a very large, high plateau with scenery of great natural beauty. The plateau can be reached more easily by following the panoramic road that goes up to **Perdasdefogu** and leads to **Monte Cardiga**. The presence of military vehicles and futuristic radar stations around Perdasdefogu hints at the presence of the Italian Air Force: you may even see or hear rockets blasting off while passing the area's spectacular *tacchi* – the high limestone plateaux often separated by deep canyons, reminiscent of Spaghetti Western film landscapes.

GATEWAY TO OGLIASTRA

Ogliastria was one of eight Sardinian provinces until 2016, when the number of provinces was reduced to five and Ogliastra was assimilated to the province of Nuoro. The region of Ogliastra has been dubbed an *isola nell' isola* – "an island within an island" – as its mountains and rugged coastline cut it off from the rest of the world. This characteristic has meant that, like the dramatic *tacchi*-studded landscape, its culture and traditions are largely untouched.

The gateway to what is now the larger province of Nuoro is **Tertenia** 🄬, which lies in the middle of a largely uninhabited region divided into three main districts: Sapala, Quirra and Villamonti. There are many springs in the vicinity, as well as a mountain torrent, the Sibiri or Rio Sibi, and a number of mountain peaks such as the San Giovanni. Between the two regions of the Sarrabus and the Ogliastra, at the southern end of the Jerzu district, you may be lucky enough to come across a *petra fitta*, a monolith usually in the form of a phallus, or a flat, altar-like *petra de s'altari*.

ANCIENT MONUMENTS

There are a number of well-preserved nuraghi in the region around

The European bee-eater (merops apiaster) can be seen in many parts of the island in the summer before it heads south to Africa for the winter.

The road towards Tertenia.

⊘ TORRE MURTA DIGS

Near **Torre Murta** the intriguing remains of an ancient settlement dating from the 3rd millennium BC, including a *domus de janas*, can be found. In 1966, an archaeologist discovered the ruins of a Phoenician settlement. It is likely that the site of the Acropolis of Sarcopos, a Phoenician-Carthaginian temple-fortress, must also have stood near here. The Latin *Itinerarium* of Antoninus, written at the beginning of the 3rd century AD, refers to the town of Sarcopos as being situated near Porticenses (Tertenia) and Ferraria (San Gregorio).

North African pottery finds in the area date from the 6th and 7th centuries AD; local clay artefacts indicate that the area was inhabited during Vandal and Byzantine times.

Tertenia; some of the best examples are the **nuraghe su Concali** and the **nuraghe Longu**, along the coast of the Marina di Tertenia south of the coastal tower of Sarralá.

Travellers interested in churches will enjoy visiting those of the Beata Vergine Assunta, Santa Lucia, San Pietro, Santa Sofia or Santa Teresa. Ideally, time your visit to coincide with one of their festivals, such as *Vergine Assunta* (Assumption) in August or the festival in honour of St Sebastian (January). The festivities attract visitors from the surrounding villages as well as foreign tourists.

WINEMAKING COOPERATIVE

Further to the west, a few miles from the SS 125 between Tertenia and Bari Sardo, on a long ridge surrounded by hilly country, lies the slightly larger town of **Jerzu** ⓭. A noble Cannonau vintage is produced in its vineyards; in former times the farmers themselves would make the wine, but nowadays this is undertaken almost exclusively by the cooperative wine

Jerzu is built on several levels up the hillside, and vineyards cling to the steep slopes around the town.

cellars. The neighbouring countryside is mostly mountainous. The cone-shaped **Punta Corongiu** affords a spectacular view of the Tyrrhenian Sea; on clear days one can even see the summits of Villacidro on the other side of the island, towering above the smaller mountain peaks and wooded slopes.

Jerzu's most important festival of the year is the **Sant'Antonio di Padova** held on 13 June in honour of St Anthony of Padua, to whom one of the town's churches is dedicated. Other buildings of note which are worth a quick visit include the churches of St Sebastian and St Erasmus.

ULASSAI AND BARI SARDO

The picturesque town of **Ulassai** ⓮ is situated in a canyon which formed itself between two *tacchi*. Of great interest for its beautiful concretions is the **Grotta Su Marmuri** (Apr–Oct, 60-minute guided tours, hours vary; tel: 0782-79859 for details), part of the limestone massif at the back of the village. The grotto has a large

⊘ VILLAGRANDE STRISCAILI

Further north, towards the wild, untouched Gennargentu mountain range and Sardinia's highest peak, Punta La Marmora (1,834 metres/6,000ft), there are fabulous opportunities for outdoor pursuits, relaxation and discovering the generous hospitality of some of the healthiest people on earth. Due to a unique blend of simple diet, unpolluted water and air, a shepherd's life of hard graft and some favourable genes thrown in, the people of Ogliastra have a better chance than most to live to 100. Indeed, the region has one of the highest concentrations of centenarians in the world: at Villagrande Striscaili the highest level of male longevity in the world was recorded for those born between 1880 and 1901.

Deep in the ancient Bosco di Santa Barbara, a vast woodland in Villagrande Striscaili, you'll find Hotel Orlando, where you can discover Ogliastra's secrets of longevity and revel in its simple pleasures. Traditional, beautifully presented Ogliastra cuisine is served, and a spit for wild boar roasts caters for groups who dine on granite tables under ancient trees. Concerts, outdoor theatre, yoga classes, art shows and various craft events add vibrant cultural life. There are also a variety of packages available (www.hotelorlando-sardegna.com).

entrance and long caves where the constant 12°C (53°F) temperature requires the use of a pullover even in summer. Contemporary artworks by Maria Lai (1919–2013) that explore myths and mountain life can be seen scattered around Ulassai's landscape, as well as in an old railway station building, the **Museo Stazione dell'Arte** (www.stazione dellarte.com; May–Sept 9.30–11am, 1–2.30pm, 6–7.30pm, Oct–Apr 9.30–11am, 1–2.30pm, 4–6pm). Continuing towards Gairo in the Rio Pardu Valley you come across the ghost village of **Osini Vecchio**, abandoned in 1951 after landslide damage.

Further north on the SS 125 is **Bari Sardo** . The origin of the name lies in its *abbari* (marshy ground). Historically the town enjoyed considerable importance; in former times it was famous for flax and the manufacture of linen. Today the town derives most of its income from cattle breeding and agriculture, the best products being its red and white wine, and various types of fruit: lemons, oranges, pears, plums and apricots. In the mountains there are still many species of wild animals: rabbits, ring and turtle doves, partridges and wild boar. The stretch of coast near **Marina di Cea** has become popular with tourists.

LANUSEI AND OAK FOREST

The little town of **Lanusei** ⑯ lies away from the coast, perched on the eastern foothills of the Barbagia surrounded by mountains. Now a bishopric and the seat of the local courts, Lanusei is the proud setting of the first Salesian-Sardinian foundation (a Catholic order known for its charitable works established by the followers of St John Bosco), and there are a number of interesting aristocratic buildings. The town also has numerous schools and colleges, lending it a youthful vibe. A handicraft fair is held in summer on the main square. In the

Duomo (Cathedral of St Mary Magdalene; daily) are some interesting paintings and canvases of Delitala, an important 20th-century Sardinian painter.

The **church of Santos Cosma e Damiano** (dedicated to two brothers, the patron saints of doctors, who were canonised following their martyrdom in the 4th century) is in the neighbourhood, on the way to Bosco Selene. This is the town's surrounding holm oak forest, which, at 1,000 metres (3,280ft) above sea level, has some commanding views of the valley below as it descends to the sea, and numerous walking trails. The **Bosco Selene Archaeological Park** (tel: 0782-41051 for hours) consists of two *tombe di giganti* and part of a large Nuragic village.

TORTOLÍ

Tortolí ⑰ lies further to the north in a small, fertile plain surrounded by agriculture. In former times the marshes and lakes surrounding Tortolí increased the risk of malaria infection

Hiking in the Jerzu hills.

⊙ Tip

At Arbatax port you can hire a *gommoni* speedboat and tour guide Marco Nonnis to explore the spectacular coastline of limestone cliffs, grottoes and pristine beaches of the Golfo di Orosei. Tel: 338-422 8788; www.velamarearbatax.it.

and gave the town a reputation for being an unhealthy place to live. Times have changed – tourism, the port, the industry of nearby Arbatax, a new airport and the fertile surrounding countryside have all helped make Tortolí one of the liveliest towns in the Ogliastra region – as witnessed by its numerous schools, restaurants, shops and hotels.

To the south of Tortolí flows the river of the same name, its banks a haven for various species of water bird, including cranes and flamingos, whose more usual homes are Andalusia, the Camargue and the lagoons of Cagliari.

ARBATAX AND A STEAM TRAIN

A few miles further on is **Arbatax** ⓲, a well-known seaside resort buzzing gently with commercial, ferry and leisure vessel traffic, with connections to the Italian mainland as well as other ports on the island. Industrial drilling platforms are produced in the port of Arbatax, and this industry, along with tourism, has brought the district regular employment and prosperity. There are a dozen or so sandy beaches around Arbatax, ranging from long, curvy, family-orientated **Spiaggia di San Gemiliano**, to intimate **Porto Frailis**, backed by rocks and the luxury hotel of La Bitta.

The small **Trenino Verde** (Green Train; tel: 070-265 71; www.treninoverde.com), formed by a 1930s steam locomotive and two vintage carriages, leaves Arbatax and follows the winding narrow-gauge railway track built in 1894 until it reaches Mandas, where you can jump on a regular train to get to Cagliari. The railway was built so that the heart of the wild southern parts of the island could be accessed and the rich mineral deposits and forests of the region could be exploited commercially. As the Trenino Verde slowly climbs through the mountains, heading through some of the wildest landscapes on the island, it sometimes stops to avoid wild animals on the track, reminiscent of D.H. Lawrence's train journey described in his book *Sea and Sardinia*, written in 1921.

Ancient shoreline defence.

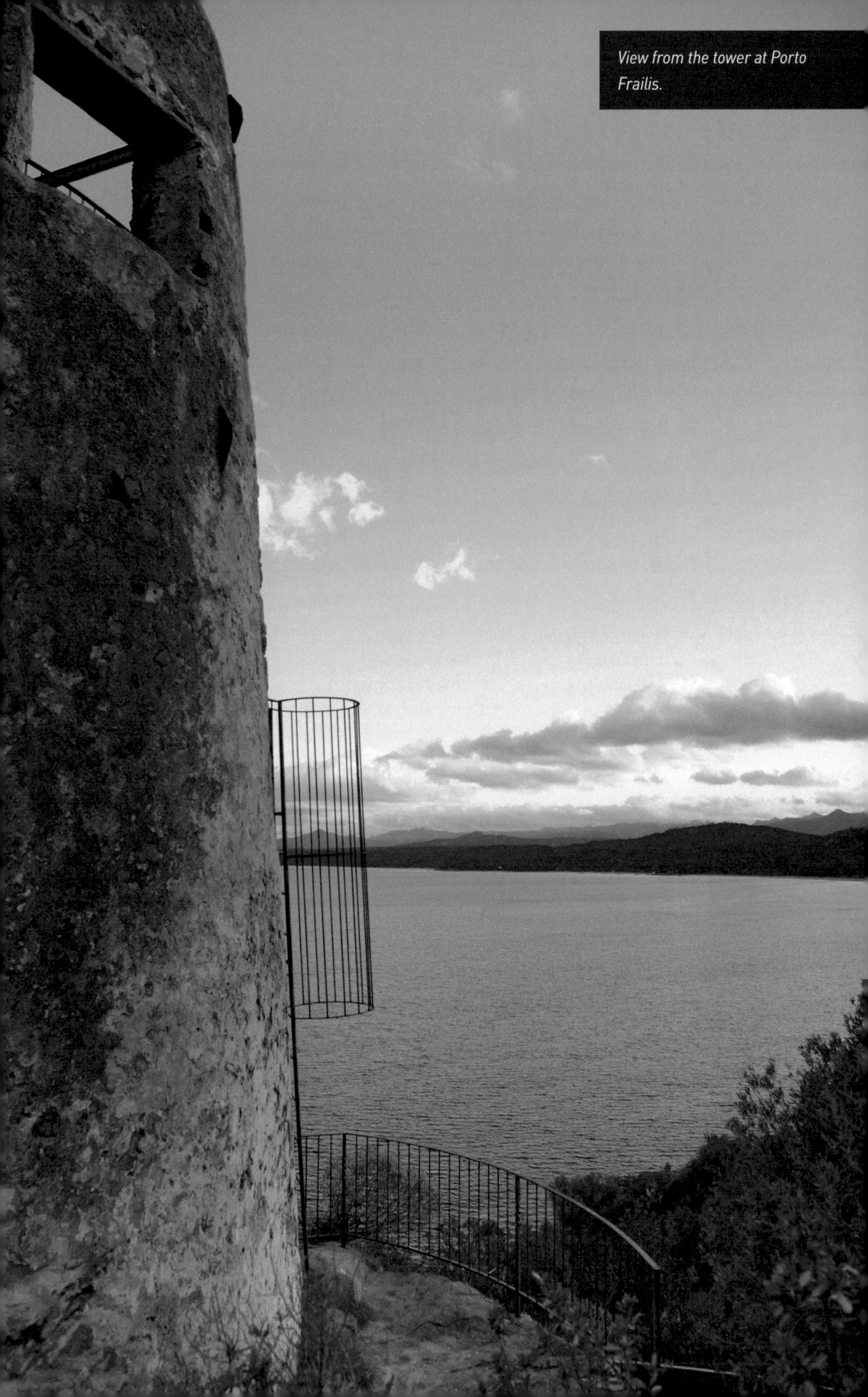

View from the tower at Porto Frailis.

GOLFO DI OROSEI TO OLBIA

Covering one of Europe's wildest and most spectacular coastlines, the Golfo di Orosei, this tour heads deep into the limestone mountains where ancient traditions flourish, then via beguiling bays to tourist boom town Olbia.

Map on page 124

All along this stretch, as far as busy Olbia, there are beautiful bays and ancient villages where intriguing traditions and festivals flourish. From Arbatax and Cala Gonone you can charter boats for memorable day-trip adventures along the incomparable Golfo di Orosei, Sardinia's wild, untouched coastline. As well as challenging walks in the limestone mountains – some paths lead down to isolated coves – there's abundant wildlife, including nimble-hoofed mouflon (wild sheep), and awe-inspiring natural features. From Oliena north to Orosei and Posada the rolling hills of the Baronia produce excellent wine, olives and almonds.

A charming little village by the sea, **Santa Maria Navarrese ❶** forms part of the community of Baunei. It developed around the church of the same name which has an olive tree in its courtyard said to be over 1,000 years old. According to legend, the church was founded by one of the daughters of the King of Navarre in gratitude for being saved from a shipwreck. The church stands on the site where she reached land. The town lies on the southern coast of Montesanto and contains hotels, restaurants and holiday villas.

Its environs are wild and untouched and stretch in the east as far as the cliffs overlooking the Tyrrhenian Sea. Goat and pig herds still wander among the holm oaks, arbutus and the shrubs of the Mediterranean *màcchia* (scrub), to feed on the profusion of berries and acorns.

The town of **Baunei ❷** is known for its hard-working population. Today, few local residents pursue the area's traditional occupations of woodcutting or weaving; most are employed in jobs associated with tourism, the manufacture of sweets or wine production.

Boat tours from Cala Gonone can take you to the Grotte di Cala Luna.

DRAMATIC COASTLINE OF COVES AND CANYONS

The vast landscape surrounding Baunei is exceptional – rugged limestone mountains, untouched by development, fall dramatically into azure waters. It is here that you begin to understand how the geology of Ogliastra defines this province's character and how isolation has preserved its traditions. It is enclosed by mighty natural barriers: the Supramonte mountains and the Codula di Luna river to the north, the Gennargentu mountains to the west, and the hills of the Salto di Quirra to the south. The coastline looks like a huge mountainous amphitheatre looking out towards the Tyrrhenian Sea.

The coast is characterised by high cliffs, false inlets carved into the malleable limestone and pristine beaches with crystalline water. The **Altopiano del Golgo** (1,000 metres/3,280ft) is a large depression in the limestone rock covered by a flow of basaltic lava, where the enormous **Golgo Ravine** (295 metres/967ft) opens up. Not far away is the simple church of San Pietro di Golgo,

built in the 18th century, and surrounded by rustic *cumbessias* (pilgrim's houses).

From the plateau it is possible to walk down the **Codula de Sisine**, a 4km (2.5-mile) narrow limestone canyon of great natural beauty formed by the Supramonte di Baunei that ends at Sisine beach surrounded by majestic cliffs. The **Cala Goloritzè** is dominated by l'Aguglia, an enormous pinnacle reaching 100 metres (328ft) high, popular with free-climbers.

From Baunei the main road, the SS 125, continues northwards. On one side is the **Gola su Gorroppu**, a spectacular canyon 500 metres (1,640ft) deep and 4km (2.5 miles) long in its most spectacular part. On the other side is the **Genna Silana Pass** (1,017 metres/3,336ft at its highest point). You can follow the Gola su Gorroppu on foot, but in the final section it is necessary to use ropes to get over some vertical cliffs and ponds, so a local guide is essential.

The path that leads down the large canyon of Cala Luna, the Codula di Luna, is about 8km (5 miles) long and starts from the Supramonte di

⊘ Tip

Bring protective shoes (preferably aqua shoes) for clambering over rocks and tiptoeing on pebbly beaches, especially for day-long boat trips on the Golfo di Orosei.

Pristine beach near Baunei.

⊘ GOLFO DI OROSEI BOAT TRIP

The 36km (22.5 miles) of rugged coast between the Porto di Arbatax and Porto Cala Gonlone is a must-see. Boats can be chartered from both ports, preferably with a guide, as local knowledge and skill is needed to negotiate hidden sea caves and rocky shoreline. Pack a lunch, drinks, swimming costumes and sun protection for an unforgettable day out.

Beyond the otherworldly brick-red granite turrets of the Rocce Rosse of Capo Bellavista, and L'Isolotto dell'Ogliastra, the limestone wonders begin to unfold. Gulls, shearwaters, shags and other seabirds encircle the towering cliffs, and wild mouflons and goats move amid blotches of *màcchia* scrub. Around each jagged corner the limpid waters of various hues of blue and green ripple over white pebbles. Small craft and gleaming super yachts drop anchor, and tanned bodies wade to the shore carrying supplies. Towards Cala Gonone charter boats ferry day-trippers to Cala Sisine and Cala di Luna. Away from the numbers, in the intimate coves of Porto Pedrosu, Cala Goloritzè and Cala degli Innamorati, you may see a diver plunging the shallower depths to spear fish and collect *ricci* (sea urchins).

Boat companies include Cala Luna (tel: 0784-93133; www.escursione-calaluna.it) and David e Golia (tel: 338-958 3436; www.davidegolia.it).

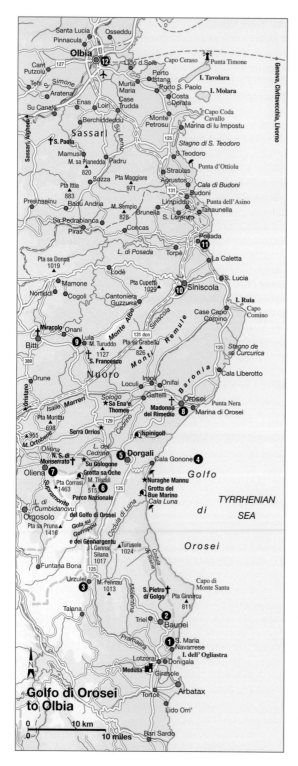

Genova, Chirtavecchia, Livorno

Sassari, Alghero

Oristano

**Golfo di Orosei
to Olbia**

0   10 km
0   10 miles

Urzulei. It takes about three hours to walk the easy-to-follow path, which passes through *màcchia* scrub and the entrances to many caves. The village of **Urzulei** ❸ is on the left-hand side, clinging to a wooded hillside and sheltered from northerly and southwesterly winds. It lies at the foot of **Punta is Gruttas**, in the midst of varied terrain where the shepherds allow their flocks to roam wild. Continuing towards Dorgali, beyond Urzulei the road is full of tortuous bends, more than compensated for by the awe-inspiring views.

GONONE AND LUNA BEACHES

Barely 2km (1 mile) before Dorgali, there is a road tunnel through the Monte Bardia. The views as you exit the tunnel are magnificent: a gentle limestone hill falls away towards the sea. Juniper, rosemary and other aromatic Mediterranean plants blossom under ancient holm oaks. Spreading out in the distance, **Cala Gonone** ❹ is a former fishing village with views extending across glistening emerald waters – nowadays it is a sizeable town with hotels, villas, flats, apartment houses and campsites.

Cala Gonone is the starting point for boat trips along the 40km (25 miles) of wild cliffs, bays and beaches. Grottoes with little sandy beaches are visible at sea level, but many of the most magical sea caves are kept secret by local guides.

The most famous grotto of all is the huge **Grotta del Bue Marino**, renowned for its spectacular caves which are thought to extend for about 8km (5 miles), although only 1km (0.5 mile) of the caves is open to the public. The grotto was also home to Sardinian monk seals until the 1950s, and along this stretch nests the elusive Eleonora falcon.

The most popular beach in the area is **Cala Luna**, described as one of the most beautiful beaches in the Mediterranean because of the flowering pink oleanders that reflect themselves in the tiny fresh-water lagoon behind the beach. The beach is surrounded by six grottoes and high rocks. A daily boat service allows you to reach parts of the coast which are otherwise only accessible by long and tiring walks.

DORGALI AND NURAGIC VILLAGES

Dorgali ❺ extends along the foot of the Monte Bardia, which protects the town's inhabitants from the sea breezes. Cattle farming and agriculture have been practised here since earliest times; the vineyards of the nearby community of Oliena to the west are famous for their noble Cannonau vintages. Dorgali itself thrives on a flourishing handicrafts industry: cork, wood, wool, gold and silver items are all produced by a variety of medium-sized firms, most of them are also involved in local tourism.

The principal sights in and around the town include the impressive Nuragic village of **Serra Orrios** (tel: 0783-96721; daily 9am–noon and 3–7pm), 11km (7 miles) northwest of Dorgali near the SS 125. This is one of the best-preserved Nuragic villages in Sardinia, dating from the 10–12th centuries BC. The 70 round huts in the village are grouped in six clusters, each with a central well. A small temple area has also been discovered. About 15km (9 miles) northwest of Dorgali is the Marreri Valley, near the village of La Traversa. On the road that connects Dorgali with the SS 131 you will see signposts to the giants' tomb of **Sa Ena'e Thomes**. The tomb has a high stela carved in granite.

Heading north from Dorgali, about 4km (2.5 miles) on the right-hand side of the SS 125 you will see a sign for the **Grotta di Ispinigoli** (tel: 0784-927 236; hours vary greatly). The cave contains a 38-metre (125ft) stalagmite – the highest in Europe. Some interesting archaeological finds dating from the time of the Phoenicians have been discovered here.

Four km (2.5 miles) from Dorgali, on the road that connects the SS 125 with Cala Gonone and not far from the tunnel, is the turn-off for the **nuraghe Mannu** (Area Archeologica del Mannu; tel: 0784-927 230; Apr–Sept daily 9am–1pm and 3–6pm), an excavated site and

The giants' tomb of Sa Ena'e Thomes, one of the best preserved on the island, dates from around 1800 BC.

Inside the Grotta di Ispinigoli.

⊘ FROM SMALL ACORNS

The residents of Uzulei and Baunei still bake *pan'ispeli* – acorn bread, at one time prepared all over the island – which was even mentioned as a Sardinian staple by Pliny the Elder in the 1st century AD. The local recipe for the dough goes something like this: soak some clay and wood-ash particles in water, then decant and pour the water into a large pot. Place the pot on the stove and add some shelled acorns (the ash particles act as a leach and remove the bitter taste from the acorns, while the clay softens them). A smooth paste will gradually form. Stir continuously, and cook until it is dark red, almost brown in colour. Allow the mixture to cool and solidify. Place the dough in the sun to dry. The acorn bread has a slightly nutty taste.

If you are visiting the Su Gologone spring, bring some food with you and enjoy lunch at one of the picnic tables in the eucalyptus wood surrounding the spring.

The mighty Supramonte mountains.

in a panoramic position over Cala Gonone. Archaeological finds dating from Palaeolithic times have also been discovered in the **Grotta Corbeddu** in the Lanaittu Valley, which during the 19th century was used as a shelter for the bandit of the same name.

THE VALLE LANAITTU TO OLIENA

The gateway to the Supramonte, the Valle Lanaittu, is covered by holm oaks and juniper bushes, which provide shelter for the mouflon that roam the hills. At the top of **Monte Tiscali** ❻ (515 metres/1,690ft) a wide crater opens up and inside is the Nuragic village of **Tiscali** (tel: 0784-927 200; daily 9am–5pm, May–Oct until 7pm). The name has become synonymous with the European internet provider of the same name, founded by Renato Soru, the left-leaning governor of Sardinia (2004–9). Discovered in the 19th century, Tiscali consists of a number of round dwellings with limestone walls. It is thought that the village was inhabited up to the time of the

Roman invasion and its high walls and surrounding terrain acted as natural defences. To get to Tiscali, take the turn-off on the right near Su Gologone and leave your car about 2km (1 mile) after Grotta sa Oche following the main dirt road. Follow the red-and-white marks on the rocks to the chasm of Tiscali; the walk to the crater village takes a little over 1.5 hours.

Returning to the SS 125 towards Olbia, a few kilometres past Dorgali you can turn off towards pretty **Oliena** ❼. The little town lies in a lovely setting at the foot of Punta Corrasi, separated from Dorgali by the Valle Lanaittu. The most noteworthy sight in Oliena is **Su Gologone**, a spring situated near the hotel and restaurant of the same name. Gushing in a torrent from the limestone cliff, it is the most important spring in Sardinia, flowing at 400 litres (106 gallons) of water per second before joining the Cedrino river.

The beauty of the surrounding countryside, coupled with the hospitable nature of the inhabitants of Oliena, is famous in Sardinia. In and around the

town are numerous late Romanesque and Pisan-style churches, all completed before the 14th century. The town centre is dominated by the **Chiesa di Santa Maria** (daily); at Easter this is the scene of one of the most popular religious ceremonies in Sardinia. **S'Incontru** (The Encounter) marks the meeting between the Virgin Mary and the resurrected Christ. The brightly coloured costumes, shawls and filigree jewellery for which the town is famous are all on display during the festival. The ancient churches of **Santa Croce** and **San Lussorio** are worth a visit; from 21 August the latter forms the setting for a popular festival combining both sacred and secular elements.

The Jesuits played a key role in the town's history. They were responsible for establishing the **parish church of St Ignatius Loyola** (daily), named after their founder. In the church offices is a varied collection of paintings and old manuscripts.

During the 16th and 17th centuries, the Jesuits painstakingly undertook the development of 16,000 hectares

(39,500 acres) of mountainous countryside; some of this was later sold off to local farmers, but 4,000 hectares (9,900 acres) are still in the possession of the society today. Thanks to their skills and their diligence, Oliena is now a thriving agricultural community, although it's best-known as a producer of olives and wine, notably Cannonau.

FROM OLIENA TO OROSEI

The SS 129 to Orosei is bordered by hills covered with olive and almond trees. Lowland stretches occur from time to time, mostly given over to viticulture except when the local livestock farmers use them as grazing for their animals, principally sheep. Now and again the way leads through rough countryside, where the parched clay soil supports oleander, *màcchia* scrubland vegetation, arbutus and the thorny Sardinian gorse, the flowers of which blossom in spring and early summer, covering the landscape in a magnificent carpet of yellow.

The valley of the **Cedrino river** is marked by a mighty dam constructed to prevent the regular destruction caused

Olive, oak and juniper trees grow in abundance around Oliena.

Standing at the entrance of the Nuragic village of Tiscali.

The church of Rosario, one of three churches in the centre of Orosei.

Orosei.

by flooding when the river bursts its banks. On one occasion, however, the dam was unable to contain the deluge; the waters devastated the valley and the ancient villages of **Galtellì**, **Loculi**, **Irgoli** and **Onifai**. Of the four settlements, Galtellì lies on the right bank; Loculi, Irgoli and Onifai are on the left. Galtellì was the most important town in the region until the Middle Ages, and was the bishopric until 1496. However, the ravages of malaria and frequent pirate raids meant that for a long time its population lived in poverty.

The houses and churches of the four villages, especially those of Irgoli and Galtellì, bear silent witness to a peasant culture and its religion, displaying fine examples of a formal but modest Mediterranean architectural style: tiled roofs, courtyards, archways, and belfries which – large or small – seem to cling to the ground rather than soar heavenwards. A good example of a 17th-century house is **Casa Marras** in Galtellì, which has been transformed into an **ethnographical museum** (tel: 0784-90005; May and Sept, Oct–Apr 10am–noon, 4–6pm, June–Aug 9.30am–12.30pm, 4.30–7.30pm).

THE HISTORIC CAPITAL OF OROSEI

Located on the final section of the SS 129 is the small town of **Orosei ❽**, with an elegant, bustling centre and whitewashed stone buildings overlooking colourful courtyards. The former capital of the Baronia region, the town had its golden age under Pisan rule, when it developed into an important harbour on the Cedrino river. Malaria and the silting up of the river caused its decline.

Three churches stand on the central Piazza del Popolo; the **Chiesa del Rosario** has a Baroque facade, while the parish church of **San Giacomo Maggiore**, at the top of a large flight of steps, is surmounted by an unusual group of small domes.

Not far from here are the *"palatzos Betzos"*, ancient homes belonging to noble families. Among them is the **Museo Don Nanni Guiso** (tel: 0784-996 273; by appointment), an eclectic

museum displaying surprising miniature theatres from the 18th century, antique books on Sardinia, old costumes and drawings of important Italian artists.

The **church of Sant'Antonio Abate** is enclosed in a large courtyard with a Pisan tower, and contains 15th-century frescoes. Every year on 16 January a big bonfire is lit at the centre of the courtyard in honour of the patron saint. Further celebrations are held in the **parish church of San Giacomo** in honour of Nostra Signora del Mare (Our Lady of the Sea) in the second week in May. Orosei is clearly prospering, not only from tourism – its long sandy beaches (including Cala Liberotto and Cala Ginepro) are a big draw – but also from agriculture and a steady income from its marble quarries.

About 30km (19 miles) inland from Orosei near the Monte Albo woods, in the region of Barbagia, is the village of **Lula** ❾, where the important sanctuary of San Francesco di Lula stands. According to tradition it was founded by bandits in 1600, who believed that Saint Francis was their protector.

Near the sanctuary is a church and a number of *cumbessias* (pilgrims' houses). It's an evocative spot, and becomes very lively in the first week of May when thousands participate in a pilgrimage to the shrine, and food and wine is aplenty.

SINISCOLA AND LIMESTONE CLIFFS

North of Orosei the SS 125 follows the coast. The invitingly clear sea here is as unpolluted as it looks. After driving for a short while through pine groves and characteristic Mediterranean vegetation, you will reach the twin villages of Capo Comino and Santa Lucia, before arriving in **Siniscola** ❿, and its coastal suburb, La Caletta, with its own harbour and a pretty beach.

During the latter part of the 20th century, tourism and a number of small industries – including a lime kiln and a cement works – have resulted in a more rapid population growth rate in Siniscola than in any of the other towns or villages within the province of Nuoro, apart from the regional capital, Nuoro itself. Today Siniscola has some 11,000 inhabitants.

In earlier times Siniscola was the seat of the barons of Monte Albo, under whose jurisdiction also lay the towns of Lodè and Torpè in the interior and Posada and San Teodoro on the coast. The defensive towers, Santa Lucia and Caletta, and the fortified wall around the town, were built following persistent raids by Turks in the 16th century. On the main street, Via Sassari, stands the 18th-century church of San Giovanni Battista, decorated with a fresco cycle showing the life of St John the Baptist.

Not far from Siniscola lie the mountains **Remule** and **Monte Albo**. What these mountains lack in height they more than make up for by their awe-inspiring, strangely shaped limestone cliffs. At dawn they greet the day with

⊙ **Fact**

Nobel Prize-winning writer Grazia Deledda described Orosei's festival of Nostra Signora del Rimedio amid the tensions of stifling family life in her novel *Canne al Vento* ("Reeds in the Wind").

Marble quarry in Orosei.

The name of Posada's Castello della Fava translates as "bean castle". It gained its name during the time of the Moorish invasion.

a shimmering pale pink hue; by midday they are a dazzling white; and as dusk falls they are suffused in a blaze of crimson.

POSADA'S TOURIST BOOM

Further north, perched on top of a limestone hill, is the town of **Posada** , dominated by the 12th-century ruins of Castello della Fava. Stairs lead to the top of the castle's tower, from where there is a panoramic view of the surrounding countryside, much of it planted with fruit trees, the sea and the Posada river. The town itself is worth exploring; follow the winding alleyways and steep stairways until you come across delightful small squares, all reminders of Posada's medieval roots.

Posada and San Teodoro further up the coast, together with Budoni between the two, have experienced rapid economic growth in recent decades, mainly thanks to the tourist boom. There are numerous hotels, apartments and rooms in private houses to accommodate the hordes of

Lighthouse on the coast of Olbia.

visitors who come every summer to the beaches between Siniscola and Olbia.

THE ROAD TO OLBIA

The coast between Posada and Olbia has some of the finest beaches on the east coast. The remaining stretch of the SS 125 as far as Olbia is some 35km (22 miles) long and leads through one of the most enchanting regions in the whole of Sardinia, past the Cala Coda Cavallo, the Spiaggia di Salinedda beach, and a succession of bays – Cala Ruia, Cala Suaraccia and Cala Purgatorio to the foothills of Monte Petrosu and the picturesque beaches of Porto Taverna, Porto San Paolo and Porto Istana.

Olbia ⑫ has a modern airport and a flourishing port, and is the main arrival point for people staying on the Costa Smeralda – except for those arriving by yacht. Thanks mainly to the growth in the tourist industry, Olbia has expanded rapidly in the past two decades. Its first population boom occurred in the 1920s, when a group of foreign industrialists

developed local cheese production and mussel farming.

Despite its Greek name (*olbius* means happy), the town was not founded by the Greeks. There is no doubt that the Carthaginians once lived here; when the Romans conquered Sardinia (238 BC), Olbia ceased to rely purely on its economic value, and acquired military power as well as strategic importance. In those days the town was connected to the rest of the island by three roads; they served as highways for the legions as well as for the transport of goods.

Later, during the Christian era, these roads were a great aid to the Christian missionaries in their progress to convert the islanders. But the town's golden age occurred under the Romans. In 1904 a hoard of money was found in the necropolis; the 871 gold coins bear the portraits of 117 different Roman families and include 312 different currencies. The break-up of the Western Roman empire during the 5th century BC marked the beginning of a long period of decline in the fortunes of Olbia. The town repeatedly fell prey to Arab raids from the 8th century onwards, and many of its inhabitants fled to the interior.

It was not until the turn of the millennium that it began to flourish again, initially as the first capital of the *giudicato* of Gallura, and later under Pisa, when it acquired the status of a free city. During this time the town was rechristened Terranova, a name which it bore until 1939.

Olbia is now a modern city and usually passed through on the way to somewhere else. In 2013, the town was severely hit by floods caused by Cyclone Cleopatra. Worth a visit, however, is the Romanesque **Basilica of San Semplicio** (daily 7.30am–1pm, 3.30–6pm, summer until 7pm), built between the second half of the 11th century and the beginning of the 12th century. It contains frescoes of the same period that represent two bishops (San Semplicio and San Vittore) and a fragment of a fresco depicting only the heads of a group of people.

> **◎ Tip**
>
> A huge four-day festival is held in Olbia in mid-May, involving a solemn procession, the Palio della Stella horse race and *Sagra delle Cozze* (a feast of mussels cooked *alla marinara*), all of which commemorate San Simplicio's martyrdom in the 14th century.

Isola di Tavolara, a marine reserve.

◎ BEACHES, BAYS AND ROCKY ISLANDS

The most beautiful beaches to be found along this stretch of the east coast are **Su Tiriarzu** at Posada, **Budoni**, the sandy beach of **l'Isuledda** on the peninsula of the same name, and the beach of **La Cinta**, a narrow strip of sand 3km (2 miles) long that separates the coastal marsh of San Teodoro from the sea, not far from the mighty foothills of Punt'Aldia.

Lurking offshore, amid the primordial granite coastal landscape, are the sculpted granite silhouettes of **Isola di Molara** and **Isola di Tavolara**. Tavolara, a limestone mountain island 4km (2.5 miles) long and just 1km (0.5 mile) wide, towering to the height of 565 metres (1,850ft), can be reached either by private boat (enquire among the local fishermen) or by one of the small ferries which leave from Porto San Paolo.

To the west soar the shimmering red-and-white granite peaks of the mountains of the interior, while in the foreground groves of holm oaks and cork oaks stretch out before them, rising above an undergrowth of myrtle, arbutus and buckthorn. Here and there blackened stretches resembling a lunar landscape are the result of fires which regularly afflict Sardinia during the summer months.

To have and have not,
Costa Smeralda.

COSTA SMERALDA

This stretch of coastline in the northeast of the island was transformed over half a century ago into the most exclusive tourist resort in the Mediterranean.

Main attractions

Porto Cervo
Cala di Volpe
Porto Rotondo

If you drive directly north from Olbia Airport you will reach the place where Sardinia is at its most beautiful, the **Costa Smeralda ❶**, or Emerald Coast. Here the sea shimmers in hundreds of shades of aquamarine, your lips taste of salt, and your hair is tousled by a breeze fragrant with the scent of the *màcchia*, a heady mix of forest, aromatic rosemary and lavender.

High, wind-eroded cliffs, wild mountain terrain, 80 stunning bays and a string of idyllic coves make this 55km (35-mile) coastal strip in northwest Sardinia one of the most attractive holiday destinations in the world. It is also one of the most exclusive. It was discovered at the start of the 1960s by His Highness Karim Aga Khan. Although scarcely out of his teens at the time, he was able to see the untamed potential of this craggy shoreline. Along with his wealthy friends, he set about creating a holiday resort for people just like him. In his own words: "This is obviously a place for people with above-avarage material for possessions - I wouldn't even want to have the others here as guests".

CARDINAL RULE

The Aga Khan's **Consorzio Costa Smeralda** was a non-profit organisation

which committed itself to a harmonious relationship between nature and man. One cardinal rule was that no villa, hotel or apartment block could be visible above the tops of the typically small holm oaks and tamarisks. All telephone wires and electric cables run underground, while waste water from the villas, the hotels and even the yacht harbour is processed by the most expensive treatment plant in the world. If a boat-owner is caught emptying his chemical toilet into the harbour or into some lonely bay, he can expect hefty

Map on page 134

Fabergé shop in Porto Cervo.

fines and, if he reoffends, banishment from the marina.

In recent decades, land prices on the Costa Smeralda have soared incessantly. In 2003 Tom Barrack, of the US property development group Colony Capital, outbid a coalition of Sardinian and Italians and bought Smeralda Holding, owner of a portfolio of properties on the coast including the Porto Cervo marina for €290 million. However, Sardinian law stymied his plans for new hotels as legislation passed in 2004 prohibits development within 2km (1.25 miles) of the coast. In 2012, he sold Smeralda Holding for €750 million to Qatar Holding, so what previously belonged to Aga Khan's is now owned by the emir of Qatar. The new owners have plans for four new hotels and a water park.

BOATS AND FESTIVALS

A private yacht is the ultimate status symbol on the Costa Smeralda. Excluding *ferragosto* (15 August), when Italian high society swoops

Rustic craftsmanship with character.

in from Milan and Rome, hiring a boat or obtaining a mooring in the harbour is easy enough – but paying for it might be more of a deterrent. The Costa Smeralda **marina** was completed in 1975, and altogether there are 650 berths for boats between 12 and 55 metres (38–176ft) in length. The best skippers in the world converge here – nowhere else in Europe will yacht owners have so little difficulty finding experienced yachting crews to help them win one of the Costa's many regattas.

Every fortnight in summer there are major competitions, including the Premio Offshore: the race for the fastest motor boats (known as "cigars"). Less glamorous, but all the more entertaining for it, is the spectacle of Is Fassonis Regatta. This takes place on the first Sunday in August as the sun sets over the water at Santa Giusta. The boats used are Phoenician in origin and made of the cane husks found around this area.

BEACHES AND GOLF

If you don't have access to a private yacht then you can still visit some of the beautiful bays on the Emerald Coast. You can enjoy diving in style: head for the sheltered **Petra Manna Beach** or **Capriccioli Bay** on windy days. You will need a boat, however, to get to the gorgeous **Spiaggia Rosa**, where the soft sand has a rose tint (also see page 141 for details of the Maddalena Islands).

The sea is not the only attraction of the Costa. International golfers regard the **Pevero Golf Course ❷** (above the Cala di Volpe hotel; www.peverogolfclub.com) as one of the loveliest and most challenging (18 holes, par 72) in the world. It was designed by Robert Trent-Jones on a raised spit of land; from each hole players enjoy spectacular views of the coast and the sea. There is also an excellent restaurant and a luxurious indoor and outdoor swimming pool. Those who are not content with the swimming, sailing and golfing facilities can practise their tennis on one of the nine courts at the plush **Porto Cervo Tennis Club**.

PORTO CERVO

Little happens in **Porto Cervo ❸**, the focal point of the Costa Smeralda, before late afternoon, but at sunset the beautiful people flock for a sundowner on the **Piazzetta** or to shop at the designer boutiques at the **Sottopiazza**. The atmosphere at Porto Cervo is glamorous but a little surreal, with luxury shops on one side and spectacular private yachts on the other. Anyone can wander around the pristine streets, but only the super-rich can afford to stay for longer than a drink or a bite to eat.

There are few cultural attractions in this area; culture is not the main appeal here. However, the pretty **Stella Maris church** built on a hill above the marina is worth a visit. Designed in 1968 by architect Michele Busiri Vici, the whitewashed church contains the *Mater Dolorosa*, a painting by El Greco, a valuable 16th-century organ from Naples, a

Detail on Stella Maris church, Porto Cervo.

German altar cross from the same period, and two outsize Polynesian shells which serve as baptismal fonts.

EATING AND DRINKING

You can eat and drink pretty well on the Costa Smeralda, but one thing is quite clear: apart from a few notable exceptions it is no mecca for gourmets. Fish, eel, *spaghetti aragosta*, roast suckling pig from the barbecue and smoked wild boar ham are popular, and everything is accompanied by warm *pane carasau*.

The Terrace Bar at Hotel Cervo, overlooking the piazza of Porto Cervo, serves as a meeting place for the whole resort and is popular for *aperitivi*. However, in terms of nightlife, Porto Cervo doesn't have much to offer. To the south on Romazzino Bay – where many of the swankiest pads are found – is the chic **Sottovento**, an expensive and exclusive nightclub (www.sottoventoclub.it). North of Porto Cervo towards Baia Sardinia lies Ritual, the training ground for the new generation of the Costa's millionaires. Those who prefer more peace and less stress should take their after-dinner *digestivo* in **Il Portico** on the Piazzetta. The bar is very attractive and decorated in Moroccan style.

For more pleasant beaches, try the sheltered **Cala di Volpe** ❹ and Cala Liscia Ruja. Alternatively, you can continue south to **Porto Rotondo** ❺ (a miniature Porto Cervo), only 20 minutes from Porto Cervo by car, or 10 by boat. Built in 1963, though less attractive architecturally, it is also a stylish resort. It lies in a little bay, with tiny piazzas, a handful of designer boutiques, a small harbour and two white sandy beaches. In summer the cafés and restaurants are crowded with visitors. The pretty granite church of San Lorenzo, up the steps leading off the central Piazzetta San Marco, was designed by the architect Andrea Cascella. An open-air theatre which holds concerts during the summer months is nearby.

Porto Cervo Marina.

A windy day on Pevero Beach.

GALLURA AND THE NORTH

This itinerary takes in Gallura's dramatic coastline, the islands of Maddalena, the town of Stintino and then travels through the interior of the region.

Map on page 140

A journey through the Gallura, in the northeast of Sardinia, is a full and varied experience. The island's most extensive oak woods surround Monte Limbara and the little town of Tempio Pausania, and the shores of the Costa Paradiso form part of one of its loveliest stretches of coastline. What's more, at Arzachena there are two of Sardinia's best-preserved *tombe di giganti* (giants' tombs).

Gallura's principal characteristic is defined by the granite rocks that determine its landscape. The countryside is punctuated with *stazzi*

(traditional houses). These are low, elongated buildings usually formed by three aligned rooms: the central room is both the entrance and dining room, with a bedroom on each side. Placed at the centre of a vast land, *stazzi* are surrounded by the necessities of family life (a kitchen garden, an orchard, vineyard and maybe a small patch of wheat) and grazing ground for cattle. Built from the 18th century by shepherds that were looking for new lands to settle, they slowly transformed themselves into farms, which are still inhabited.

THE GOLFO DI ARZACHENA

The fashionable atmosphere of the Costa Smeralda fades as one drives away from Porto Cervo, but the first place of any size on the Golfo di Arzachena is the elegant seaside resort of **Baia Sardinia**. Just across the bay, however, the small fishing port of **Cannigione** has a more down-to-earth feel.

The steep cliffs surrounding **Arzachena ❶** lend the little town the appearance of a village in the Dolomites rather than one on a Mediterranean island. However, the rapid development of the Costa Smeralda over the past decade has brought economic benefits and considerable change to the town and neighbouring regions. In the vicinity are many interesting prehistoric settlements.

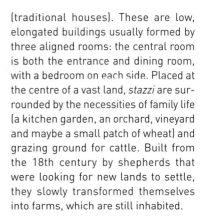

Giants' tomb at Arzachena.

ARZACHENA'S ARCHAEOLOGICAL SITES

For some 3,500 years the Gallura was inhabited by groups of semi-nomads and shepherds, and around Arzachena are a number of important remains from the time of the Nuragi. Archaeologists now call this civilisation Arzachena Culture. The main prehistoric sites – Li Muri, Li Lolghi and Lu Coddu Ecchju (in Italian, Li Longhi and Lu Coddu Vecchju) – can be reached by taking the SS 427 towards Calangianus for about 3km (2 miles), then the right turn towards Luogosanto; a dirt track is signposted to "Coddu Ecchju".

At **Lu Coddu Ecchju** (tel: 0789-83401; daily 9am–one hour before sunset) is one of the best-preserved *tombe di giganti* in existence. A stela, 4 metres (13ft) high and subdivided into two sections – a square unit and a half-arch – stands sentinel in front of the grave. Through the semicircular opening at ground level, which repeats the contours of the stela, sacrificial offerings could be presented to the dead person. Flat stone slabs positioned vertically form a semicircle demarcating the ceremonial and sacrificial arena.

On a hill a few kilometres further on, also marked by a signpost on the Luogosanto road, are the stone box graves of **Li Muri** and **Li Lolghi** (Lu Coddu Vecchiu; tel: 0789-83401; daily 9am–one hour before sunset). These witnesses to the Nuragic epoch were found each to be holding a single corpse buried in a squatting position. The graves themselves were surrounded by concentric circles of stones. The *tombe di giganti* of Li Lolghi comprise 14 huge slabs of granite, under which lay 100 bodies.

The traveller approaching the region via the SS 125 from Olbia will find the **Nuraghe Albucciu**. It is signposted about 3km (2 miles) before Arzachena. The nuraghe itself is not constructed in the familiar tower form – it is one of the very few corridor nuraghi in Sardinia. Close by stands the **Temple of Malchittu**, which formed part of the settlement. The **Roccia Il Fungo** (Mushroom Rock) is a weathered granite rock near Arzachena. Like the spectacularly

Figs and wild fennel drying in the sun.

Garibaldi memorial on La Maddalena.

⊘ GIANTS' TOMBS

Built in the Bronze Age, there are 321 *tombe di giganti* (giants' tombs, namely megalithic gallery graves) in Sardinia, all of which are aligned south to southeast to ensure their residents would catch the rising sun which symbolised rebirth. Whilst many have the appearance of large cairns, flat stone slabs positioned vertically form a semicircle demarcating the ceremonial and sacrificial arena. The best examples still have their stela: the large slab, up to 4 metres (13ft) high, which commonly has a semicircular doorway cut into it. These stelae were adorned with carvings: Lu Coddu Vecchju has the most ornate carvings. The inside chamber, which lies north to northwest to catch the setting sun, is a square or rectangular burial unit.

GIVSEPPE GARIBALDI

LA MADDALENA

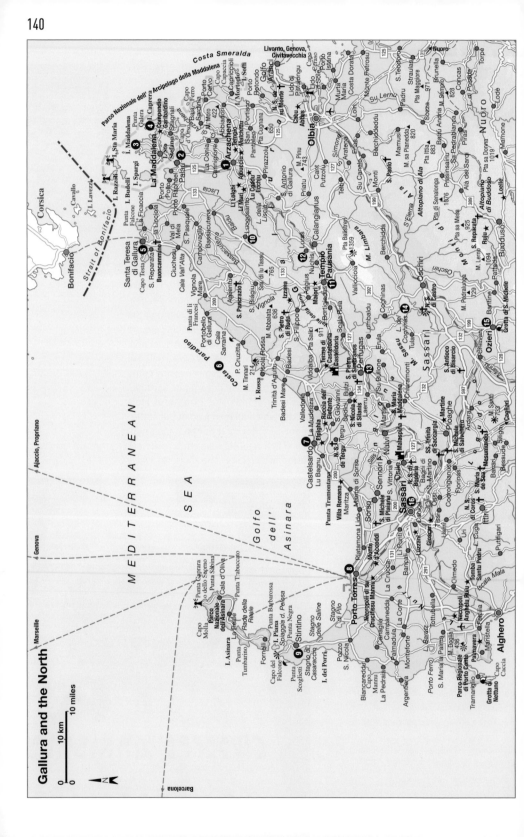

Gallura and the North

shaped Roccia dell'Elefante (Elephant Rock) near Castelsardo and the Roccia l'Orso (Bear Rock) near Palau, it features on many postcards.

PALAU

Continuing along the SS 125, you pass first through the little port of Palau and then through **Capo d'Orso**, where a weathered cliff formation, the Roccia L'Orso, resembles the eponymous bear. **Palau ❷** itself is a little coastal town dominated by its harbour, from which ferries leave regularly for Caprera and La Maddalena. It is easy enough to find boats to take you to any of the offshore islands (just ask around at the quay; the fishermen will advise), but at Palau Mare in Palau's Via Nazionale you can hire everything you might need to explore the archipelago independently.

LA MADDALENA

The island of **La Maddalena ❸** is the largest in size – almost 50 sq km (19 sq miles) – in the archipelago, and the only one with an urban centre, also called La Maddalena. Lying only a few kilometres from the mainland, together with the other islands of the archipelago, it represents what remains of the land link that once existed between Sardinia and the island of Corsica.

La Maddalena has enjoyed a higher profile thanks to Silvio Berlusconi having one of his infamous holiday villas here.

The town of La Maddalena has a prosperous, laid-back charm, with 18th-century pastel-hued villas surrounding graceful piazzas. Highlights include chic shopping on Via Garibaldi, a bustling daily indoor market (mornings) at Piazza Garibaldi and the parish church of **Santa Maria Maddalena**, which contains two silver candlesticks and a crucifix donated by Horatio Nelson in 1804, as thanks to the island's residents during the admiral's lengthy campaigns against Napoleon's fleet.

Driving around the island on the Strada Panoramica, there are plenty of opportunities to stop, take photos and admire the weathered, otherworldly sculptural shapes of huge

The town of La Maddalena.

The belltower of the church of San Vittorio in Santa Teresa di Gallura.

Sandy cove on the island of La Maddalena.

granite boulders. Between stops and walks along stunning beaches you can visit the **Museo Archeologico Navale Nino Lamboglia** (Maritime Museum; Giardino, Strada Panoramica; tel: 0789-790 633; 9.30am–12.30pm and 3.30–6.30pm, by appointment) which contains the remains of a Roman cargo ship dating from the 2nd century BC.

OTHER ISLANDS IN THE ARCHIPELAGO

The fame of the other large island, **Isola Caprera** ❹, is largely due to its famous resident, Giuseppe Garibaldi (1807–82), for whom it was home for many years, the refuge to which he always returned, and the place where he died. Garibaldi created a model farm on the island; his memorial museum, the **Compendio Garibaldino** (www.compendiogaribaldino.it; Mon–Sat 9am–8pm, Sun 9am–2pm), has the air of a place of pilgrimage, and is well worth visiting.

The Maddalena archipelago is formed by seven major islands, of which **Budelli** is also well known thanks to its **Spiaggia Rosa** (Pink Beach), made famous by the 1965 film *Il Deserto Rosso* (Red Desert), directed by Michelangelo Antonioni. Its sparkling rosy-hued grains of sand (the ancient remnants of a protozoan sea creature) were so attractive to visitors that they would grab a handful to take home – so much so that today the grains are protected by law.

The stop-off point on the island of **Santo Stefano** is the Spiaggia del Pesce beach; most of the rest of this former US military base is still off limits. Thanks to their advantageous strategic position, the islands often played an important military role in the past and a controversial one at that. The island of Santo Stefano was from 1972 a US nuclear submarine base, set up as a technical and logistical base to monitor Soviet activity. The US navy base was dismantled in 2008, an indication of the shift in relations between Europe and Russia. The Italian navy remains in La Maddalena, albeit with a much reduced presence.

BACK ON THE MAIN ISLAND

Santa Teresa di Gallura ❺ lies at the northernmost tip of Sardinia. Its harbour is the starting point for ferries across to Corsica. The twin approach roads – the SS 133 from Tempio and the SS 200 from Castelsardo – both pass through attractive countryside. The most noteworthy sights here are the bizarre rock formations along the cliffs near **Capo Testa**. From the **Torre Longosardo** there is a spectacular view of the wild and often inaccessible coast of the Gallura, whose waters and seabeds provide ideal conditions for deep-sea diving and the white cliffs of Bonifacio. Also in the vicinity of Capo Testa are two quarries dating from Roman times.

PARADISE COAST

The road from Santa Teresa to Castelsardo has one of Sardinia's most stunning stretches of coastline. The steep precipices typical of the northern coast force the road inland. Running parallel to the coastline, it follows a serpentine course through untouched *màcchia*. The reddish peaks of the Monte Pitrighinosu and the Monte Puntaccia stand on the horizon.

The sparsely populated area between the SS 200 and the SS 133 has a wild charm. Along the lonely stretch of road to **Tempio** you will see cork oaks, their trunks, with patches of freshly peeled reddish bark, gnarled and misshapen by the wind. Some 10km (6 miles) past Santa Teresa, the **Spiaggia di Rena Maiore** and the **Cala Vall'Alta** are good places to stop for a swim.

The best-known stretch of coast here is the lovely **Costa Paradiso** ❻, which consists of several little *villagi* (holiday villages), hidden away in dense thickets. Inevitably, development comes at a price. Legislation in 2004 has halted building within 2km (1.25 miles) of the coast, but for a region heavily dependent on tourism and largely owned by rich foreigners, this law is repeatedly challenged.

The two smaller beaches of the **Baia Trinità** are open to the public; overlooking them is the **Isola Rossa**.

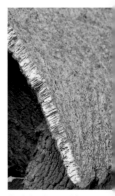

Cork is obtained from the stripped bark of cork oak trees which grow in the region.

Dramatic rock formations envelop the Capo Testa.

From here there is also a long sandy beach stretching almost as far as the rocky promontory overlooking the town of Castelsardo.

CASTELSARDO

Perched on a cliff, **Castelsardo** ❼ offers a mixture of Sardinian folklore and kitsch. It was founded in 1102 by the Genoese Doria family. First known as Castel Genovese, the settlement's name was changed after the Spanish conquest to Castel Aragonese; in 1796 the King of Sardinia gave it the present name of Castelsardo.

Nowadays, during the summer months at least, the town is usually too full of tourists to make a visit here entirely pleasurable, but the castle hill has managed to retain its attractive atmosphere and it is worth venturing up its steep, narrow alleys.

The fortress at its summit houses the **Museo dell'Intreccio Mediterraneo** (Via Marconi; www.mimcastelsardo.it; daily Apr and Oct 9am–7pm, May–June and Sept 9.30am–9.30pm, July–Aug 9am–12.30am, Nov–Mar

10.30am–4.30pm), which displays a collection of basketwork and weaving. Other attractions in the town include the **Cattedrale di Sant'Antonio Abate**; inside is a 16th-century altarpiece, *Madonna with Angels*, by a 15th-century painter known as the master of Castelsardo.

If you're in Castelsardo at Easter, you'll witness Lunissanti (Holy Monday), generally regarded as one of the best Easter festivals on the island, when people dressed in hooded costume proceed through the torch-lit streets. Interspersed with ancient rituals and traditional songs, the ceremony has retained all its original medieval character.

Outside the town, on the twisting road to Perfugas, lies the **Roccia dell'Elefante**, a curiously shaped outcrop of rock which resembles a young elephant with its trunk raised.

ALONG THE COAST

Continuing south, the SS 200 follows the outline of the coast once more. Some 15km (9 miles) from Castelsardo

Cheeky mural on a cake shop (pasticceria).

it arrives at the **Punta Tramontana**. By taking the route via **Sorso** and **Sennori**, you can quickly reach Sassari. The SS 200, however, carries on along the coast through the *pineta* (pine forests), beyond which lies the **Platamona Lido**, the favourite beach of the inhabitants of Sassari. Over 20km (12 miles) long, the beach stretches as far as the industrial port of Porto Torres. Its backdrop of pine groves makes for an attractive setting, but the proximity of Sassari has somewhat marred its beauty. Campsites alternate with discotheques and beach cafés.

PORTO TORRES

It makes no difference from which side you approach **Porto Torres** ❽; it is an unattractive little town dominated by vast oil refineries. Since Roman times it has been famous as the home of seafarers; even in those days the inhabitants conducted lively trade with the mainland. Nowadays container ships and tankers have taken over. The principal port in northern Sardinia, Porto Torres is one of the main gateways to the island, with ferry links to Civitavecchia and Genoa.

The town has impressive remains from its early Roman history – ruins of the original trading post and the former Turris Libisonis, the Roman colony founded in 27 BC. Near the present railway station lie the **Terme Centrali** (Roman Baths), with mosaics dating from the 3rd–4th century AD. There is also a seven-arched bridge from the same period and a museum, the **Antiquarium Turritano** (Via Ponte Romano 99; tel: 079-514 433; Thu–Tue 9am–7pm) that contains finds from archaeological excavations in town and on its outskirts. The **Basilica di San Gavino** (tel: 0348-899 6823; Apr–early May and Oct 9am–1pm, 3–6pm, early May–Sept 9am–1pm, 3–7pm, rest of year by appointment) was completed in the year 1111; it houses the tomb of the martyr of the same name and is one of the most important Romanesque buildings to be found on Sardinia.

Following the main highway to Sassari, the SS 131, you will arrive at the

The harbour at Porto Torres.

⊘ **Fact**

The 15-metre (50ft) high L'Olivastro di Luras, located by the small church of Santa Baltolu in Luras, is thought to be the oldest tree in Italy – French scientists think it could be 4,000 years old.

sanctuary of **Monte d'Accoddi**, (Tue– Sun from 9am), an early altar shaped like a truncated pyramid with a large access ramp. Similar to a Mesopotamian ziggurat, it dates to approximately 2500 BC. It is the only structure of this kind to be found in the Mediterranean area.

UP TO STINTINO

The most northwesterly point of the island is a small triangle of land bounded by the towns of Porto Torres to the north and Alghero to the south. The drive from Porto Torres to Stintino passes through fertile, sparsely populated farmland; unfortunately vast chemical complexes dominate much of the landscape.

Stintino ❾ is a small, unaffected place consisting of holiday cottages, a few hotel complexes and two marinas. Founded at the end of 1800 by fishermen and shepherds forced to abandon the island of Asinara, the town is a major tourist destination. The **Pelosa beach**, at Rada dei Fornelli between Capo del Falcone and the island of Asinara, is regarded as being among the most beautiful beaches in Sardinia. In August, the Regata della Latina, with vintage boats and colourful yachts, is worth seeing.

The island of **Asinara** was expropriated in 1885 to set up a hospital and a penal colony. In its recent history the Fornelli prison on the island was used to confine Italian *brigatisti* and *mafiosi*. The penal colony was closed in 1997 and the island became a national park, the **Parco Nazionale dell'Asinara**. Although access is still restricted, you can arrange a guided tour of the island to see the wildlife (contact the tourist office, see page 234).

Just before Stintino lies the Tonnara Saline, formerly an important tuna fishing station which has now been converted into a complex of holiday homes. The former mining village of **Argentiera** has little miners' cottages and a preserved main shaft.

NORTHEAST GALLURA

Parts of Gallura consist of gentle countryside punctuated by large heaps

⊘ THE CORK OAK

Cork harvesting is still an important part of the Gallura regional economy, as visible in the forests around Calangianus. French traders introduced industrial cork processing to Sardinia in the 1830s. Spread across what remains of the once-magnificent woodland that cloaked the island is a species of oak tree found only in the Western Mediterranean: the *Quercus suber* or cork oak. Extensive woods of cork oaks are found in Giara di Gesturi and Gallura. The many dialect names for the cork oak – *suberju, suelzu, suveliu, suergiu, suaru* or *cortigu, ortigu, orteghe* – are derived from the Latin *suber* or *corticulum* – "cork" or "bark".

The thick cork bark protects the tree from damage, cold, heat and drying out. A cork oak can produce bark until it is about 125 years old if the peeling is done correctly. Peeling requires considerable skill and experience to avoid harming the bright-red cambium, the growing surface for the next layer of cork. When stripping is done properly, the bark is peeled from a cork oak for the first time when the tree is around 15 years old. A tree will be peeled about eight times during its lifetime, usually at intervals of nine to 12 years, or until the quality of the cork declines below an acceptable level. The sections of stripped bark are transported to the factories in Tempio and Calangianus, where they are graded according to quality. The poorest quality is processed straight away into cork waste for the building industry, where it is used as insulation material. The elastic cork from later peelings is left to mature in the open air for at least six months. During this process the sun and rain, heat and cold removes most of the red powder and other impurities from the cork's pores and makes it lighter in colour. The cork is then soaked in enormous vats of hot water for about an hour, which removes the tannic acid and causes the cork to swell up so that it gains the requisite elasticity. Bottle corks are then stamped out from the sheets of bark, which are pressed flat as they dry.

The cork industry is worth hundreds of millions of euros to the Sardinian economy, but the trend towards screw tops and plastic stoppers means cork is less in demand, resulting in falling prices and a decline in farmed cork oak. Environmentalists and Sardinians are urging the wine industry to show corporate responsibility towards this sustainable, environmentally friendly natural resource, and is seeking government action to preserve the economic viability of cork production.

of granite blocks, inselbergs (granite towers) and cork tree woods. To the southwest of Arzachena, the village of **Luogosanto** ⑩ (350 metres/1,148ft above sea level) is typical of the region, in a verdant setting surrounded by pinkish-grey rocks. Continuing south, **Aggius** lies at the foot of the impressive granite mountains (Monti di Aggius) and is connected via a panoramic road to the **Valle della Luna**, a vast plain with an incredible scenery of weathered granite blocks, piled one on top of the other.

The chic little town of **Tempio Pausania** ⑪ lies at the heart of the Gallura, at the foot of the granite peak of **Monte Limbara**. Irrespective of the direction from which you approach this area, you cut through dense oak forests unlike any to be found elsewhere in Sardinia. Tempio Pausania itself lies at an altitude of 555 metres (1,820ft), giving it the air of a mountain resort – an impression underlined by the town's atmosphere. Worth a visit are the 15th-century cathedral and **Museo Bernardo de Muro** (daily 8am–7pm; free), dedicated to the famous tenor who was a native son of the town.

About 10km (6 miles) east of Tempio is **Calangianus**, the cork capital of Sardinia. Nearby is **Luras** ⑫, which is worth stopping at to see the **Museo Etnografico** (www.galluras.it; daily), a three-storey traditional house crammed with objects from the locality. The recreated traditional Sardinian bedroom is deeply evocative of a time now lost.

Leaving Tempio and travelling towards Sassari, the road No.127 crosses the Coghinas river, the natural border between Gallura and the subregion of Anglona, and reaches **Perfugas** ⑬. The oldest man-made lithic tools of Sardinia, dating back to the Palaeolithic period, have recently been found in this area. The **Museo Archeologico e Paleobotanico** (Via Nazario Sauro; tel: 079-564 241; Tue–Sun June–Sept 9am–1pm, 4–8pm, Oct–May 9am–1pm, 3–7pm) displays many of the prehistoric and Nuragic objects found in the region.

Mural of Stintino fishermen catching tuna during the matanza.

LAKESIDE PICNIC

Following side roads through a mountainous area, you will reach the **Lago del Coghinas** , the second-largest lake in Sardinia. It was dammed in 1927 and provides one of the island's main supplies of drinking water. The journey is delightful if you don't mind the serpentine nature of the road. A good place to have a picnic is at the site of the Romanesque church of **Nostra Signora di Castro** (daily) because of its position dominating the plain and Lake Coghinas. It was built in the second half of the 12th century and was the seat of the bishopric of a medieval hamlet until 1505. Passing through **Oschiri** and taking the SS 199 you will finally arrive in **Ozieri** ⑮, a prosperous and attractive little town with some handsome neoclassical houses, lying on a fertile plain supporting crops and cattle farming.

PREHISTORIC FINDS

Not far from Ozieri lies the **Grotta di San Michele** (tel: 079-787 638; guided tours Tue–Sun summer 9am–1pm and 3–6pm, winter 9am–1pm and 2–5pm), the scene of some of Sardinia's most important archaeological finds. The name of the town was given to the prehistoric period which they represent, which is now known as the Ozieri Culture. Part of the excavated material can be seen in the **Museo Archeologico** (Convento delle Clarisse; tel: 079-785 1052; Tue–Fri 9am–1pm, 3–7pm, Sat–Sun 9am–1pm, 3–6pm), housed in the 17th-century cloisters of the convent annexe of the church of San Francesco.

In the same square is an interesting 16th-century noble house. The **Cattedrale dell' Immacolata** (daily) has a neoclassical facade and an interior with Gothic vaults. There is also an important polyptych, the *Madonna di Loreto*, the work of a 6th-century Sardinian artist known as the master of Ozieri. The nearby village of **Pattada** is the best place to buy a genuine hand-crafted shepherd's knife. If you are not yet tired of winding roads you could tackle the lonely, sinuous and unforgettable stretch of road from **Buddusò** to **Bitti** and **Nuoro**.

Hand-crafted Sardinian shepherds' knives make an excellent souvenir (although remember not to carry them in your hand luggage on your return).

⊙ THE SHEPHERD'S KNIFE

The shepherd's knife, a potent symbol of a lost pastoral world, is still a significant accessory; although they may not be strictly necessary for their work, many a Sardinian factory worker or bank employee considers his knife as part of his identity. Designed for daily use, these days shepherd's knives have become sought-after collector's items.

Sa resolza or sa resordza (the Sardinian shepherd's knife) comes from the Latin word *rasoria*, referring to knives with a swivelling sheath, and only the very finest knives have their blades protected by a sheath of wood or horn. The test of a good knife, if you are a man, is to spit on the back of one's hand, rub hard and then check whether the knife will give a close shave.

The very best knives with a classic pointed blade *a foll'e murta* – "like a myrtle leaf" – are made by true master craftsmen who will only work to order. As recently as 50 years ago, such knives were commonly produced in pastoral communities all over the island – Arbus, Guspini, Gavoi, Fonni, Santu Lussurgiu and Pattada, to name a few. Nowadays, however, good-quality knives are really only produced in the traditional manner in the last two of these villages. Knives from Pattada are considered to be the ultimate in Sardinian craftsmanship.

The view over to La Maddalena from Capo d'Orso.

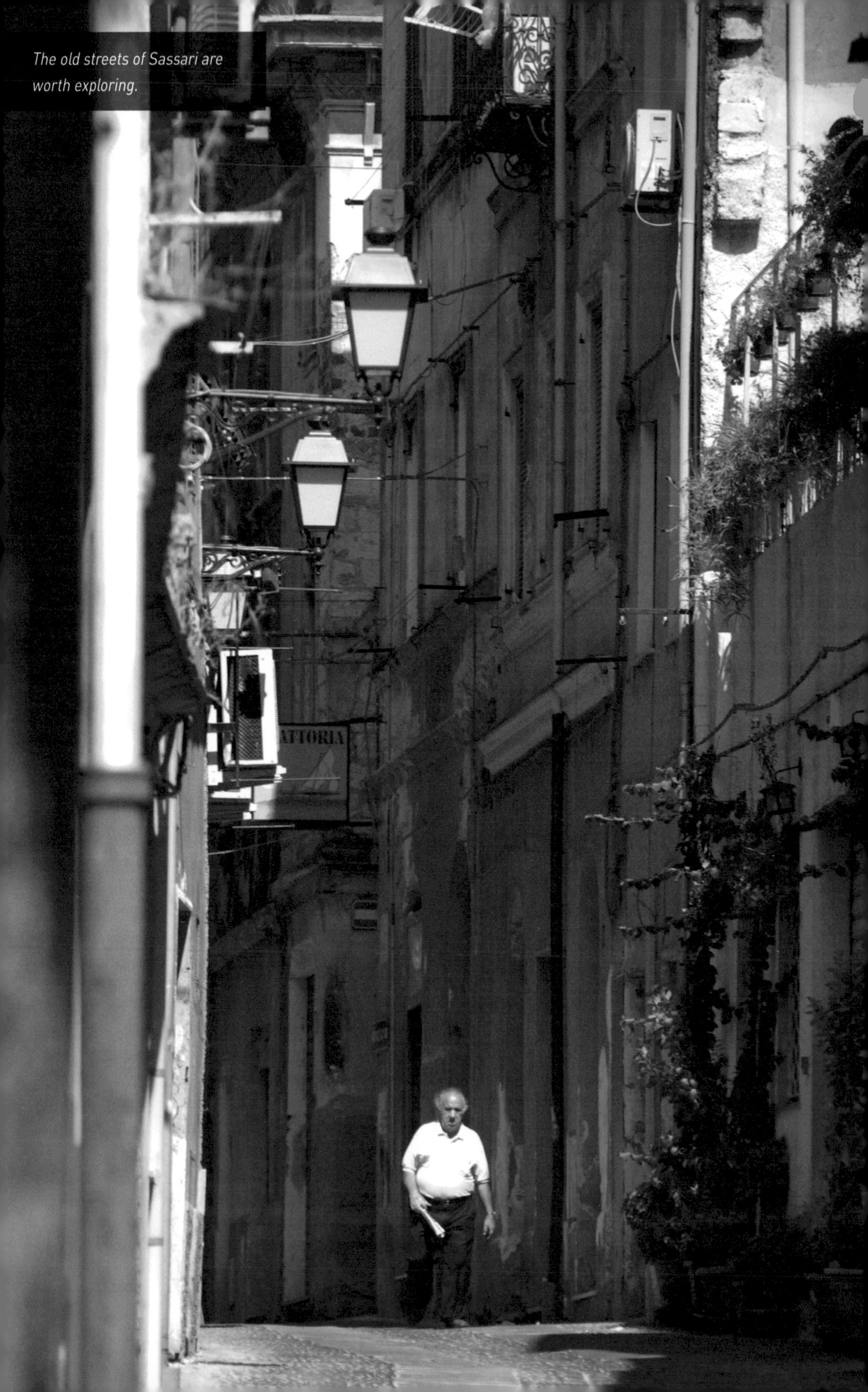

The old streets of Sassari are worth exploring.

SASSARI

If you arrive in Sassari at the end of a tour of Sardinia, you will probably feel as if you have returned to the Italian mainland without actually crossing the sea.

Sardinia's second-most important city, **Sassari** has a long history of raids and conquests, but also of stubborn resistance which perhaps shows in its urban, worldly countenance. In fact, a great deal of mainland blood flows through the veins of its inhabitants. In the early 13th century the merchants of Genoa and Pisa – both cities of international importance in medieval times – transformed an insignificant peasant village in the hinterland of Porto Torres into a flourishing commercial town.

Even today, the citizens of Sassari are proud of being a "community of shopkeepers". Trade enabled them to free themselves from the dependence on Porto Torres which had dogged their existence since Roman times. Their only regret is that throughout their long history they have never quite managed to oust Cagliari from its position as the most important town on the island. During the 17th century it was a close-run thing, as Sassari almost managed to overtake its arch-rival in the south. In 1617 the University of Sassari received its charter, three years before that of Cagliari. Such was the town's prosperity that private citizens donated enough money to build or renovate nine churches and monasteries. However, the plague in 1652 and the subsequent fall in population shattered the hopes of Sassari's

Pretty Sassari square.

inhabitants. It seemed that thereafter their town was fated to remain the perpetual runner-up.

THE MODERN CITY

Today, with its population standing at nearly 130,000, Sassari is again able to show that it is at least as good as the capital. Three of the most famous Sardinian politicians of post-war times – Communist Party leader Enrico Berlinguer, and former presidents Antonio Segni and Francesco Cossiga – were all natives of Sassari.

Main attractions
Piazza d'Italia
Museo Nazionale G.A. Sanna
Piazza Tola
Duomo
Pinacoteca Nazionale di Sassari
Museo della Brigata Sassari

Maps on pages 140, 152

Bust of Giuseppe Garibaldi.

In the sphere of arts, too, Sassari succeeded in finding its own individual style. Many of the churches are the work of local stonemasons, known as *picapedras*, who gave the basic architectural styles imported from the mainland a popular, Sardinian touch. This tendency also applied to the sculptors of Sassari, who during the 17th century adorned the town's numerous new churches and monasteries with countless statues and altars. They also carved the *candelieri*, enormous wooden pillars shaped like candles which every year on 14 August are carried through the Old Town from the Piazza Castello to the church of Santa Maria di Betlem (St Mary of Bethlehem) by the members of the various craftsmen's guilds. The *I Candelieri* (Feast of Candles), whose origins appear to lie way back in the 13th century, has remained an authentic folk festival, drawing many expatriate Sassaresi home each year.

During the *Cavalcata Sarda* (usually held in May), however, the local population prefers to leave the town to foreigners and tourists. The Cavalcata, one of Sardinia's best-known festivals, draws from surrounding villages and features a horseback parade of riders in traditional costume who later take part in a daring horse race. Over the weekend, folk groups perform traditional songs and dance in the Piazza d'Italia.

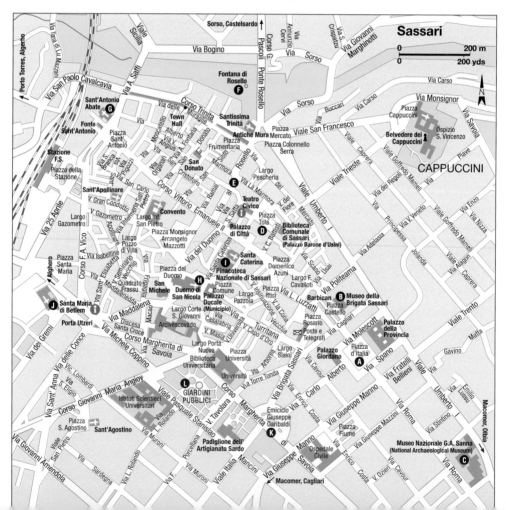

THE PIAZZA D'ITALIA

The spacious **Piazza d'Italia** , covering an area of precisely 1 hectare (2.5 acres), is framed by elegant 19th-century buildings such as the **Palazzo della Provincia** and the neo-Gothic **Palazzo Giordano**. For an entertaining look at Sassari life, visit the square during the evening *passeggiata*. Some 150 years ago, sheep still grazed on this piazza, in whose numerous banks and administrative buildings the financial and political fate of the town is now decided. Until well into the 19th century there seemed no necessity to expand the urban area beyond the limits set by the 13th-century city walls. For 600 years, under the Spanish and the Piedmontese, the entire area was compressed within an area of only 30 hectares (75 acres).

Providing a link between the Old Town and the newer districts is the **Piazza Castello**, which lies to the north of Piazza d'Italia. In the 1870s, whilst new buildings in the architectural style of the Italian mainland were sprouting up on the Piazza d'Italia, on the Piazza Castello they were demolishing the fortress after which it is named. The castle was built in 1330 by the Aragonese; for centuries afterwards it served as a symbol of foreign rule and oppression. Recent archaeological excavations have revealed two **Barbican** passageways which are now open to the public (http://turismosassari.it; Tue and Sun 10am–1pm, Wed–Sat 10am–1pm and 4.30–7.30pm).

TWO MUSEUMS

The military barracks attached to the castle house the **Museo Storico della Brigata Sassari** (Piazza Castello; tel: 079-208 5308; Mon–Fri 8am–4.30pm, Sat 8am–1pm; free). The museum is dedicated to the Sardinian regiment, famous for their bravery, who endured heavy losses during World War I fighting against the Austrians. The museum's collection has a reconstruction of sandbag trenches alongside military items and poignant memorabilia from the conflict.

There is one more essential site to see before making a tour of the historic Old Town: the **Museo Nazionale**

> ### ⊙ Tip
> The Palazzo di Città houses the city's tourist office (Via Sebastiano Satta 13; tel: 079-200 8072) as well as the City Museum, showcasing Sassari's drama, festivities and sights, and Teatro Civico.

Piazza d'Italia is surrounded by neoclassical buildings.

The Baroque facade of the church of Sant' Antonio Abate.

Sculptural detail on Sassari's Duomo.

G.A. Sanna (Via Roma 64; http://turismosassari.it; Tue–Sat 9am–8pm). Housed in the immaculately ordered galleries of a handsome neoclassical villa, the museum presents a summary of the most important aspects of the island's archaeology. The **ground floor** is dedicated to a complete vision of the island's prehistory and history up to medieval times; a room is dedicated to the prehistoric altar of Monte d'Accoddi (about 2500 BC), followed by showcases that display objects coming from *tombe di giganti* (giants' tombs) and natural caves (from the Neolithic to the Bronze Age, 6000–1800 BC). The **upper floor** focuses on the Nuragic civilisation and includes a collection of 2,000–3,000-year-old bronze statues, among which is the realistic bronze ox found in the sacred well of Perfugas. There is also a collection of imported Etruscan and Greek pottery and equally fascinating pieces of gold and silver Carthaginian and Roman jewellery, which is still worn with traditional Sardinian costumes.

THE HEART OF THE OLD TOWN

Through the middle of the Old Town runs the **Corso Vittorio Emanuele II**, built upon the old Porto Torres–Cagliari Roman road. The town's long-standing residents still call it the Plath de Codinas (the Street of Stone) because it was once lined with elegant palazzi and the residences of wealthy merchants. At no. 35 is the **Teatro Civico**, a grand 19th-century neoclassical theatre built upon the medieval Palazzo di Città – it now houses the City Museum (http://turismosassari.it; Mon–Sat 9am–2pm and 4–8pm) dedicated to the history of Sassari with backstage glimpses of thespian life.

Apart from the Corso, the citizens of Sassari have given other streets and squares local dialect names. The **Via La Marmora**, which runs parallel to it, is lined with crumbling stucco facades known to locals as the Carra Longa; leading off the Corso is the Carra Pizzinna (today's Via Battisti), which links up with the Carra Manna (the Piazza Tola). The dialect names – "little bushel" and "large bushel" – refer to the fact that these official market measures were

once in use here. Rising above **Piazza Tola** ⒟ is the monument to the influential historian Pasquale Tola (1800–74), who sits above the market stalls. Tola's bequeathed book collection forms the core of the **Biblioteca Comunale di Sassari** (Piazza Tola 1; information about exhibitions and cultural events tel: 079-279 380), housed in the imposing 16th-century Palazzo d'Usini on the piazza.

The most popular street in the Old Town is the **Via al Rosello** ⒠. The silversmiths after whom the alley was named are a rare species today. You'll see the odd cobbler and carpenter at work, latter-day representatives of a once-thriving craft tradition. The picturesque Via al Rosello leads to a spring and the **Fontana di Rosello** ⒡, the island's most famous monumental fountain (http://turismosassari.it; Tue–Sun 9am–5pm, May–Aug until 7pm). The 12 stone lion's heads adorning the Renaissance fountain are surrounded by statues symbolising the four seasons. The statue in the middle of the fountain represents a divinity called Giogli, and a statue of San Gavino rides a horse at the arched summit.

Returning via the **Ponte Rosello** you'll come to the **Nuovo Mercato**, the New Market, where fresh fish from the Gulf of Asinara is on sale every morning. To the west is the elegant church of **Sant'Antonio Abate** ⒢ (daily). Dating from the early 1700s, this Baroque church, with its harmonious proportions, dominates the tree-lined Piazza Sant'Antonio.

SASSARI'S CATHEDRAL

Continuing along the Via al Rosello and across the Corso, you will come to the Cattedrale or **Duomo di San Nicola** ⒣ (daily). The towering, ornately carved Baroque facade (c.1700) was added to a Gothic structure which was itself built onto an 11th-century Romanesque church. After exploring the restored Gothic interior, head to the Museo del Tesoro in the sacristy which contains fine statuary, reliquary, silverware and other pious treasures. There are many churches near the Duomo: opposite stands the desecrated Manneristic Chiesa di San Michele.

Inside Santa Maria di Betlem.

⊘ PINACOTECA NAZIONALE ARTWORKS

Opened in 2008, the Pinacoteca Nazionale di Sassari displays a fascinating collection of artworks dating from the medieval period right up to the mid-20th century. Here are a few highlights to look out for. Among the religious paintings on the ground floor (piano terra) is a 13th-century cross with intriguing geometric patterns and a *Madonna con Bambino* (1473) by Bartolomeo Vivarini (examine the dainty hands). A mesmerising mix of the sacred, allegorical, saintly and erotic fills rooms III–IV of the first floor (primo piano). Francesco Solimena's (1657–1747) *La Resurrezione di Lazzaro* is all brooding Baroque drama. The mythological, religious and pastoral combine in dreamy Arcadian scenes in Sala IV, while portraits of the Italian aristocracy line Sala V. Next door, nymphs frolic amid the plump flesh and ecstatic gestures of gods Venere (Venus), Giove (Jupiter) and Semele. The second floor (piano secondo) rooms (XII–XIX) feature the Ottocento and Novecento, starting with the works of Sardinian Giovanni Marghinotti (1798 –1865) – full of delicate portrait features and romantic heroism – to the emotive etchings of Mario Delitala (1887–1990), who explored sacred and folkloric themes (Via S. Caterina–Piazza del Comune–Via Canopolo; http://musei.sardegna.beniculturali.it; Tue–Sat 9am–6pm).

A statue in the Giardini Pubblici overlooking the pleasant grounds.

Statue of Vittorio Emanuele II on Piazza d'Italia.

ART, CHURCHES AND A PARK

On Piazza del Comune is the grandiose **Palazzo Ducale** (Ducal Palace), built for the Duke of Vallombrosa from designs of Valino between 1775 and 1805. It has housed the town hall since the early 20th century. Now it's also home to a branch of the City Museum, the **Duke's Rooms and Cellars** (http://turismosassari.it; Tue–Fri 9.30am–1pm and 4.30–7.30pm, Sat 9.30am–1pm). Excavations in 1985 and 2006 unearthed five cellar rooms probably dating back to the 16th century.

Following the main road in front of the palace is the Jesuit College of Canopoleno built between 1559 and 1605, together with the annexed church of San Giuseppe. In 1617 it became the first university in Sardinia. The Jesuit college now houses the **Pinacoteca Nazionale di Sassari** ❶ (Via S. Caterina–Piazza del Comune–Via Canopolo; http://musei.sardegna. beniculturali.it; Tue–Sat 9am–6pm), an important collection of around 400 artworks exhibited over three floors (part of the collection is being restored at the time of writing).

On the far side of the broad expanse of the **Piazza Mazzotti** rises the church of the Convento Cappuccini, which houses a number of altars carved by local artists.

Across the **Corso Vico**, outside the city walls, stands the church of **Santa Maria di Betlem** ❶ (daily), with its striking silver dome. This much-venerated church is where the huge 3-metre (10ft) wooden candles used in the *I Candelieri* festival are stored. On 14 August they are carried here in procession. Inside the cloister is a 14th-century fountain which once supplied the town with water.

Passing along the **Via Maddalena** and the **Via Turritana** in the Old Town, where there is a succession of modest inns and restaurants, you will arrive in the bustling **Via Brigata Sassari**, named after the heroic Sardinian brigade which saw action during World War I. Continuing across the semicircular **Emiciclo Garibaldi** ❻, dominated by the statue of Giuseppe Mazzini (1805–72), the politician instrumental in the unification of Italy in 1861 – you will soon reach the **Giardini Pubblici** ❶ (Municipal Park), a refreshing place to cool down and unwind.

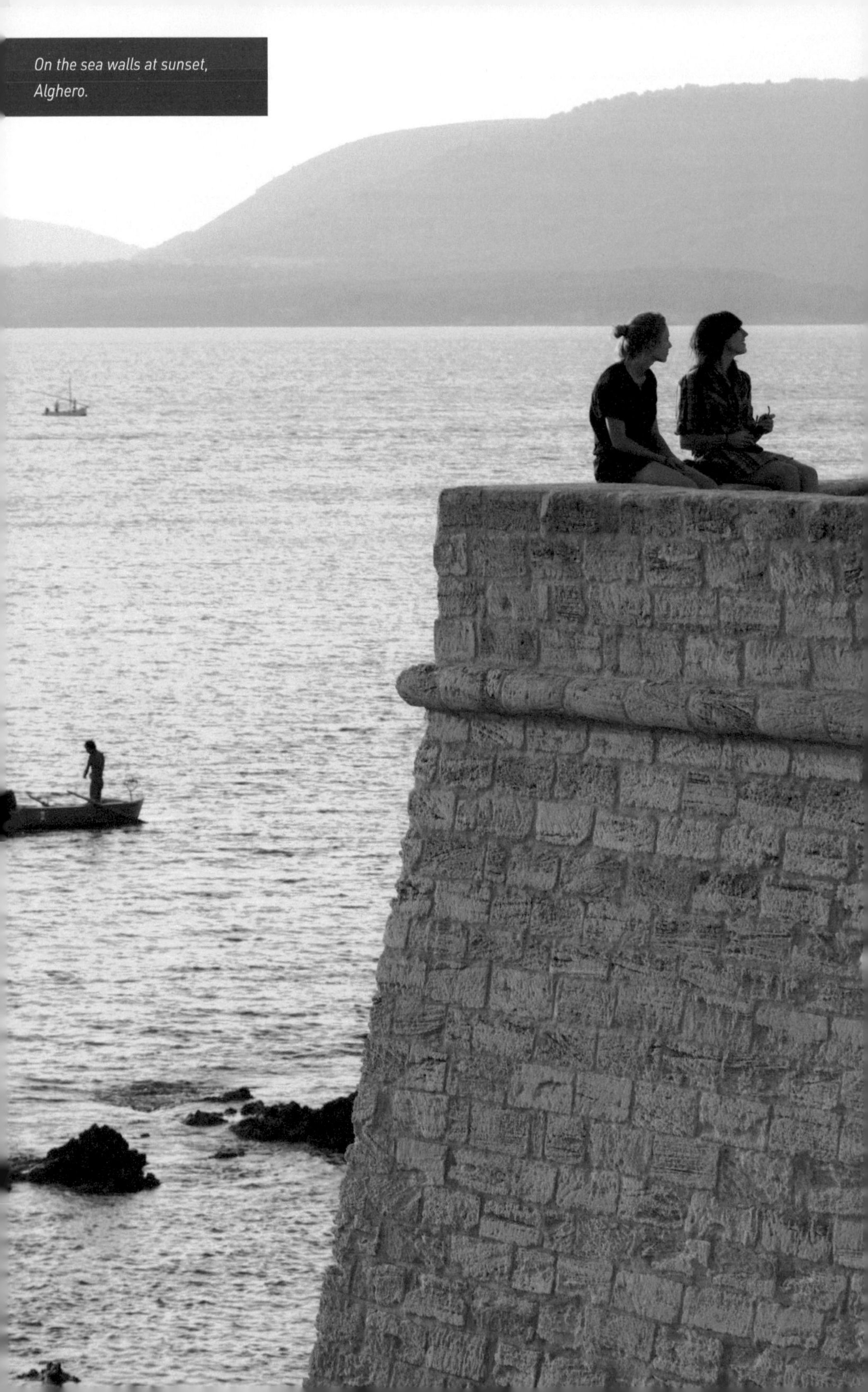
On the sea walls at sunset, Alghero.

ALGHERO TO ORISTANO

There is much to explore along the western coast of Sardinia: nature reserves, caves, hiking trails, Romanesque architecture, splendid towns, Roman remains and, of course, beaches.

Strongly influenced by Spanish culture, **Alghero** ❶ has the most Spanish feel of any Sardinian town. The city is generally considered to have been founded in 1102. However, long before the dawn of the Christian era the Phoenicians set up a trading post on this exposed bay in western Sardinia. In the early Middle Ages Arabs kept a base here from which they set out on their raids of southern France. It was not until the 12th century that settlers fortified the little peninsula on which the Old Town remains huddled to this day.

SPANISH LOYALTY

It was at this time, too, that the place received its somewhat inauspicious name, Alghero, which translated means "full of algae". For 250 years the Doria family from Genoa was in power here, but in 1353 they were forced to cede the town to the forces of Aragon. With the first Aragonese-Catalan officials came Catalan settlers. Following an uprising against harsh Aragon rule, the resident Sardinians and Ligurians were all driven out of Alghero, and were replaced from 1372 by settlers from Barcelona, Valencia and Mallorca.

Alghero was transformed into an urban fortress in which only citizens loyal to the regime were allowed to live. The town was closed in on all sides by walls, towers and bulwarks (the fortifications on the landward side were demolished during the 19th century to provide work for the inhabitants of a nearby penal colony). The citizens were not allowed to travel further than about 3km (2 miles) beyond the city boundaries, as far as a number of churches in the surrounding countryside. The dominant influence in Alghero was from the Iberian peninsula, and the Catalan language is very much alive and thriving.

Main attractions
Alghero
Grotta di Nettuno
Valle dei Nuraghi
Bonorva
Santu Lussúrgiu
Nuraghe Losa
Oristano
Tharros
Is Arutas
Bosa

Map on page 160

Fortified Alghero.

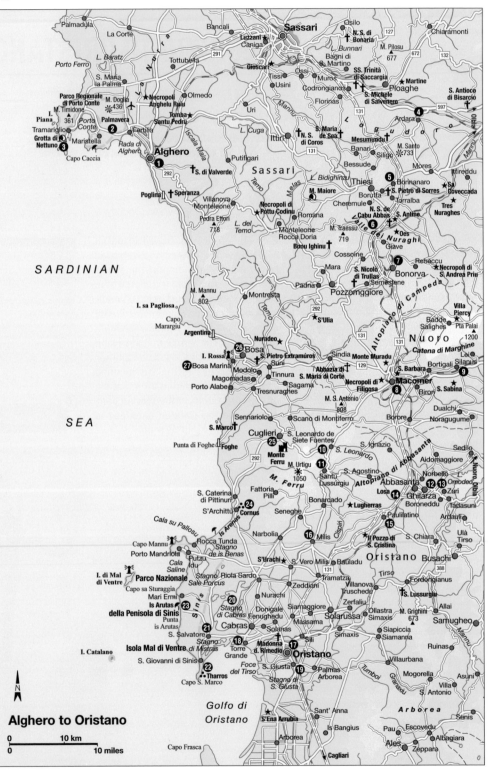

Palmadula

La Corte

L. Baratz

Porto Ferro

S. Maria la Palma

Bancali

Caniga

Luzzani ★

Sassari

Osilo

N. S. di Bonaria †

127

Chiaramonti

132

M. Pilosu 677

672

Tottubella

291

Gioscari ★

Tissi

Ossi

Muros

Bagni di S. Martino

SS. Trinità di Saccargia †

Martine ★

Ploaghe ★

Codrongianos

Usini

S. Michele di Salvenero †

S. Antioco di Bisarcio †

Parco Regionale di Porto Conte

Necropoli Anghelu Ruju †

M. Doglia ☀ 436

Olmedo

Uri

Florinas

597

I. Piana

M. Timidone 361

Palmavera ●2

Porto Conte

Tomba Santu Pedru ★

Fertilia

Tramariglio

Maristella

Grotta di Nettuno ●3

Rada di Alghero

Alghero ●1

Capo Caccia

292

S. di Valverde †

Poglina

Speranza †

Putifigari

S. Maria de Sea †

N. S. di Coros †

Ardara

●4

Mesumundu †

S. Santo ☀ 733

Siligo

Banari

Bessude

Mores

Mireddu

S A R D I N I A N

S E A

Sassari

L. Cuga

Ittiri

Temo

Melas

M. Maiore ●

Thiesi

L. Bidighinzu

●5

Bonnanaro

Borutta

S. Pietro di Sorres †

Cheremule

Torralba

Sa Coveccada ★

Tres Nuraghes ★

Villanova Monteleone

Necropoli di Pottu Codinu †

Romana

N. S. de Cabu Abbas †

S. Antine ★

Pedra Ettori 718

L. del Temo

Monteleone Rocca Doria

M. Traessu 719

●6

Oes

Giave

Valle dei Nuraghi

Bonu Ighinu †

Cossoine

Rebeccu

●7

Necropoli di S. Andrea Priu †

Villa Piercy

I. sa Pagliosa

Capo Marargiu

M. Mannu 802

Mara

Padria

S. Nicolò di Trullas †

Pozzomaggiore

Bonorva

Semestene

Badde Salighes

Pta Palai

1200

Argentina

Montresta

Temo

292

S'Ulia

131

Altopiano di Campeda

131

Nuoro

Catena di Marghine

Lei

Nuradeo ★

●26 Bosa

I. Rossa

Sindia

Monte Muradu

129

S. Barbara ★

Bortigali

Silanus

●9

●27 Bosa Marina

Modolo

S. Pietro Extramúros ★

Suni

Tinnura

Abbazia di †

Necropoli di Filigosa †

Macomer

●8

S. Sabina ★

Biron

Magomadas

Sagama

S. Maria di Corte †

Porto Alabe

Tresnuraghes

M. S. Antonio 908

Scano di Montiferro

Borore

Noragugume

Dualchi

Sennariolo

S. Marco ★

Cuglieri

●25

Punta di Foghe

Foghe

S. Leonardo de Siete Fuentes

●10

S. Leonardo

S. Ignazio

Sedilo

Aidomaggiore

Nuoro-Dòlia

Norbello

S. Caterina di Pittinuri

S'Archittu

Cornus ●24

292

Monte Ferru ★

M. Urtigu 1050

M. Ferru

●11

S. Agostino

Santu Lussurgiu

Altopiano di Abbasanta

Abbasanta

●12 ●13

Omodeo

Zuri

Tadasuni

Ardauli

Fattoria Pilli

Bonàrcado

Losa ●14

Ghilarza

Bonneddu

Paulilatino

●15

Ulà Tirso

Cala su Pallosu

Is Arenas

Rocca Tunda

Seneghe

Lughèrras ★

Il Pozzo di S. Cristina ★

S. Chiara

Capo Mannu

Stagno de is Benas

Narbolia

●16

Milis

Cispiri

Oristano

Busachi

Porto Mandriola

Putzu Idu

Cala Saline

S'Urachi ★

S. Vero Milis

Bauladu

131

Tirso

388

Fordongianus

I. di Mal di Ventre

Parco Nazionale

Capo sa Sturaggia

Mari Ermi

Stagno di Sale Porcus

Riola Sardo

Zeddiani

Tramatza

Villanova Truschedu

Zerfaliu

S. Lussurgiu †

Allai

Is Arutas

della Penisola di Sinis

Punta is Arutas

●23

Stagno di Cabras

●20

Nurachi

Donigale Fenughedu

Siamaggiore

Massama

Ollastra Simaxis

Solarussa

Simaxis

M. Grighini 673

Samugheo

●21

Cabras

S. Salvatore

Stagno di Mistras

Solanas

Sili

Simaxis

Siapiccia

Siamanna

Ruinas

Asuni

I. Catalano

Isola Mal di Ventre

●18

Torre Grande

Madonna d. Rimedio

●17

Oristano

Villaurbana

Mogorella

Villa S. Antonio

S. Giovanni di Sinis

●22 Tharros

Capo S. Marco

Foce del Tiro

S. Giusta

●19

Palmas Arborea

Stagno di S. Giusta

Tumboi

Granaxiu

Mannu

N

Alghero to Oristano

0   10 km

0   10 miles

Capo Frasca

Golfo di Oristano

S'Ena Arrubia ★

Arborea

Sant' Anna

Is Bangius

Arborea

Pau

Ales

A r b o r e a

Escovedu

Sènis

Albagiara

Zeppara

Cagliari ★

ALGHERO OLD TOWN

The Old Town of Alghero covers barely one-tenth of today's total city. It is, however – apart from the beaches and hotels located beyond the city limits – the only part of the town worth exploring. Surrounded on three sides by towers and fortifications, the best introduction to the town can be gained from a walk along the old **battlements**.

Setting out from the massive round **Torre dell'Espero Reial** (the Tower of Royal Ambition), you can stroll past the lively **Piazza Sulis** in the southeast, fringed by cafés and trees, to the half-ruined but still impressive Forte de la Magdalena lying right beside the harbour in the north. En route is the octagonal **Torre de Sant Jaume** (St James's Tower) and the circular **Torre de la Polvorera**, which is situated on the northwesterly tip of the peninsula. From the fortifications along the **Lungomare Marco Polo** there are spectacular views across the Bay of Alghero as far as Capo Caccia. Finally, via a narrow battlement walk, you reach the 16th-century **Forte de la Magdalena**, where fishermen repair their boats. Locals take their evening stroll along the three-sided seafront promenade, especially the **Lungomare Colombo** to the south, which is overflowing on public holidays. The fascinating alleys of the Old Town, tall and narrow like dark mountain gorges, lead off the promenade. The Old Town itself is best entered through the **Porta a Mare**, the Sea Gate, on the north side. Another entrance is in the **Porta a Terra**, the original main entrance to town. The door still bears the stone coat-of-arms of the crown of Aragon and used to be closed at dusk.

View of the Duomo di Santa Maria.

DUOMO DI SANTA MARIA

The **Duomo di Santa Maria** (Cathedral of Our Lady; Mon–Tue and Thu–Sat June–Aug 10.30am–1pm, 7–9.30pm, Apr–May and Sept–Oct 10.30am–1pm and 4–6.30pm) is reached by crossing the long, funnel-shaped main square – the **Piazza Civica**. Its style evolved over 200 years, from the mid-16th to the mid-18th century; unsurprisingly, the result, a late Baroque-Manneristic

Boats at sunset in Alghero's harbour.

⊘ A CHURCH AND A COW

Santissima Trinità di Saccargia (Church of the Trinity of the Spotted Cow; daily), one of the finest Romanesque churches, stands near the village of Codrongianos, 15km (9 miles) from Sassari. According to legend, a gentle, pious cow played a significant role in the church's foundation – though, with its distinctive walls of alternating layers of dark basalt and light limestone, in fact it resembles a zebra more than a cow. Inside, the apse contains the only extant cycle of 13th-century frescoes in Sardinia.

Only 3km (2 miles) away is the 12th-century **Chiesa di San Michele di Salvènero** (daily), which retains some of its Romanesque-Pisan charms despite alterations at the beginning of the 20th century.

Alghero is famed for its fresh seafood. Stop at the market in Via Sassari for lobster, sea urchins and squid, or try the local restaurants.

The battlements of Alghero Old Town.

superstructure on top of the late Gothic main building, lacks unity. Attached to the Duomo is the **Museo Dioces-ano d'Arte Sacra** (tel: 079-973 3041; July–Aug Mon–Sat 10.30am–1pm and 6–9pm, Apr–June and Sept–Oct Thu–Tue 10.30am–1pm and 5–8pm, Jan–Mar Fri–Sun 10.30am–1pm and 4.30–7.30pm, Dec Thu–Tue 11am–1pm and 4.30–7pm) inside the church of Nostra Signora del Rosario. On display is a collection that forms the town's liturgical treasure.

In front of the cathedral, on either side of the **Via Sant'Erasmo**, lies the former Jewish quarter; the Jews formed an essential part of the community in every trading centre of international importance during the Middle Ages and often rose to positions of influence. In the middle of the 15th century, with the necessary permission of the King of Aragon, Alghero's Jews raised the required finance for the construction of the **Torre des Hebreus** (The Jewish Gate). It provided a second point of access to the town on the landward side; until well into the 19th century it was closed every evening at dusk with the traditional cry "All those outside must stay outside!".

Fanning out behind the cathedral are the most elegant streets of the Old Town: **Via Umberto**, in which the aristocracy and clergy resided under the rule of Spain and Savoy, and the **Via Carlo Alberto** (Carrer Major), now filled with upmarket shops. Dominating the end of the street is the sumptuous Baroque **Chiesa di San Michele** (daily), built by the Jesuits. Its coloured majolica dome rises above the exquisitely restored monastery complex of San Francesco (built during the 14th and 16th to 17th centuries); during the summer months the Romanesque cloisters form an atmospheric setting for classical music concerts. Some of the alleys of the Old Town have a distinctly southern flair, with a less restrained feel reminiscent of Naples. This is for good reason, as for centuries Alghero was the capital of the Mediterranean coral industry, and attracted Neapolitan fishermen specialised in the hazardous business of fishing for coral.

⊘ UN'ISOLA LINGUISTICA

Although you become accustomed to the coexistence of two languages in Sardinia – Italian and Sardinian with its myriad of dialects – the situation in Alghero is considerably more complicated; it is often referred to as *un'isola linguistica* – a linguistic island. Here you will hear Catalan in addition to Italian, which virtually all Sardinians speak perfectly even if it is not their mother tongue, and the archaic-sounding Sardinian, which is comprehensible only to the initiated. The visitor will often hear local inhabitants using Catalan in conversation, and will notice that it is used with increasing frequency on the streets, in the squares and, for some reason, in relation to buildings of interest to tourists. Perhaps the local inhabitants think Prassa del Pou Vel, Carrer de Bonaire and Les Quatre Cantonades sound more inviting than **Piazza Civica**, **Via Umberto** and **Via Carlo Alberto**. In the general wake of all stronger minorities, the citizens of Alghero have revived an interest in their Catalan roots, founding parties to promote the interests of their minority culture and various folklore groups to breathe new life into their traditional folk music. It is not surprising, therefore, that the town's most famous culinary speciality is Catalan-style lobster.

The combination of this influx from Campania, linked to the Catalan influence, has given the townspeople their characteristic bonhomie. Nowadays only a small proportion of the coral used in the decorative items on display originate off the Sardinian coast. The coral reefs have long been depleted.

EXCURSIONS FROM ALGHERO

Moving north from the town and passing the Bombarde beach, you come to the Nuragic complex of **Palmavera** ② (tel: 079-994 4394; Apr and Oct 9am–6pm, May–Sept 9am–7pm, Nov–Mar 10am–2pm; guides available). This is surrounded by a village of round huts that includes one used as a meeting house, with a stone bench along its perimeter that could seat over 40 people.

Continuing along the same road, the bay of Porto Conte, the ancient Roman **Portus Ninpharus**, appears in front of you. It's the only true natural port in Sardinia, where Charles V's fleet was harboured on its way to Tunis; it is closed on one side by the promontory of Capo Caccia, which houses the **Grotta di Nettuno** ③ (Apr–Oct 9am–7pm, Nov–Mar 10am–3pm). To get to the grotto you can either take a Linea Grotte di Nettuno (tel: 079-978 961; www.navisarda.it) or Frecce della Grotte (tel: 368-353 6824; www.grottedinettuno.it) motor boat (pricey), sailing boat (magical) or bus (cheapest and most comfy when the water is choppy), all from Alghero port. Once inside the cave, the tour brushes the seawater lake, Lago La Marmora, through atmospheric chambers filled with multicoloured rocks hewn into otherworldy stalactite and stalagmite forms, with names like Grand Organ and Cupola.

North of Porto Conte is the inaccessible **Cala dell'Inferno** (Hell's Bay), set in a limestone cliff shaped by erosion and surrounded by *màcchia* bush. From Porto Conte to the north it is easy to reach Argentiera and Stintino.

Taking the road through Sassari, you reach the **Via Carlo Felice**, the SS 131, which passes through a region full of historical interest and several Romanesque churches. The majority of them were constructed between the 12th and 14th centuries by Tuscan master craftsmen – often at the behest of the wealthy mainland merchants who imported large quantities of minerals, coral, hides, cattle, cheese, salt and cereals from Sardinia.

FROM ARDARA TO BORUTTA

About 15km (8 miles) further along the road is the village of **Ardara** ④, a fascinating stop for anyone interested in the house of Hohenstaufen (a dynasty of German kings in the 12th and 13th centuries). Here, in 1239, in the **Santa Maria del Regno** (the Black Cathedral; daily) – built of black basalt in about 1100 – Enzo, the son of the Hohenstaufen Emperor Frederick II, celebrated what was to prove a short-lived marriage to Adelaida. Since his wife's dowry included a sizeable proportion of the island,

> **Tip**
>
> A magical way to experience the natural wonders of Capo Caccia – including trips to the Grotta di Nettuno often accompanied by dolphins – is aboard the handsome *Andrea Jensen* sailing boat which sails from Alghero (tel: 3389-708 139; www.ajsailing.com; charge includes lunch).

Sunset over the west coast.

ROCK OF AGES: SARDINIA'S KARST CAVES

The enormous variety of rock types makes Sardinia a dream destination for geologists and cavers, and creates the landscapes that appeal to the rest of us.

Karst formations – which are shaped by the action of water on soluble bedrock – cover a relatively small area of Sardinia (only about 6 percent of the island, mainly along the coast) compared with the more extensively occurring metalliferous rocks and granite. But it's the karst formations

Stalactite formations of the Grotta di Ispinigoli, near Dorgoli.

and their eerie underground worlds that are the main attraction for most travellers.

A STUDY IN KARST

Sardinia's karst limestone was created almost 500,000 years ago (Palaeozoic Era). Erosion by sea action has created an amazing range of grottoes, each with a completely individual character, making them attractive to geohydrologists, palaeoclimatologists, biologists and everyday punters. A Golfo di Orosei boat trip with an expert local guide is a chance to swim in many such magical sea grottoes.

The study of Sardinia's caves didn't start until the 1950s. In 1954 a British team of explorers discovered and investigated the Grotta di Nettuno on the Capo Caccia, a formation of red limestone rising 180 metres (600ft) above the sea. Today, over 100,000 people a year clamber into the bowels of the earth via the Escala Cabirol, the so-called Deer's Steps. Many more visit by fishing boat from Alghero harbour. The cave contains a small lake (La Marmora), which – like the lake in the Grotta del Bue Marino in Cala Gonone near Dorgali (see page 124) – provides a perfect miniature example of the vast underground lakes of Europe. Passing through the chambers you encounter strangely shaped stalactites and stalagmites formed by the drip-dripping of mineral-rich water over millions of years. It is thought that these, along with other caves on the island, had religious significance during the Ozieri period.

CHANCE DISCOVERIES

More often than not Sardinia's caves were discovered by accident: some by engineers seeking karst springs to increase the island's scarce water supplies, others by miners after lead and zinc, and even some by workers collecting *guano* (seabird excrement) for use in fertilisers.

During the 19th century, General Alfonso La Marmora made a detailed study of the island's caves. Scientifically based speleology has been applied to Sardinia only since the end of World War II. Only a small proportion of Sardinia's caves have been studied, but for the visitor after other-worldly experiences, there are plenty of underground worlds to explore.

in the form of the *giudicati* of Torres and Gallura, Enzo proclaimed himself King of Sardinia. He soon abandoned both his wife and the island (he seems to have been unable to stand life on this rough and lonely island for any length of time), but he refused to relinquish his royal title, which he held until his death in a dungeon in Bologna, where his enemies kept him prisoner for 23 years.

In the same cathedral is Sardinia's largest retable: a polyptych measuring 10 by 6 metres (32 by 20ft), painted in 1515 by Giovanni Muru, hanging behind the main altar and formed by various wooden panels.

ROMANESQUE CHURCHES

From Ardara, continuing east on the SS 597 there are two other important Romanesque churches: **Sant' Antioco di Bisarcio** (daily), built in 1065–1153, with an unusual asymmetrical facade, and **Nostra Signora di Castro** (daily) situated in a panoramic position.

Heading south from Ardara, after 20km (12 miles) the highway rejoins the Carlo Felice Superstrada at the farming village of **Bonnanaro ❺**. The effects of the steady migration from the land during the past decades have been particularly noticeable here. The settlement has given its name to an advanced culture (the Bonnanaro Culture, 1800–1600 BC) which preceded the Nuragic period. It must have been an austere civilisation based on the bare essentials of life – in keeping with the harsh, unyielding nature of the island interior – and yet, according to archaeological evidence, it was sufficiently sophisticated for the performance of complicated surgical operations such as trepanation, the drilling of the skull.

Another Romanesque church lies in the vicinity of Bonnanaro. **San Pietro di Sorres** (daily), in the village of **Borutta**, stands dramatically perched at a height of 520 metres (1,665ft) on a little

plateau. Its location amid the bleak limestone landscape is breathtaking.

Situated on a limestone plateau nearby is a largish village, **Thiesi**, whose inhabitants make a living from arable and livestock farming. A mural on the building of the local middle school by Aligi Sassu, a well-known artist of Sardinian extraction who lived in Thiesi, represents *S'annu de s'attaccu* – "the Year of the Attack" – 1800, when the Duke of Asinara launched an attack on the villagers who refused to deliver his feudal dues. This illustrates the part played by chauvinism and exploitation in Sardinian history. Those of the island's politicians who support Sardinian autonomy accuse the Italian state of these same attitudes.

VALLEY OF NURAGHI

From Thiesi, a road crossing pretty countryside passes under the Carlo Felice Superstrada and leads into the **Valle dei Nuraghi ❻** near **Torralba**. The name sounds as though it is a slogan coined by the tourist office, but it is authentic. The hollow

In this area are some of the best-preserved Megalithic remains on the island.

Nuraghe di Santu Antine.

In the heat of summer, you will see lizards darting into rock crevices as you approach.

"Royal palace" at the Nuraghe di Santu Antine.

contains a large number of mysterious Megalithic Nuragic constructions. The finest, the **Nuraghe di Santu Antine** (www.nuraghesantuantine.it; daily Apr–Oct 9am–8pm, Nov–Mar 9am–5pm), stands in the middle of the valley. Its main tower, now some 17.5 metres (56ft) high, may well have measured as much as 20 metres (68ft) before the top courses of stones were dismantled during the 19th century to build the village well in Torralba.

The nuraghe is of a highly complex construction; built of layers of basalt blocks, it includes – apart from the 3,500-year-old main tower – three lower and less ancient subsidiary towers arranged in a clover-leaf shape. In later times, the local population was so impressed by the nuraghe that it called it Sa Domu de Su Rei, the Royal Palace. Strangely enough, the king referred to was actually the Roman emperor Constantine, who is revered throughout the island as a courageous fighter of holy wars and a protector of the Sardinian people.

You can discover more about the Nuraghe Santu Antine – its labyrinthine interior structure of walls, corridors and rooms as well as the remarkable construction of the main tower, which consists of 28 courses of stone blocks, mounted upon each other without the use of mortar – at Torralba's **Museo dei Nuraghi** (www.nuraghesantuantine.it; closed for restoration), where excavated items and other interesting exhibits are on display.

Also famous for its nuraghe, as well as its attractively coloured hand-woven carpets, is **Bonorva ❼**, a small agricultural market town lying further to the south. One of the most famous sites is the **Sant' Andrea Priu** necropolis (daily), a prehistorical ipogeic tomb formed by 18 rooms that in Palaeo-Christian, Byzantine and medieval times was used as place of worship. Frescoes discovered on the walls are in the process of being restored. Other ancient ruins lie at an altitude of approximately 650 metres (2,080ft) on the **Su Monte** plateau. Here the Nuragi must have made their last desperate

stand against the incursions of the Carthaginians.

MACOMER

In 1478 yet another Sardinian dream of maintaining the island's independence was shattered near the little town of **Macomer ❽**, which lies some 15km (10 miles) further southwards. The soldiers of Leonardo Alagon, Margrave of Arborea, were defeated by a vast army sent by the new rulers from Aragon. It was this Spanish victory that broke the last remaining pocket of resistance on the island. Macomer lies on a trachyte ledge which slopes away to the south. The panorama from the town sums up the island's geological history. It stretches from the basalt plateau in the foreground to the granite and limestone mountains of the interior on the horizon.

The town itself has a welcoming atmosphere: as an ancient trading centre and road junction, Macomer has a long tradition of hospitality. The area was settled in ancient times by the Nuragi, who were followed by the Carthaginians and the Romans. The roads radiating from Macomer follow tracks used since time immemorial: east through the village of **Silanus ❾**, with the Byzantine-Romanesque **Chiesa di Santa Sabina** and the nuraghe of the same name, and west through **Sindia** with its nearby Romanesque-Burgundian Cistercian abbey church to Bosa.

SPRING WATER AND EXTINCT VOLCANOES

Alternatively one can take the road to Santu Lussúrgiu, which runs through the hills to the southwest of Macomer; after 15km (10 miles) of lonely countryside one reaches the hamlet of **San Leonardo de Siete Fuentes ❿**, whose *siete fuentes* (seven springs) rise in a shady park. In summer people come to take the waters, which have a mildly diuretic effect. The parish church, the Chiesa di San Leonardo, built of dark-coloured trachyte rock, dates from the 12th century. It was originally constructed in Romanesque style, but

Limoncello, a popular Sardinian liqueur made with lemon zest, is usually served as an after-dinner drink.

Rooftops of Santa Lussúrgiu.

The warm water for the Roman baths at Fordongianus flows from the local hot springs.

Rugged Sardinian landscape.

extensive Gothic additions were built at a later date.

Along the barren rocky cliffs of the Monte Ferru is an extinct volcano, and the region's topography shows scars of past eruptions. In fact, the market town of **Santu Lussúrgiu** spreads out across a former crater. Livestock farming is the main source of livelihood for the inhabitants, and its handicrafts are closely linked with sheep rearing: the women weave rugs and blankets from the wool, and the men produce the sharp knives which they need for shearing in the spring. The town also has a reputation for excellent woodcarving, a skill which in days gone by occupied the shepherds in the long days and weeks as they grazed their flocks.

From Santu Lussúrgiu to Abbasanta the road descends the barren slopes of the Monte Ferru and then passes between an endless succession of *tancas*. These plots of land demarcated by stone walls are an essential characteristic of the Sardinian countryside, giving it a geometric chequerboard appearance. When the land was parcelled out during the 19th century to enable more peasants to become landowners, the construction of these walls marked a revolution in land use. For thousands of years – since the earliest days in the island's history – the Sardinians enjoyed common land that was worked by the community as a whole. From this point on, however, this quasi-communist concept of property ceased to exist.

ABBASANTA CHURCHES AND A MUSEUM TO GRAMSCI

In the tiny village of **Sant'Agostino**, modest cottages and guesthouses for pilgrims, known as *muristenes*, are clustered round a solid basalt church. The same dark stone was used for the buildings forming the heart – the oldest part – of **Abbasanta**. This village possesses a pseudo-Renaissance parish church which lends it a certain dignity.

Ghilarza , which today forms part of the Abbasanta built-up area, appears to have a much more urban

air, an impression due in part to the large number of churches within the town limits. They include **San Palmerio, San Giorgio, Santa Lucia** and the **Carmelo**. In addition there are several picturesque medieval country churches in the vicinity.

The small **Casa Museo di Antonio Gramsci** (tel: 0785-53075; Fri–Sun 10am–1pm, 4–7pm) on the Corso Umberto in Ghilarza provides an insight into the life of the Marxist writer, philosopher and politician. Gramsci was born in 1891 in the village of **Ales**, attended the school in Ghilarza for 10 years and died in 1937 in Rome after enduring a lengthy prison sentence for his anti-Fascist views. His writing left a lasting philosophical and political legacy – not least in the resurgence of the Partito Communista Italiana (PCI) following World War II.

From Ghilarza it's a stone's throw to the tiny hamlet of **Tadasuni**, where the local priest has founded a museum of traditional Sardinian musical instruments, the most complete of its kind.

ZURI AND ROMAN BATHS

The village of **Zuri**  is also worth a visit. During the 1920s, when the Omodeo Dam was under construction, the entire settlement was moved to its present site. Not only the inhabitants but also the lovely Romanesque-Gothic parish church of **San Pietro** was relocated: the pink trachyte blocks were painstakingly dismantled, one by one, and then reconstructed here.

The village of **Fordongianus** to the south offers the only possibility to visit the ruins of Roman thermal baths where hot water still flows (www.forumtraiani.it; daily 9.30am–1pm and 3–5.40pm). The name comes from the Latin Forum of Traiani, an important Roman settlement which controlled the movements of the local population from the mountains to the east. Not far below, **Samugheo** has an important Textile Museum, the **Museo Unico Regionale dell'arte Tessile** Sarda (http://murats.it; summer Tue 10am–1pm and 5–8pm, Wed–Sun 9.30am–1pm and 5–8pm, winter Tue 10am–1pm and 4–7pm, Wed–Sun 9.30am–1pm and

Sheep provide the milk for Sardinia's most famous export – pecorino cheese.

For something different, visit Tadasuni's museum of traditional musical instruments.

⊘ MUSICA SARDA

Tadasuni's priest, Don Giovanni Dore, founded its **Museo degli Strumenti della Tradizione Sarda** (Museum of Traditional Sardinian Musical Instruments; Casa Parrochiale, Via Adua 7; by appointment only, tel: 0785-50113; free); his indefatigable enthusiasm led him to make a study of the sophisticated construction techniques employed in the seemingly primitive musical instruments of Sardinia – above all, the *launedda*, the shepherd's flute, the *serraggia* fiddle and the *tumbarinu* drum.

Don Dore's demonstrations provide the best introduction to the island's musical tradition. Although this music is still performed at folk festivals, the archaic tone patterns make it largely inaccessible to the uninitiated.

Architectural detail in Oristano.

Red-tiled rooftops of Oristano.

4–7pm), showcasing the skills of the local artisans.

NURAGHE AND WATER TEMPLES

Before leaving this densely populated region on the edge of the basalt plateau of Abbasanta, it is well worth making a slight detour to view the well-preserved **Nuraghe Losa** ⑭ (tel: 0785-52302; 9am–one hour before sunset), located some 3km (2 miles) southwest of Abbasanta. The ivy-clad ruins exude a nostalgic air; naturally enough, in this volcanic area, the walls are constructed of dark basalt blocks. The main 12-metre (40ft) high tower dates from the middle Bronze Age (approximately 14th century BC) but has been built upon many times since – as have the later subsidiary towers and exterior walls.

The Nuraghe Losa, the fortress of Santu Antine near Torralba, and the settlement Su Nuraxi near Barumini are all quite different constructions, and represent excellent examples of the nuraghe – some 7,000 in all – which can be found all over Sardinia. Some are in good condition, but many are decayed almost beyond recognition. The nuraghe lend the landscape an aura of archaic melancholy, in which all attempts at progress seem out of place. All the more powerful, therefore, is the impact of the Nuraghe Losa, standing on a small rocky outcrop just a stone's throw from the noise and frenzy of the traffic ploughing up and down the Carlo Felice superstrada below.

Visitors are frequently surprised by the obvious parallels between the religious rites of the Nuragi and those of present-day Christianity. Three thousand years ago, the Nuragi used to gather to celebrate their festivals around **Il Pozzo di Santa Cristina** (Water Temple of Santa Cristina; www.archeotour.net; 8.30am–dusk), which lies a few miles south of **Paulilatino** ⑮ on the stretch of the Carlo Felice between Abbasanta and Oristano.

The elegantly constructed well shaft of the ancient sacred spa is surrounded by walls which archaeologists believe to be the remains of former pilgrims'

huts called *muristenes*. Housed in a handsome 19th-century *palazzina* in the centre of town, the **Museo Archeo-logico-Etnográfico** (www.archeotour.net; Tue–Sun summer 9am–1pm and 4.30–7pm, autumn and winter 3–5.30pm, spring 3.30–6.30pm; entrance with Water Temple ticket) has a collection of finds from Santa Cristina as well as artefacts recreating the pastoral lives of peasants. The rural **Chiesa di Santa Cristina**, situated not far from the ruins of the nuraghe spa temple, is similarly encircled by simple dwellings for worshippers. Here, as so often on Sardinia, there is no clear distinction between the pagan and the Christian. To sample the potent mixture of the secular and the sacred, and the warmest Sardinian hospitality, it is best to visit during the town's ancient feasts, that coincide with the planting and harvest of crops: the nine-day rites of Santa Cristina in May or San Serafino in October.

On the road to Oristano, one more detour remains – a short side-trip to **Milis** ⓰. On the edge of the village stands the Romanesque **Chiesa di San Paolo**, dating from the 12th–13th centuries. The houses are surrounded by the citrus orchards which the French poet Paul Valéry described in his *Sardinian Journey*.

There are plenty of opportunities for horse-riding in this region.

ORISTANO – THE SMALL CAPITAL

Regardless of the direction from which you approach the town of **Oristano** ⓱, it is easy to fall under the impression that you are entering an overgrown village rather than the capital of Sardinia's smallest province. The town has become the focal point of western Sardinia, a region it governed during the period of the medieval *giudicati*. Until well into the 15th century the town was the capital of the judicature of Arborea, which was subjugated by the rulers of Aragon later than the other three *giudicati*. It is possible that the Aragonese were in no particular hurry when it came to conquering this province – the ruling family of Arborea was itself originally of Catalan descent, although they had been resident on Sardinia for many years. The dominant personality of the

Statue of Eleonora d'Arborea in the piazza of the same name, Oristano.

Wild flowers grow amongst the thick, shrubby vegetation of the màcchia.

The Cattedrale di Santa Maria Assunta in Oristano.

house of Arborea was the *Giudichessa* Eleonora, who died in 1404.

HISTORIC CENTRE

Eleonora's seat of government is commemorated in the main square, **Piazza Eleonora d'Arborea**; during the 19th century it was also decided that a somewhat pompous statue should add to the tribute. Surrounded by figures of lions, Eleonora strikes an elegant pose. Today, people gather here, especially in the evening, to meet their friends and lovers, lick ice creams, exchange gossip or just to see and be seen.

Dominating the Piazza Eleonora is the **Palazzo Comunale** (town hall). It is a former Piarist monastery, whose (desecrated) church, with an unusual oval ground plan, now serves as the local council chamber. A stone throw's away, at Piazza Eleonora 19, is a tourist information point (tel: 0783-36831; Mon–Thu 8.30am–1pm and 3pm–6pm, Fri 8.30am–1pm). Despite the increase in population to over 31,000 over the past 30 years, Oristano has none of the sophisticated flair of Cagliari, Sassari or even Alghero, but its compactness adds to the charm of the *centro storico*.

From **Piazza Roma** you enter the pedestrian area in the historical centre, once completely surrounded by medieval walls of which today only the **Torre di Mariano II** (Torre di San Cristóforo), built 1291, remains. It once served as the main gate to the city. The small pedestrianised area has new, upmarket shops.

Lining Via Parpaglia are elegant buildings, including Palazzo Arcais, with its wrought-iron balconies, and Palazzo Parpaglia, which houses the **Antiquarium Arborense** (www.antiquariumarborense.it; Mon–Fri 9am–8pm, Sat–Sun 9am–2pm and 3–8pm). This museum features a wonderful art gallery, with some interesting 16th-century altarpieces in Catalan style, and a large and wide-ranging archaeological collection, including Roman, Neolithic and Nuragic artefacts from the excavations at Tharros and Sinis. There is also a large reconstruction of Tharros in the 9th century AD.

THE CATHEDRAL

The **Cattedrale di Santa Maria Assunta** (daily) was built in a mixture of architectural styles; of the original complex, dating from the 13th century, only the Gothic Cappella di Rimedio in the right aisle remains. Parts of a Romanesque ambon, created by Pisan craftsmen and used as a chapel balustrade, are now displayed in the first chapel of the right aisle. Nino Pisano, whose name indicates that he, too, was a native of Pisa, carved the coloured Gothic wooden statue of *The Annunciation* in the cathedral, as well as a statue of St Basil standing in the nearby church of St Francis. Nino Pisano was a craftsman who lived and worked during the 14th century, when Pisa was still anxious to maintain its links with the *giudicato* of Arborea and its capital.

THE SPANISH INFLUENCE

Next to the Duomo is a good example of 18th-century architecture, the **Seminario Tridentino** (daily), and along the same road is the church of San Francesco, with a neoclassical facade, where you will find the *Crocifisso di Nicodemo* (Crucifix of Nicodemus) in a side chapel. The colourful wooden crucifix is generally considered to be one of the finest examples of Spanish sculpture.

Following in the footsteps of the Pisans and other Tuscans, who had been instrumental in encouraging the skills of Romanesque church builders on the island, the new Spanish colonial rulers began to show their determination to excel in the realm of the arts as well. The best way of establishing contact with the people and buying their loyalty was undoubtedly via the churches and the art treasures they contained; they enabled them to impress and surreptitiously influence the masses.

Also clearly of Spanish origin is the **Sartiglia** (www.sartiglia.info), a spectacular competition for mounted riders which takes place on the last Sunday before Lent and on Shrove Tuesday. Cervantes describes a *Sortija* of this kind (even the name is very similar) in his world-famous picaresque novel, *Don Quixote*. The event is a riding

Much of the countryside in the west is planted with vineyards.

The Corinthian columns at Tharros, the symbol of the town.

competition between two leading riders and their attendants, masked and wearing typical Spanish dress, with lace mantilla and top hat. Lances at the ready, they are required to gallop at and pierce a hanging star. Magical powers are ascribed to the two leading riders, who are known as *componidoris*. It is said that the success of the next harvest can be predicted from the number of times they manage to strike the star.

AROUND ORISTANO

Seven kilometres (4 miles) west of Oristano, built on a once marshy isthmus, is **Torre Grande** , an Aragonese tower which lends its name to the beguiling beach beside its cylindrical hulk. A 2km (1-mile) promenade lined with cafés and *gelaterie* makes it popular with families and couples.

To the south of Oristano the **Campidano** is a vast alluvial plain, in part still covered by coastal marshes and lagoon. The fertile alluvial soil and the abundance of water make this a very important region for Sardinian

Beach of Capo San Marco.

agriculture, and excellent vegetables, rice and wines are produced here. In the inner part of the plain, villages have an agriculturally based economy, while fishing is the major activity for communities living near the lagoons, for example Santa Giusta and Cabras.

The cathedral of **Santa Giusta** , 3km (2 miles) south of Oristano, was built when Pisan influence on the region was at its zenith, not only in politics but also in the arts. Standing imposingly on a hill, the 12th-century trachyte basilica, a jewel of Pisan Romanesque architecture, with Arab and Lombard elements, served as a model for many churches in Sardinia. The interior, with its triple nave, is supported by granite and marble columns which are far older than the church itself: they were lifted from the Carthaginian-Roman settlements of Tharros and Othoca (a common practice at the time). Latest archaeological investigations indicate that Othoca, once a prosperous town, must have been located on the site of the present village of Santa Giusta.

BIRD PARADISE UNDER THREAT

Santa Giusta lies between two coastal marshes which are havens for island wildlife. The first, the **Stagno di Santa Giusta**, covers an area of some 900 hectares (2,200 acres) and is well stocked with fish. There are, however, many pressures on the wildlife, especially from heavy industry and the fishing sector. In 2009, the Sardinian regional government authorised a culling of cormorants wintering in Oristano's lakes *(stagni)*. This measure was in contravention of European law and has enraged environmentalists.

The second lake, the **Stagno Pauli Maiori** (Big Swamp), is in fact smaller than Santa Giusta. It lies to the east, with its dense reeds, interspersed with tamarisk, providing a home for mallards, coots, marsh harriers, bitterns and the rare purple heron. Ruddy shelduck, which are already extinct in mainland Italy, can still be spotted in parts of the **Stagno di Cabras ⓴**, a lake lying to the west of Oristano. Its vast size – 2,000 hectares (5,000 acres)

– helps to make it one of the most fascinating ecological wetlands in the whole of Europe.

Although it is directly linked to the sea, the lake displays a relatively low level of salinity; for this reason, the flamingos prefer the saltier waters of the **Stagno di Mistras** to the west. In autumn they settle in their hundreds – even thousands – when they migrate from the Camargue in the south of France to spend the winter months in Sardinia. A wealth of unexpected discoveries awaits nature-lovers in the region surrounding Oristano. You can hire a local guide for a tour of the Stagno di Cabras. Until recently, the fishermen here used *fassonis* – narrow, one-man boats made of reeds similar to those that are still used on parts of the Nile and Lake Titicaca.

SILENT CHURCHES

Those heading from Cabras to **San Salvatore ㉑** will feel themselves transported into another world as they approach the village isolated between the lagoons. For most of the year the

Prickly pears grow in abundance.

village-sanctuary is utterly deserted, but it comes to life during the summer months when tourists arrive, and at the beginning of September when pilgrims from the surrounding villages come to take part in the nine-day *Sagra di San Salvatore* (Festival of the Redeemer).

During the festival they live in *cumbessias* (pilgrims' houses) praying, eating and sleeping in the company of the other visitors over a period of several days. The statue of Christ is borne in procession from Cabras to the church of San Salvatore, accompanied by youths in white robes, running barefoot.

It is noteworthy that here, too – as in Santa Cristina near Paulilatino – a Christian place of pilgrimage coincides with a pagan holy site. Beneath the present building lies a *hypogaeum* (ancient burial chamber; tel: 347-818 4069; irregular times, call for details; donation expected) constructed by the first inhabitants of the area, the Nuragic, as a water temple. Carthaginians used the three underground cellars as storerooms for their wares (the flourishing trading centre of Tharros lay only 5km/3 miles away); the Romans used them as a dungeon, and from the 4th century AD the Christians turned them into a catacomb church, which they decorated with monochrome wall paintings with divinities related to water worship: Venus, Mars, Eros, nymphs; the Punic writing of the word *rufus*, meaning "heal", is also frequently seen.

Not far from San Salvatore, the church of **San Giovanni di Sinis** also has a long history. A simple 6th-century building was extended into a triple-naved edifice during the 9th–11th centuries, or possibly even earlier; the barrel vaulting of the roof rests on short, massive pillars. The stone blocks needed for the conversion were brought from nearby Tharros. From the 11th century onwards the once-magnificent Phoenician and Carthaginian trading city served only as a quarry – not only for the extension of San Giovanni in Sinis, but also for **Christano**. Here magnificent medieval buildings were constructed using marble and stone blocks already hewn

Interior of San Giovanni di Sinis.

into the appropriate shapes and often decorated with splendid carvings.

THARROS

At the southernmost tip of the Sinis peninsula lie the evocative remains of the Punic-Roman town of **Tharros** ㉒ (tel: 0783-370 019; archaeological site: summer 9am–7pm, till 8pm in Aug, winter 9am–5pm). It was founded by Phoenician merchants during the 8th century BC, who built their protected mooring spot upon an earlier Nuragic village. It achieved incomparable prosperity before passing to Carthage in 510 BC, who transformed it into a naval base and Punic city. It passed into the hands of the Romans after the First Punic War (241 BC), who extended it considerably, adding basalt pavements, sewers, temples and aqueducts.

During the 8th and 9th centuries the inhabitants started to leave the town – possibly because of the Saracen raids which were an almost daily occurrence, but conceivably also because of the malaria which had reached epidemic proportions in a marshy district of the peninsula. Later, during the 11th century, when an attempt to resettle Tharros ended in complete failure, the new and rapidly growing town of Aristanis (Oristano) finally wrested supremacy from its declining neighbour. Its stones were thereupon plundered to build churches and other buildings in the new town across the gulf.

SINIS PENINSULA

The Sinis peninsula lies between Capo Mannu in the north and Capo San Marco in the south. The beach of **Is Arutas** ㉓, northwest of San Salvatore, consists of glittering round grains of quartz, and is now a protected zone after visitors started to take sand home as a souvenir. Nearby **Sa Mesa Longa** is a popular beach with families – a long rocky platform calms the surf here, creating a beautiful marine pool for paddling and swimming. Further to the north, by the **Capo sa Sturaggia**, the coast becomes steeper as it plunges seawards down yellowish-brown cliffs. Here the flocks of cormorants reign supreme, building their nests on the rocky crags.

⊙ Tip

Weekend visitors to Bosa Marina shouldn't miss the opportunity to enjoy spectacular coastal views from the terrace of the Torre Aragonese (tel: 0785-368 000 for hours).

Seaside activities on Putzu Idu's beach.

A short distance further on is **Putzu Idu**, which has become a popular place to buy a holiday home for people living in Oristano, although the inauguration of the **Parco Nazionale della Penisola di Sinis** (Sinis Peninsula national park) has put an end to the uncoordinated building proposals which threatened the area. **Santa Caterina di Pittinuri** is an unpretentious modern seaside resort situated on an attractive rocky inlet, near which interesting examples of coastal erosion, such as the rock arch **S'Archittu**, are in evidence. Near the town lie the ruins of **Cornus** , probably founded by the Carthaginians during the 5th century BC.

During the First Punic War the native Sardinians and the Carthaginian immigrants, among whom relations had not always been convivial, joined together in an anti-Roman alliance – but this did not prevent their being defeated by the legions of Rome. Cornus remained a town of some importance even in Roman times; in about AD 1000 it was nonetheless abandoned by its inhabitants, who probably found a new place to live in Cuglieri, 15km (10 miles) away.

The road to **Cuglieri** climbs along the sides of Monte Ferru. The town has been the seat of old religious orders, a bishops' headquarters and the site of an important seminary. In days gone by there were no fewer than three monasteries in this farming village, and in **Scano di Montiferro** nearby. The region also has other remains bearing witness to even older civilisations: *tombe di giganti* and the ubiquitous nuraghi, of which there must have been three (hence the name) in **Tresnuraghes**.

From here it is worthwhile climbing down to the crystal-clear sea and the enchanting coastal strip. The leafy branches invariably lying on the village streets of **Flussio** and **Tinnura** tend to remind visitors of preparations for Palm Sunday. In fact, they are fronds of bog asphodel grass, spread out to dry before being woven into attractive basketwork, which is then offered for sale in the doorways of the houses along the main street. Passing through Suni, with its

Exploring Tharros.

☉ THARROS'S STOLEN PUNIC TREASURES

It was a Punic custom to bury the dead with rich funeral gifts: exquisite gold jewellery, precious stones, valuable glasses and fine pieces of pottery. Many such items can be seen in the principal archaeological museums of the island, especially in the Museo Archeologico Nazionale in Cagliari (see page 102) and the Museo Nazionale G.A. Sanna in Sassari (see page 153). But as organised excavations did not begin until recent times, some archaeological treasures inevitably fell into the hands of plunderers. An English aristocrat, Lord Vernon, removed the contents of 14 graves during the 19th century; and neither Charles Albert (1798–1849), the King of Savoy and Piedmont-Sardinia, nor the French novelist Honoré de Balzac (1799–1850), could resist the temptation to take a few precious "souvenirs" home with them. Of the magnificence of former days, only ruins and the remains of walls are left – the best-preserved dating from Roman times. Visitors with little experience of archaeological sites may find it difficult when confronted with these ruins to imagine a living town with temples, public baths, streets, shops and a colourfully mixed population. But anyone can appreciate the magnificent setting of the ruined city on its narrow peninsula jutting out into the Gulf of Oristano.

characteristically squat houses, the road continues downhill into Bosa.

BOSA

The little town of **Bosa** ㉖ lies on the banks of the Temo, the only navigable river in Sardinia. Thanks to its attractive urban architecture and the gentle green of the surrounding countryside, Bosa is one of the most attractive towns in Sardinia.

It was founded by the Phoenicians and settled by the Romans before being ruled by a succession of Tuscan nobles. The town has two major districts: Sa Costa and Sa Piana. A residential area grew up and formed a link between the two districts; the main characteristic of Sa Piana is that the buildings are rather higher and the alleys narrower than in any other town on the island.

The district of the town known as **Sa Costa** clings with a succession of parallel rows of houses to the side of an 80-metre (260ft) hill, the summit of which is crowned by the **Castello Malaspina** (or Castello di Bosa; www.castellodibosa.com; Mar–Nov daily, Dec–Feb Sat–Sun only, hours vary greatly so tel: 340-395 5048 for times), which was built by the Malaspina family in 1112 and later extended by the rulers of Aragon. This district has no church of its own, since the residents were dependent on the castle in religious as in other affairs. They were permitted to use the castle chapel, **Nostra Signora di Regnos Altos**, where in recent years a cycle of 14th–15th-century frescoes of the Catalan school was discovered. If the church is open, climb to the top of the ramparts for a magnificent view. Beneath the maze of cobblestone alleys and stairs which make up the streets of Sa Costa, the former free town of **Sa Piatta** sprawls across the plain by the river. The **Corso Emanuele II** contains some elegant patrician houses and the imposing **Cattedrale** (daily), which has a 16th-century marble statue of *Madonna col Bambino*.

There is a small, picturesque river port by the bridge over the Temo river, and beyond the bridge extend the unusual terraced houses of **Sas Conzas** – former tanneries which present a fascinating example of industrial architecture of a bygone age.

Fisherman and his boat on the River Temo.

In idyllic isolation on the left bank of the Temo, 2km (1 mile) from the town centre, stands the Romanesque-Gothic **Chiesa di San Pietro**. Constructed in the 11th century, the church formerly served as the cathedral of Bosa. As the presence of the necropolis indicates, it occupies the site of the Roman town.

Be sure to take a gentle stroll up to the fortress – wandering aimlessly through the Sa Costa district before climbing a further 111 steps between olive, fig and almond trees to the summit of the castle hill. In the alleys of Sa Costa black-clad women produce beautiful embroidery and sell it outside their homes – although the women are supposed to sell all their exquisite needlework to cooperatives, which then sell it at set prices in the tourist towns. Along with gold and silver filigree work, coral jewellery and woodcarving, this so-called *filet de Bosa* is eloquent proof of the craftwork tradition still practised here.

Bosa is beautifully situated on the River Temo.

The nearby seaside resort of **Bosa Marina** has a beach of darkish sand containing a high proportion of iron which is said to possess healing properties in the case of rheumatic illnesses. Today the beach is a more popular venue for windsurfers, and equipment can be hired locally in the summer months.

About 10 minutes' drive from Bosa is the pleasant hillside village of **Magomadas**, where you can enjoy a good lunch at Riccardo).

From Bosa a road leads northwards in the direction of Alghero. It passes through an austere landscape with eroded slopes and strangely formed trachyte rocks. Skirting round the villages of **Montresta** and **Villanova Monteleone**, it then descends to the plain of Alghero via a series of vertiginous bends and switchbacks. Since the 1960s Bosa and Alghero have also been linked by a new coastal road. Nonetheless, the stretch of coastline made accessible by this road arouses a wonderful sense of solitude more intense than almost anywhere else on the island; driving or hiking through the region is a real pleasure.

THE SOUTHWEST

From beautiful, remote countryside to sand dunes and beaches via prehistoric settlements and former mining towns – this area is an eclectic mix.

The southwest mixes natural beauty in its beaches, dunes and geological marvels – including limestone caves and a "Geopark" – with the relics and scars of a fascinating history. Costa del Sud and Costa Verde sand dunes and granite outcrops are still largely untouched, bar a few lavish resorts and golf courses, while the splintered rocks of Isola di Sant'Antioco and Isola di San Pietro possess lots of charm and seafood. At Carbonia and Iglesias, rich seams of lead, zinc, silver, copper and iron have been mined for millennia by successive foreign rulers. Vestiges of exploitation, conflict and culture left by Neolithic Ozieri, Nuragic, Phoenician, Roman, Spanish, Fascist and Italian hegemonies can be explored on hilltops and museums, and down mine shafts.

The alluvial plains known as the Campidano divide the southwest from the rest of the island – and are crossed by two motorways (autostrade): the north–south A131 and the A130 west to Iglesias.

Leaving Cagliari on the SS 195, heading southwards towards the **Capo Malfatano**, you pass the lagoon of the **Stagno di Santa Gilla ❶**, an area of international importance which has managed to survive despite creeping industry and aircraft noise. The lagoon and ancient Macchiareddu salt flats extend over 4,000 hectares (9,800 acres)

and have been used since Nuragic times for the production of sea salt.

ROMAN CITY

About 30km (18 miles) from Cagliari is Pula, and on a small peninsula nearby stands the Roman town of **Nora ❷**. The oldest Phoenician inscription was found here, dating from approximately 1000 BC. In 238 BC Nora was chosen as the capital of the Roman province of Sardinia, largely due to its favourable location and a fine natural harbour. From the 5th century AD the town sank

⊙ Main attractions

Chia
Isola di Sant'Antioco
Isola di San Pietro
Grotte di Is Zuddas
Iglésias
Arbus
Piscinas
Arborea
Sanluri
Su Nuraxi

Map on page 184

Mosaic floor, Nora.

The Southwest

0 — 10 km
0 — 10 miles

N

SARDINIAN

SEA

MEDITERRANEAN SEA

into insignificance, to be reawakened after centuries of oblivion by archaeological excavations during the 1950s. They revealed what is thought to be a Phoenician temple to the fertility goddess Tanit, a 2nd-century Roman temple, a theatre and on the *sa punta 'e su coloru*, the Cape of Snakes, a Phoenician-Carthaginian holy place.

It is possible to take a free guided tour (also in English) of Nora's remaining excavations contained within an **archaeological site** (tel: 070-921 470; 9am–sunset). On the beach at Nora is the church where the 350-year-old May procession of *Sagra Sant' Efisio* ends. According to tradition, the underground crypt preserves the remains of the saint.

STUNNING COASTAL ROUTE

In contrast to the north of the island, the south coast of Sardinia has not as yet suffered from overdevelopment. However, there are signs of billionaire investments at the world-class **Is Molas** golf course and the massive Forte Village complex. This resort lies between Santa Margherita and Bithia, taking advantage of the 10km (6-mile) stretch of sandy beach, **La Pineta**.

Bithia ❸ is accessible via the nearby village of Chia, where you can see the Saracen Tower built in the 17th century to defend the island against the Turks. It is also the site of a Phoenician-Roman township with a temple complex, where a likeness of the archaic deity Bes, originating in Egypt, was discovered.

In **Chia** ❹ there are fine granite sand dunes that can reach up to 24 metres (75ft) and upon which ancient juniper trees grow. The wild, unspoilt topography recalls the landscape of the west coast of Scotland, but on closer exploration of the flora and fauna – lots of yellow broom instead of thorny gorse sprouting amidst the familiar granite outcrops, and bulbous exotic insects instead of midges – reveal its true Mediterranean character. A dip into the warm, shallow emerald and deep-blue waters off **Spiaggia Campana** and gorgeous **Spiaggia Su Giudeu** make it a wonderful place to relax, bathe and snorkel.

Ancient Roman remains found at Nora.

The church of Sant'Antioco stands on the site of a 6th-century church.

Sea view from Sant'Antioco.

The coastal road now becomes the Strada Panoramica della Costa del Sud, and goes past **Capo Spartivento** with views over largely unspoilt southern coastline, through a sparsely populated area to a lighthouse and then on to the **Capo Malfatano**. The rocky headlands are emphasised by additional watchtowers, such as the 17th-century **Torre Piscinni**, which was built over a Roman quarry.

Near the little hamlet of **Porto di Teulada** the road leaves the coast, skirting the **Monte s'Impeddau** (267 metres/876ft), a vast area used by NATO forces for target practice. Near **Sant'Anna Arresi**, which holds an annual international jazz festival (www.santannarresijazz.it), a little side road leads back towards the coast, to the seaside resort of **Porto Pino**. There are the many coastal marshes hereabouts: the **Stagno de Is Brebeis**, **Stagno di Maestrale**, **Stagno Baiocca**, and the **Stagno di Santa Caterina** shortly before you arrive in Sant'Antioco. Ornithologists flock here to watch flamingos, herons and cormorants. In the old ghost village of **Tratalias** ❺ stands the Pisan-Romanesque church of Santa Maria (Tue–Sun 9am–1pm and 3–5pm), built in 1213 in grey trachyte.

ISOLA DI SANT'ANTIOCO

At 109 sq km (42 sq miles), the volcanic **Isola di Sant'Antioco** ❻ is the largest island lying off the coast of Sardinia, and the fourth-largest in Italy. It is reached via a causeway; just before entering the village of Sant'Antioco itself you can see the remains of an old **Roman bridge**. Sant'Antioco is a bustling little port with a picturesque old town centre and pine tree-shaded main street, the **Corso Vittorio Emanuele**. During the Phoenician era (9th and 8th centuries BC), **Sulcis**, as Sant'Antioco was called, was one of the most important port cities in the Mediterranean area, dispatching ores mined in the region. The **Museo Archeologico** (www.archeotur.it; daily 9am–7pm) has displays of recent excavations. More relics lay in the catacombs beneath the parish church. On the way to the necropolis, in an early 20th-century farmhouse in Via Mazzini,

is the **Ethnographic Museum** (www. archeotur.it; daily Apr–Sept 9am–8pm, 1st–mid-Oct 9am–1pm and 3.30–8pm, mid-Oct–Mar 9.30am–1pm and 3–6pm).

Not far away lies the **Tophet** (Via Castello; www.archeotur.it; daily 9am–7pm), the ritual ground of the Phoenicians where their deceased children were cremated. Countless urns containing children's ashes stand on the archaeological site close to the vast **Necropolis**.

During the First Punic War, Sulcis acted as a Carthaginian naval base, which in turn led to harsh retaliatory measures by the forces of the Roman empire. Under the emperors the town regained much of its former importance, but it was plundered on several occasions by the Saracen hordes. During the 16th century virtually all the inhabitants abandoned the city. Only in the 19th century did it rise again from oblivion, a trend which has continued as a result of the local tourist industry.

CALASETTA

More attractive is the little port of **Calasetta**, which lies on the northernmost tip of the island. Founded around 1770 to house the Ligurian fishermen arriving from Tabarca in Tunisia, the chequerboard street layout and low, two-storey houses recall the Arab influence. The parish church in the main piazza has a belltower of Arab derivation, and the local popularity of couscous is a culinary relic of this time.

If you are on the island in May or early June and have the stomach for it, take a boat trip to witness the *matanza*, the bloody but dramatic ritual in which tuna fish are harpooned and hoisted on board by hand. During the *matanza*, a complicated system of nets is erected in order to lure the fish into the *camere della morte* (death chamber), in which the sea turns crimson with blood as the tuna are killed. Processing takes place in the *tonnara* (tuna factory) on the **Punta Maggiore**. The entire procedure attracts large crowds of onlookers every year.

For a less gruesome spectacle, make a visit to the **Museo d'Arte Contemporanea** (tel: 0781-887 219; May–June and Sept–Oct Fri–Sun 6–8pm, July–Aug Tue–Sun 6–9pm), housing

⊙ Eat

A mix of Ligurian, Sardinian and Tunisian influences goes into *cucina Calasettana* creation *pilau* (couscous with crustaceans) and *pè di porcu* (pig's trotters).

Relaxing in the shade in Pula.

⊙ Tip

The *Matrimonio Mauritano* (Mauritano wedding) on the first Sunday in August in Santadi represents a genuine example of traditional Sulcis country life: a wedding ceremony celebrated according to centuries'-old customs.

the Leinardi collection of Constructivist and abstract works.

ISOLA DI SAN PIETRO

Calasetta is also the starting point for the crossing to the pretty **Isola di San Pietro** ❼. Its area of 50 sq km (20 sq miles) makes it the third-largest of the offshore islands. The only place of any significance is **Carloforte**, a pleasant town overlooking the port founded in 1738 under the King of the House of Savoy, Charles Emmanuel III. As in the case of Sant'Antioco, the island was settled by Ligurians; during the 16th century many of them were kidnapped and borne off to Tunisia, but were later set free. The island has volcanic rock formations and pillars such as the Punta delle Colonne and Capo Sandalo, and myriad species of birds, among them Eleonora's falcon, named in honour of Eleonora d'Arborea who first declared that the bird should be protected in the 14th century. For years Sardinian conservationists have been lobbying to have the island declared a national park. Apart from a *grotta* in

Carloforte on the island of San Pietro.

the south, San Pietro can also offer the visitor a *tonnara* (tuna factory) in the north of the island.

THE INLAND ROUTE

Leaving Cagliari in a northwesterly direction on the SS 130, pass **Elmas Airport** and continue towards Iglesias and Sant'Antioco. To the west in the mountainous area is **Monte Arcosu** (Sat–Sun summer 8am–7pm, rest of the year 9am–6pm), the largest World Wildlife Fund Reserve in Italy, covering 3,000 hectares (7,400 acres). It is one of the last habitats for the Sardinian deer.

About 15km (10 miles) from the capital lies the pretty village of **Uta**, and some way outside the village lies the church of Santa Maria (built in AD 1140), a most beguiling Romanesque country church. A few miles south of Siliqua stands the 13th-century **Castello di Acquafredda** (www.castellodi acquafredda.it; Wed–Sun 9.30am– 5.30pm), on a volcanic outcrop overlooking the Cixerri river.

The scenic SS 293 winds around the Colle della Campanasissa,

Villaperuccio and Monte Pranu. Abandoned stations of the narrow-gauge railway criss-cross this mining region of the **Sulcis**. Visitors can park by one of the stations and walk along the routes of the former tracks. Near **Nuxis** stands a rare example of Sardinian Byzantine architecture: the country church of **Sant'Elia** (daily), dating back to the 8th century. West of here is the Montessu Necropolis.

The territory of **Santadi** belongs to the part of the island which emerged from the sea in the Lower Cambrian era. The abundance of limestone and schist have created natural caves rich in weathered rocks and crystal formations. Particularly worth a visit for their fine stalagmites and stalactites are the **Grotte di Is Zuddas** ❽ (www.grotteiszuddas.com; daily, times vary greatly, check website), 8km (5 miles) south of Santadi.

The economy of the region is based on sheep rearing and agriculture, as is demonstrated by the existence of numerous *furriadroxius*: small rural hamlets created by shepherds in the 18th century in order to protect their flocks from Saracen incursions. **Casa Museo Sa Domu Antiga** at Santadi (Via Mazzini; tel: 0781-955 955; daily summer 9am–1pm and 5–7pm, winter 9am–1pm and 3–5pm) recreates the interiors and courtyard activities of typical Sulcis peasant dwellings.

FASCIST ARCHITECTURE

The former mining town of **Carbonia** ❾ was built in just two years following Mussolini's 1936 Abyssinian campaign and subsequent international sanctions. The town is a typical example of Fascist architecture, with broad streets converging on the main square, **Piazza Roma**, where the buildings are heavy and imposing.

The sulphurous "Sulcis coal" produced was supposed to ensure self-sufficiency but was virtually useless. Sulcis's mining history is related at the **Museo del Carbone**, housed in the former mine Grande Miniera di Serbariu (www.museodelcarbone.it; mid-June–mid-Sept daily 10am–7pm, mid-Sept–mid-June Tue–Sun 10am–6pm), which ceased activity in 1967. Also worth a

Statue of statesman Quintino Sella, in Piazza Sella, Carbónia.

⊘ OZIERI REMAINS

North of the village of Villaperuccio is the site of the most important rock necropolis in Sardinia: the **Necropoli di Montessu** (daily summer 9am–1pm and 3–8pm, winter 9am–1pm and 2–5pm). Dating from the late Neolithic period of Ozieri Culture (end of the 4th to beginning of the 3rd millennium BC), it contains almost 40 *domus de janas*, the so-called "houses of the fairies", some of which retain their original red and yellow walls. Trachyte or granite menhirs litter the mountains Monte Narcao and Terrazzu. More creepy *domus de janas* chambers can be seen at **Marchiana** and **Sa Grutta**. The Museo Archeologico in Santadi nearby (Via Umberto I; www.museo-archeologicosantadi.it; Wed, Sat–Sun 8.30am–1.30pm and 3.30–6.30pm, Thu 8am–2pm) is filled with prehistoric finds, including ceramics from Montessu.

look is the **Museo Archeologico Villa Sulcis** (Via Napoli; Apr–Sept Tue–Sun 10am–7pm, Oct–Mar Wed–Sun 10am–3pm), where finds from local *domus de janas*, such as bronze statuettes and jewels, are on display.

In stark contrast to Carbonia's Fascist architecture is the important nearby archaeological site at **Monte Sirai** ❿ (Tue–Sun Apr–Sept 10am–1pm, 4–8pm, Oct–Mar 10am–5pm). The former Nuragic settlement was destroyed during the 7th century by Phoenicians from Sulcis (Sant'Antioco), who then constructed a fortress here. Today you can explore atmospheric remains of an acropolis, houses and a necropolis. Views of the industrial havoc wrought throughout the countryside plunge you back into the present. From the nearby harbour of **Portoscuso** you can take a boat to the Isola di San Pietro.

MINERS' TOWNS

Continuing along the road in a northerly direction, strike off westwards towards **Fontanamare** ⓫, soon after the **Gonnesa** turning. Driving through the district surrounding the reedy estuary of the **Torre Gonnesa**, the road eventually reaches the sea. Of the former coal port very little remains today; abandoned buildings and slag heaps take on the appearance of prehistoric ruins.

The mountains and coastline of the Sulcis and the Iglesiente show the scars of centuries of exploitation. From Fontanamare there is a breathtaking corniche leading to the mining villages of **Nebida** and **Masua**. The **Scoglio Pan di Zúcchero**, a vast rocky outcrop ("sugarloaf"), rises dramatically from the sea on the horizon. In this area there are many mines or part of mines which can be visited with specialist guides (contact Igea, tel: 0781-491 404; www.igeaspa.it), including: Porto Flavia in **Masua**, where minerals were taken from tunnels directly to ships for export; and Galleria Henry, in **Buggerru**, which clings to a cliff above the sea on Planu Sartu plateau.

The most important town in the southwest of the island is the mining town of **Iglesias** ⓬ (derived from *ecclesia*, Latin for church), at the heart

⊙ MINING

Some regions of Sardinia consist of rocks considerably older than other mountains in the Mediterranean, which means much richer mineral deposits. Sardinia's southwest (Sulcis and Iglesiente), southeast (Gerrei and Sarrabus) and Nurra in the northwest, consist of rocks with rich mineral deposits, especially lead, zinc, silver, copper and iron.

Around 4,500 years ago settlers began to extract and smelt metals (copper, lead and silver), then the Nuragic civilisation prospered from their trading links and skills in metalworking. Evidence of the degree of mining activity in Phoenician, Carthaginian and Roman times can be found in the tools and oil lamps discovered in mine shafts, as well as in vast slag heaps such as the one at Campo Romano near Iglesias. Under the Roman empire, Christians were often exiled to the mining areas of the Iglesiente. Under Pisan rule, silver casting around Iglesias (Monteponi, Campo Pisano) became prevalent. During the 13th century Iglesias, the former city of Uilla Ecclesiae, received its charter as a "silver town" with exemplary mining regulations and municipal rights under Pisan law, including that of minting its own coins. In 1343, 20 years after their conquest of Sardinia, the rulers of Aragon imported Sardinian mineworkers to Spain in order to improve the silver-mining industry.

Sardinian mining creaked back to life in the 19th century – thanks to increased mechanisation and the use of explosives. Piedmontese Mining Laws of 1848 permitted foreign investors to circumvent the property rights of Sardinian landowners. Sardinia's mining heyday waned at the turn of the last century, with falling prices and declining productivity. Mussolini ignited an artificial boom with the intention of making Italy strong and independent. It was a sham: Carbonia was founded to produce sulphurous lignite (with a combustion rate scarcely above that of peat), dubbed "Sulcis coal" by Mussolini's propaganda machine.

Visitors to Buggerru will have difficulty imagining that the mining town of 100 years ago – complete with public services and a concert hall – was the first town on Sardinia to have electricity. Indeed, there is hardly a trace left of the living and working conditions which in 1904 led to bloody unrest and the first general strike in Italy's history.

of the zinc- and lead-quarrying district. Founded in the 13th century, it was a significant silver-mining centre; the community was even awarded the right to mint its own coins. The Old Town was built according to a chequerboard plan; it is clustered around the Gothic-Romanesque **Cattedrale di Santa Chiara** (Fri–Wed) on Piazza Municipio, and filled with attractive townhouses with wrought-iron balconies. The **Museo delle Arti Minerárie** (www.museoartemineraria.it; June–Aug Sat–Sun 6–8.30pm, other times by appointment) has over 8,000 rare stones and fossils discovered during mining excavations alongside some intriguing mining equipment.

SPECTACULAR MOUNTAIN ROAD

The Iglesias to Oristano road (SS 126), with its hairpin bends, views over vast oak forests and dizzying drops, requires careful driving but is well worth the effort. This underpopulated region can compete with Barbagia in terms of remoteness and beauty. At the top of the pass, at the **Arcu Genna Bogai**, a valley vista frames the pillared **Tempio di Antas** ⓭ (July–Sept daily 9.30am–7.30pm, Apr–June and Oct daily 9.30am–5.30pm, Nov–Mar Tue–Sun 9.30am–4.30pm), where Sardus Pater was worshipped. A Roman place of worship during the 2nd century AD, it was built on the site of a much earlier Punic temple. According to Sardinian mythology, Sardus Pater is the original ancestor of the island's inhabitants. He reputedly came from Africa to populate the island, but the origins of the deity can be traced back to a Punic god. Today, only six of the pillars and the partially restored floor plan of the temple remain; its undeniable attraction is derived primarily from its enchanting site.

Following the course of the Rio Antas on the SS 126, you pass the **Grotta di su Mannau** (www.sumannau.it; Apr–June daily 9.30am–5.30pm, July–Oct daily 9.30am–6.30pm, winter by appointment only) and the small town of Fluminimaggiore. At the village of **Arbus** ⓮ to the north, the **Museo del**

In the Old Town of Carbónia.

Coltello (Museum of Knives; Via Roma; www.museodelcoltello.it; Mon–Fri 9am–12.30pm and 3.30–7pm, Sat–Sun by appointment; free) displays *s'arburesa* knives – hand-crafted clasp knives from the town – and has a reconstruction of a blacksmith's workshop.

San Cosimo is a well-preserved *tombe di giganti* by a little road leading from Arbus to Gonnosfanadiga. Heading west from the SS 126 before you reach Arbus, a side road leads down to the mining communities of **Ingurtosu** and **Naracauli**, consisting of miners' quarters (open but not secure) and management headquarters (closed to the public).

The dirt road continues down to the stunning sand dunes of **Piscinas**  that cover about 30 sq metres (almost 12 sq miles). The 100-metre (330ft) high dunes of fine sand are being continually reshaped by the mistral, a strong north wind that blows in from France. This unique ecological niche is an ideal habitat for many animals, including foxes, wild cats and rabbits, whose footprints you can usually spot in the early mornings.

Inside the Grotta di San Giovanni.

ON THE COSTA VERDE

A small winding road leads from Guspini along the ridge to **Montevecchio**. The lead and zinc mines here closed in 1960 but it's possible to explore the 1876 Liberty-style pit and view a mineral collection (www.minieramontevecchio.it; guided tours: times vary, check website). Continuing on you reach the **Costa Verde**; the name refers more to the hinterland than to the coastal margin itself, for its massive sand dunes recall a desert rather than a green and pleasant land. From **Marina di Arbus** the coastal strip is open to vehicles in both directions. Despite a law passed in 1990 forbidding development of this particular coastal strip, small fishing villages have sprouted ugly holiday complexes.

ARBOREA

Heading north again, you negotiate 30km (20 miles) of arduous bends to reach the **Golfo di Oristano**, behind which lie the **Stagno di Marceddi** and the **Stagno di San Giovanni**. Back on the SS 126 is **Arborea**, originally

⊘ SAN GIOVANNI GROTTO

The **Grotta di San Giovanni** (daily) near **Domusnovas** carves through the oldest rocks in Italy, which are over 500 million years old. A road, some 900 metres (3,000ft) long, follows the course of the river through the stunning grotto. At the end of the tunnel there is a restaurant, a bar and a picnic area. Within this vast **Foresta Demaniale Marganai** territory, at 720 metres (2,360ft) above sea level, is the Giardino Montano Linasia, 9,000 sq metres (96,900 sq ft) brimming with native plants and many other rare species. Its museum, Casa Natura, contains collections of fossils, minerals and archaeological finds (May–Sept Tue, Thu, Sat and Sun 9am–noon and 4.30–7.30pm, Oct–Apr Sat–Sun 9.30am–1pm).

called Mussolinia after Il Duce. Arborea was laid out along new-town principles in 1928 in order to populate the plain of Oristano, which had been made agriculturally viable by the construction of irrigation canals. It was decided to introduce settlers from Venetia and the plain of the Po; they defied the endemic malaria and transformed the region into fertile land. The little town possesses a few fine Art Nouveau villas and an equestrian sports centre called Horse Country.

SU NURAXI

Following the SS 131, take the exit to **Sanluri** ⑱ where, in 1409, the Aragonese troops led by Martin the Young won the battle that put an end to Sardinia's independence. The Castello di Eleonora d'Arborea houses the **Museo Risorgimentale Duca d'Aosta** (tel: 070-930 7105; July–mid-Sept Sun 10am–1pm and 4.30–9pm, Tue–Fri 4.30–9pm, mid-Sept–June Sun 9.45am–1pm and 3–7pm). The museum contains 19th-century military exhibits and Napoleonic memorabilia. On the upper floor is the

Museo della Ceroplastica, displaying miniature 16th-century wax sculptures. Also in Sanluri is the **Museo Storico Etnografico** (Via Cappuccini; tel: 070-930 7107 by appointment), attached to the Convento dei Cappuccini.

On the way to Barumini is the small village of **Villamar** ⑲. The parish church contains a large polyptych, painted in 1518, situated behind the main altar, which was the most important work of the Sardinian painter Pietro Cavaro. Just after the village, a road on the left leads to the Nuragic site of **Bruncu Sa Cruxi** (daily).

Su Nuraxi ⑳ (tel: 070-936 8128; daily 9am–dusk; guided tours every 30 minutes), about 1km (0.5 mile) to the west of Barumini, consists of a large Nuragic fortress dating from the 13th to the 6th century BC, surrounding a massive round 15th-century BC defensive tower with a well. This Unesco World Heritage site, excavated in 1949, reveals fascinating layers of construction including 200 small circular huts, Carthaginian and Roman remnants and a canal system.

The parish church at Villamar.

The Unesco World Heritage site of Su Nuraxi.

Ask at the local tourist office for horse-riding centres.

Castle ruins at Las Plassas.

WILD ANIMALS AND SPRINGS

South of Su Nuraxi, the appropriately named Marmilla (from the word for bosom) rises out of the plain. Perched on top is an ancient fortress marking the frontier between the former *giudicati* of Arborea and Cagliari. The ruins of the castle of **Las Plassas** date from the 12th century. Between Barumini and Las Plassas is the **Sardegna in Miniatura park** (www.sardegnainminiatura.it; daily 9am–7pm), where the island's most important archaeological sites and monuments are reproduced in 1:20–25 scale.

Just to the northwest of Barumini is **Tuili** ㉑, an unspoilt village, perfect for a stroll soaking up the island's old way of life. Seek out the polyptych of San Pietro, painted by the Master of Castelsardo (1500) in the parish church.

The **Giara di Gesturi**, a volcanic high plateau to the north, is famed for its 500 wild horses *(cavallini)*; the isolated table mountain is covered by myriad large and small rainwater ponds that in the spring are covered by various *ranunculi* (aquatic plants), creating a unique and enchanting landscape. The plateau has also become home to a variety of birds, some of which are migratory. It is possible to hire a guide to take you on a horseback tour of the area.

In the town of **Villanovaforru** ㉒, the **Museo Archeologico Genna Maria** (Viale Umberto; www.gennamaria.it; Tue–Sun Apr–Sept 9.30am–1pm and 3.30–7pm, Oct–Mar 9.30am–1pm and 3.30–6pm) displays Nuragic artefacts found in the nearby nuraghe complex of **Genna Maria**, 1km (0.5 mile) west of the town.

Sardinia has a number of springs which have been exploited for thermal cures. The town of **Sardara** ㉓ was famous in Roman times for its healing spas, and today they are used in the treatment of rheumatic illnesses. Sardara also contains an important sacred spa from the era of the Nuragi; it rises near the **Chiesa di Sant'Anastasia**. The **Museo Civico di Sardara** (Piazza Libertà; tel: 070-938 6183; Tue–Sun June–Sept 9am–1pm and 3–8pm, Oct–May 9am–1pm and 4–7pm) displays material ranging from pre-Nuragic pottery to objects belonging to the *Giudicati* period.

The Roman temple at Antas.

📷 THE ART OF THE MURALES

As a form of public art, murals communicate directly to a wide audience. In Sardinia they are becoming an artistic tradition.

Brilliantly coloured murals *(murales)* on satirical, political or social themes are a popular form of expression in Sardinia and can be found in many villages around the island. The tradition of mural painting in Sardinia dates back to the 1960s and reached a peak in 1975 in the town of Orgosolo in the Barbagia, when the local art teacher Francesco del Caslon and his students decided to fill the town with murals on local and universal themes. The Italian Association of Painted Towns was formed to preserve and publicise towns with murals and to promote cultural and creative links between the regions. Perhaps the most famous touristic murals are to be found in the village of San Sperate, about 8km (5 miles) northeast of Uta, which contains works by the local artist Pinuccio Sciola. The murals here are not as vibrant, numerous or political as they are in Orgosolo. Instead they are painted in the muted tones of the Sardinian countryside and represent bucolic and domestic scenes.

Fonni's murals are less overtly political than those of Orgosolo.

Another Orgosolo mural illustrating shepherds' strength of feeling against industrialisation.

Mural of a religious procession in Fonni.

Goats in Orgosolo.

Murals in Orgosolo

If you're travelling in the Barbagia region, make a detour to Orgosolo to see some of the town's 150 murals. On Via Deledda there are characters drawn from the books of Grazia Deledda. Along Via Gramsci is a mural depicting the life of the politician, one of the founders of the Italian Communist Party; at No. 60 another depicts the tragic events leading to the end of the Baader-Meinhof Group and at No.166 is a mural showing shepherds protesting against not being able to leave their pastures fallow in the spring with the slogan *"Vardamos o non vardamos?"* (To keep or not to keep?). Opposite is a mural with the message "The young want to work, not shoot" – a reference to the town's reputation for banditry. Further on is a mural protesting against noise pollution. On Via Mercato on the walls of the library are paintings by local artists; in front of the parish church is a scene from a bandit hunt, while other murals indicate strong opposition to war and militarism.

Nuoro mural on the rights of women.

Mamoida mural showing Mamuthones in the traditional costume of masks, cow bells and goatskins.

Anti-war mural in Orgosolo: "Fertilisers, not missiles".

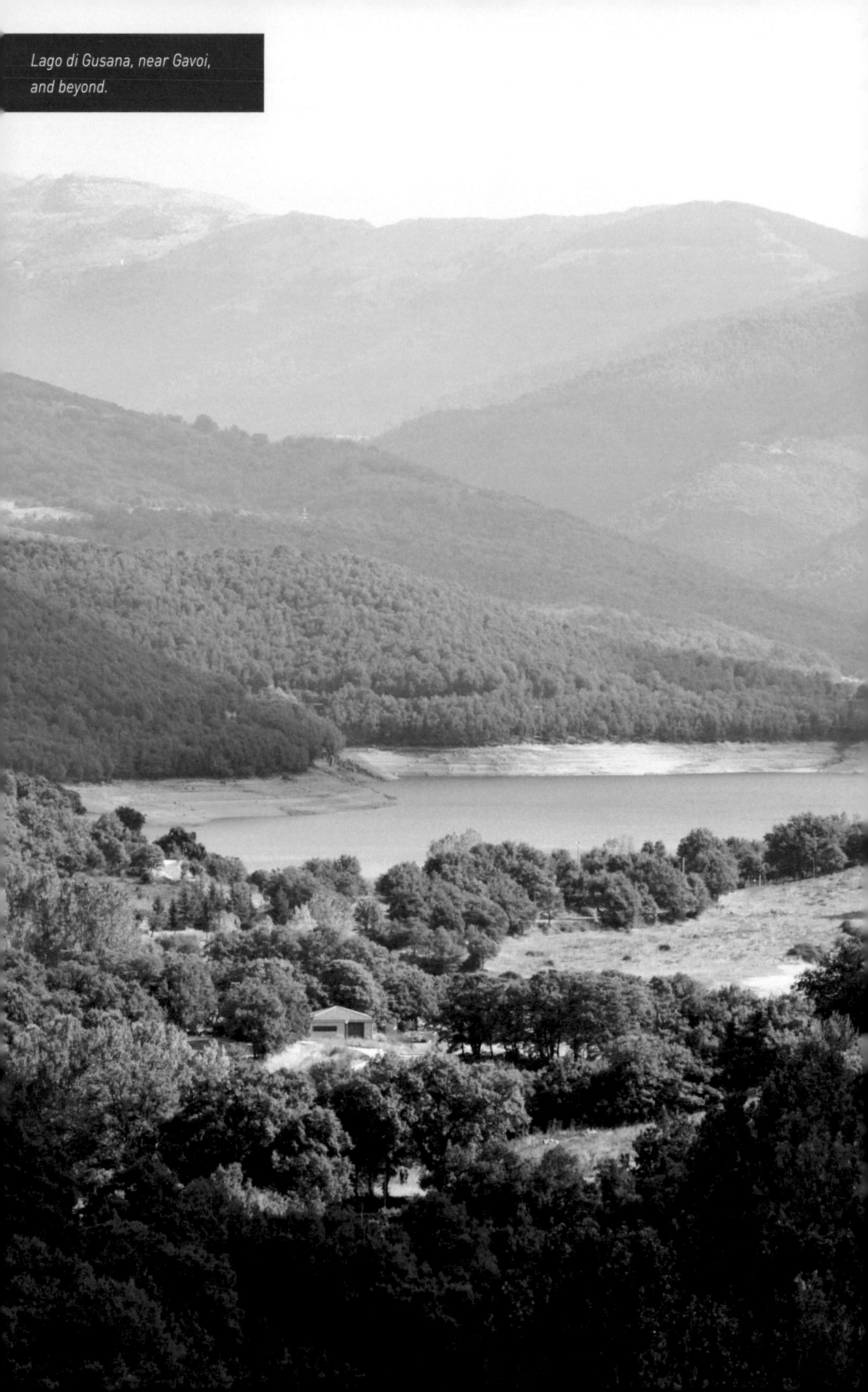

Lago di Gusana, near Gavoi, and beyond.

THE BARBAGIA

In the heart of the island, this region of rugged mountains, raw beauty and isolated villages characterises the essential Sardinia.

The Barbagia, which runs almost parallel to the mountain range of the Gennargentu, is the highest of the sub-regions of Sardinia. The name is of Roman origin and is derived from the Latin *Barbaria* or *Barbaricum*. The Roman conquerors described as Barbarians any people whose culture was based neither on the Roman nor the Greek civilisation, and whose social order and lifestyle were markedly different from their own (the people here resisted Roman colonisation for longer than those in any other Sardinian region). It was probably a *giudice* from the *giudicato* of Arborea who first subdivided the region into five sections: Barbagia di Ollolai, di Seui, di Seulo, di Belvì and Supramonte.

PREHISTORY AND HISTORY

Remains of antiquity, bearing witness to the early settlement of the area, can be found here as elsewhere in the form of the nuraghi, which date from the 15th to the 2nd century BC. Unlike those to be found elsewhere on Sardinia, most of Barbagia's nuraghi, *tombe di giganti* (giants' graves) and *sas pedras fittas* (massive standing stones) are remarkably well preserved. Examples of the last stand at Gavoi-Lodine, not far from the original Byzantine cemetery of Nostra Signora d'Itria, as well as Grillu (near Fonni) and Ovodda. Archaeologists reckon they were

worshipped as late as the 6th century AD, before local inhabitants and their chieftain Ospiton were converted to Christianity by Pope Gregory I.

Other stone relics worth visiting are the *domus de janas* (fairy dwellings), dating back to the Neolithic age (3500 BC). Legend maintains that they were inhabited by fairies or virgins; they took the form of small houses or caves hewn from the bedrock and measured about 1–2 metres (3–5ft) in height.

Ancient scientific and historical texts describe the inhabitants of the

Main attractions
Barumini
Aritzo
Tonara
Desulo
Sorgono
Fonni
Gavoi
Mamoiada
Nuoro
Bitti

Map on page 200

Sweet chestnuts.

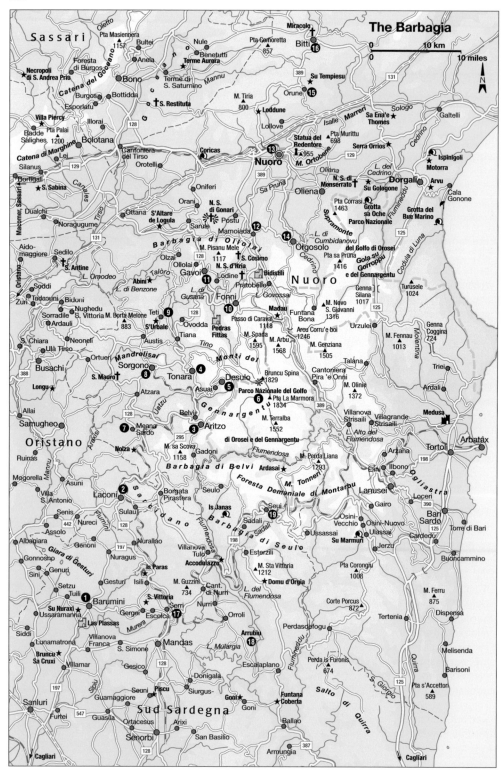

The Barbagia

0   10 km

0   10 miles

N

Barbagia as "the people from Ilion" or "the descendants of Iolaos", who bravely fought against the Carthaginian and Roman hordes in an attempt to preserve their freedom and independence. One derivation of the name indicates a link with Troy ("Ilion"), and refers to a maritime people originally from Asia Minor who had come to Sardinia in order to found their own colony. The other harks back to Iolaos, the legendary Greek hero who is purported to have reigned over a Greek colony with the assistance of the sons of Hercules.

ROMANS, CHRISTIANS AND SARACENS

When the island came under Roman rule in 238 BC, the new conquerors, while trying to bring the entire island under their sway, encountered determined resistance in the Barbagia. Under the rule of the Emperors Tiberius and Justinian a large number of exiled Romans were dispatched to quell the Barbaricini. During the 6th century AD the Barbaricini were converted to Christianity. Pope Gregory I sent Felix and Cyriacus to the

Barbagia to spread the Gospel throughout Sardinia. The Barbaricini embraced the new faith with fervour. It seems possible that their passionate enthusiasm for the new beliefs encouraged them to desecrate the symbols of their former religion, as other Sardinian tribes before them had done.

During the Saracen invasion many Sardinians fled deep into the interior of the island in the face of the brutality of the advancing foe, finding refuge with the Barbaricini and thus augmenting their numbers. Although contemporary sources provide no information on the matter, it seems possible that the inhabitants of the Barbagia, true to their reputation as indomitable warriors, may have played a decisive part in the crushing defeat of the Saracen Prince of Mogeid-al-Amiri, referred to in ancient chronicles as Museto. After the victory over Museto (AD 1015–16), the history of the Barbagia becomes progressively more integrated into that of the island itself.

It passed through the period of the *giudicati*, became the scene of violent struggles and was ruled in turn by the

⏱ Fact

Estimates put the total number of nuraghi on the island between 7,000 and 8,000; some 200–250 of these are situated in the Barbagia.

The Barbagia people converted to Christianity in the 6th century AD.

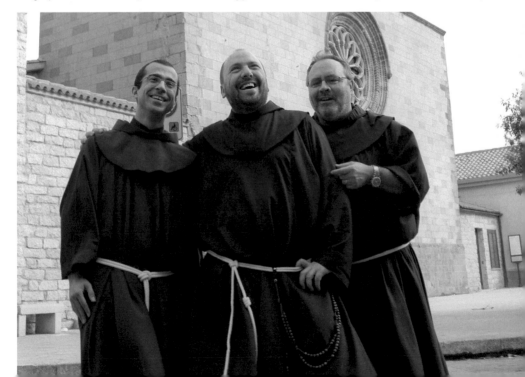

*Notices of deaths
in Fonni.*

Genoese, Pisans, Aragonese and Spanish. In the face of the frequent unjust tricks played on them, the people of the region never abandoned their guard and maintained a rebellious attitude. This can be witnessed in an episode dating from 1719, when a sudden doubling of taxes prompted the Barbaricini, and in particular the citizens of Olzài, to revolt against Spanish rule.

MOUNTAIN PEAKS

The Barbagia consists almost entirely of mountainous and hilly country, which rises towards the east as it approaches the massive ranges of the Gennargentu. Some of it is very bleak. Its highest peak is named after General Alfonso La Marmora (Italy's most senior general, 1804–1878). The summit of **La Marmora** reaches 1,834 metres (6,017ft) above sea level, while the neighbouring peak of **Bruncu Spina**, which for several months each year is capped with snow, is more than 1,829 metres (6,000ft). On a fine day with little cloud, the view from the highest peaks of the Gennargentu is overwhelming

*Mountain range in the
Gennargentu.*

and confounds the sense of bleakness that the region so often inspires. In particularly clear conditions you can see as far as the Tyrrhenian Sea on the distant horizon.

The peak of **Monte Spada** lies in the region known as **Barbagia di Ollolai**. It marks the end of an extensive mountain range which stretches eastwards as far as the **Corru'e boi** (Cattle Horn) gorge and the pass of the same name on the main Nuoro–Lanusei–Ogliastra road. Then the highland area winds on further to Monte Novo S. Giovanni in the district of Orgosolo, where the Cedrino river rises, and on as far as the limestone escarpment by Oliena and the Lanaittu Valley, which marks the boundary between the administrative districts of Oliena and Dorgali.

SPRINGS AND RIVERS

Throughout the region there are springs fed by the mountain snows. Their fresh water is popular all over the island; healing powers are even attributed to some of them, such as the springs of **S'Abba Medica** near Gavoi,

Ø RETURN TO THE LAND

Migrant workers and traders who sought employment in the more prosperous regions of the island, such as Nuoro, Cagliari, Sassari or mainland Italy, often return eventually to their native mountains, where they invest part of their savings in the construction of a new house or the renovation of an old building. Today, vegetable fields, vineyards and orchards which had been allowed to lie fallow since the 1960s are being revived by owners who have become disillusioned by jobs in the service industries or in one of the factories in the faraway towns.

The future also looks rosy for the groves of oak and chestnut trees and the large areas planted with hazelnut bushes, oak and pine woods, groves of cork oaks and the *màcchia*, where heathers, rosemary, thyme, rock roses, arbutus trees, mastic shrubs and black-berried myrtle flourish. The mastic shrub is the principal source of food for both goats and pigs; it is also used to yield an oil for household use. Myrtle berries and juniper are used to distil *mirto*, a schnapps. Not long ago there were entire woods of juniper bushes several hundred years old. Today the stands are much younger, although in the valleys of the Barbagia you may still come across an ancient specimen which is as big as a tree.

or the spring water from the **Guppunnìo** spa and the **Regina Fontium** (Queen of the Springs) in Ollolai. The most famous healing spas are those of **Monte Spada** and **Campu Maiore** in Ortueri. People come to sample them from all over the island.

Three main rivers flow through the Barbagia: the **Flumendosa**, the **Taloro** and the **Araxisi**. The Flumendosa rises in the southern gorges of the Corru'e boi, collecting the water of the eastern Gennargentu and numerous smaller tributaries from the mountains of the Ogliastra before flowing into the Tyrrhenian Sea. The Taloro, a tributary of the Tirso – the island's biggest river – has its source in the Barbagia di Ollolai, expanding between the districts of Gavoi, Ovodda and Olzai to become the lake of the same name, after which it flows across the Plain of Ottana and the central Tirso Valley before joining the main river.

HOLM AND CORK OAKS

The Barbagia still retains some of the luxuriant vegetation, especially the forests, which at one time made Sardinia one of the greenest spots in the entire Mediterranean.

In the mountains, acorn-bearing oak trees still grow up to an altitude of 1,200–1,300 metres (3,800–4,200ft) above sea level. By far the most common species is the holm oak, some of which are hundreds of years old, followed by pedunculate and cork oaks. The latter supply the cork industry, a factor in the Sardinian economy since the 19th century (see page 146).

The cork, stripped from each tree every seven to eight years, is exported in a raw and processed state. The numerous forest fires which plague the region in the hottest summer months and uncontrolled overfelling have led to a drastic reduction in the tree stocks. At the beginning of the 19th century they were estimated at 66 million. The millenary woods of Sardinia were cut down by charcoal burners from the Italian peninsula and transformed into railway sleepers, charcoal for domestic heating or wood to feed steam engines. The protests of locals

You will see evidence of the cork industry throughout the Barbagia.

Farming mural in Mamoiada.

The Barbagia is rich in wild flowers.

Sardinian honey is widely available.

went unheard, and in a few decades the island's landscape had changed.

Apart from the incalculable ecological and aesthetic damage, the fires have a deforesting effect which has led to a shortage of food for livestock. Oak trees are particularly important in the rearing of pigs, as they produce excellent meat for the manufacture of ham and sausages when fed on acorns.

CHESTNUT TREES

Sweet chestnut trees in the region used to supply excellent wood for a variety of purposes, and still do to some extent. In the old days (and occasionally still today) craftsmen used it to make items for everyday use, such as doors or windows. Stylised yet functional objects are now popular, including benches with built-in storage chests (the front panel of which is almost always decorated with illustrations of birds, flowers, leaves or the landscape of the place of manufacture). Looms, spindles, distaffs and other items for the processing of wool are also crafted from

chestnut. Tables, plate racks, kitchen furniture and beds were usually made of a softer wood, in particular that of the pear tree.

PLANTS AND FLOWERS

As far as flora is concerned, the Barbagia is especially well endowed: broom, oleaster, yew, ash, tamarisk, willow, elder, alder, poplar, holly and laurel grow in abundance. *Màcchia* shrubs – blackthorn, myrtle, arbutus and numerous other species – are one of the reasons that many visitors come to this part of Sardinia and scientists from Italy and abroad come to study the environment.

Many of the plants bear berries or wild fruits with a slightly bitter taste, for instance, the sloe. Others, such as the arbutus, produce delicious fruits; it is from the blossoms of the arbutus that bees collect nectar for the famous, pungent-tasting Sardinian honey. The fruits are red and are about the size of a morello cherry. They are eaten raw or made into jam, and are known for their laxative effect. In former times it

⊘ BITTERSWEET HONEY

Apiculture (bee-keeping) was once more widespread than it is today, but the increased number of uninhabited areas given over to protected flowering plants has led to a revival of the ancient occupation. As in the old days, walkers can once again delight in the unexpected discovery of a honeycomb tucked away in a tree hollow which one of the many swarms of wild bees has converted into a hive. You can pick up local honey in many villages. Particularly worth seeking out is the distinctively bitter *miele amaro corbezzolo*, which derives its punchy sweetness and bitter aftertaste from the *arbutus unedo* plant, called the strawberry tree in English. Honey features in many Sardinian desserts, including the classic sweet pastries *seadas*.

was common for locals to distil them to make a schnapps-like drink.

Chestnut woods and hazelnut bushes are chiefly found around Desulo, Tonara, Aritzo and Belvì. The inhabitants of these districts include the fruits of the forest in their diet to some extent, albeit less than in days gone by. Nowadays much of the produce is exported to other regions of the island. Almonds and hazelnuts are the principal raw ingredient required by the confectionery industry for the production of *torrone* (nougat with nuts), eaten in great quantities during festivals. For generations it has been manufactured in Tonara, Aritzo and Belvì.

Among Sardinia's plants and herbs are thyme, rosemary, wild lavender, gorse with its characteristic yellow flowers and sharp thorns, brambles (laden with blackberries during September), pink and red rock roses, heathers and a wide variety of forest ferns. Seemingly endless fields of daisies, corn poppies and bog asphodel make for an unforgettable sight in spring and early summer.

BIRDS AND BEASTS

A wide range of animals live in the Barbagia. Eagles, falcons, vultures, red kites, partridges, ring doves, thrushes, magpies, quail, turtle doves, snipe, blackbirds and buzzards all live and breed here. On the mountain slopes, where acorns and berries are plentiful, or even near vineyards and vegetable gardens, wild boar *(cinghiale)* may be seen. The Sardinian wild boar is a robust species which breeds easily in spite of damage to its environment. In recent years it has become a popular addition to the Sardinian menu. The most common wild animal on Sardinia and in the Barbagia used to be the mouflon, a wild short-fleeced mountain sheep. In former times it wandered the mountains in herds, but sadly today it is becoming increasingly rare. Only walkers crossing the crests of the Supramonte near Oliena and Orgosolo, or wandering through the heart of the Gennargentu may be fortunate enough to see this magnificent creature. It looks like a ram, but has the coat of a deer.

You are just as likely to encounter animals as cars on the road here.

Mural near Orgosolo known as "the greedy landowner".

LA FESTA OR LA SAGRA

Festivals play a significant role in traditional village life in Sardinia, and they are celebrated with great gusto in the Barbagia, the most rural area of the island.

Following a meagre harvest or a catastrophic year, tensions are released in a *festa* or *sagra*. As well as being celebrations, they express confidence in the future and faith in a deity. Festivals were a means of expressing all the plans, ideals and dreams conjured up by human fantasy and an opportunity to give vent to a basic melancholy. Dance is an essential component of every celebration, and usually the musical accompaniment is provided by a single instrument, the accordion. Traditionally, the dancing takes place in front of a church or at country places of pilgrimage.

The Mamuthones of Mamoiada don carved wooden masks at festival time.

GIVING THANKS

Church festivals take place either at places of pilgrimage dedicated to the saint in question or to the Mother of God, or else in the villages themselves. They often honour a local patron saint, or another saint, or the Madonna. Some pilgrims recite their prayers in *novenae*, in a cycle of nine consecutive days. By this means they fulfil a vow or thank God for His mercy. In the larger and major festivals, the faithful still sleep in the *cumbessias* (also called *muristenes*), which are peasant dwellings built in an arc or a circle around the church.

Many village and country festivals are still observed with great ceremony, sometimes even with pageantry. Wealthy men and women of good reputation assist the priest, and are given titles – although this is an image-building exercise for the organising families or clans.

EAT, DRINK AND BE MERRY

Entertainments include the game of Morra, the *ballu tundu*, the "national" dance of Sardinia, poetry competitions, guitar competitions and horse racing *(un palio)*. The entire contents of kitchen and cellar will be wheeled out as hosts try to outdo each other in their hospitality. *Torrone* (nougat) can be purchased, along with cow bells and a variety of small kitchen utensils of wood, copper or bog asphodel leaves manufactured in Tonara, Desulo, Aritzo, Belvì, Isili, Ovodda or Ollolai.

BEST FESTIVALS

Many festivals occur in spring, when the shepherds and their flocks return from the plains of the Campidano or the Nurra, and in summer, when workers come home to see their families.

The most attractive festivals in the western Barbagia are the *Feste-Fiere* (the church dedication festivals): in Samugheo this is dedicated to St Basil (13 August); *Ortueri* (8 September) celebrates the nativity of the Virgin Mary; and in Sorgono the *festa* is for St Maurus Abate (1 June). In Sorgono the *Assunzione della Barbagia Vergine* (the Assumption of the Virgin Mary) and the Festival of the Redeemer *(Salvatore)* on 9 November are celebrated with due style. In the Barbagia di Seulo, the festivals of St Mary Magdalene, and that of Corpus Christi, in mid-June, and St John the Baptist (23–4 June) are legendary.

A JOURNEY INTO THE BARBAGIA

An expedition into the Barbagia is recommended to every foreign visitor; it is a truly wild spot which even many Sardinians haven't explored. That being the case, travelling round the area is not as straightforward as the more tourist-oriented coast; the roads are winding, and sometimes little more than dirt tracks and road signs are limited.

The more adventurous can use public transport, but it is slow and unreliable – a private car will obviously give you a greater degree of independence. The SS 131 from Siniscola to Nuoro has been improved and is now of motorway standard, but has remained toll-free; by taking it, you can soon reach Nuoro, one of the possible starting points for a tour of the Barbagia. The following route, using **Cagliari** – with the largest harbour and the principal airport – as the point of departure, is only one of the many possibilities available. It is very difficult to organise a single itinerary that covers the Barbagia, because of the great morphological variability of the

region. Deep valleys, high plateaux and mountain peaks and ridges, which are at times difficult to get over, take turns to provide the dominant geographical feature. In some places there is no asphalt road, only a dirt track to follow.

After leaving Cagliari on the Carlo Felice (SS 131), you will soon arrive at the right-hand turning of the SS 197 between **Serrenti** and **Sanluri**. Here a detour is recommended to the remarkable nuraghe complex of **Barumini** ❶ and the **Giara di Gesturi**, a vast table mountain of basalt which is as geologically interesting as it is picturesque, and which is the home of wild Sardinian ponies (see page 194).

After about 10km (6 miles) on the SS 128 you reach the village of **Laconi** ❷, which is still in the **Sarcidano** but lies on the edge of the Barbagia. The largest town in the Sarcidano, Laconi enjoys an attractive situation. It is the birthplace of St Ignatius of Laconi, and the saint's meagre possessions are preserved in the house where he was born, **Casa Natale di Sant'Ignazio** (tel: 0782-867 064). Apart from the 16th-century

Driving around the Barbagia's tortuous roads is not for the faint-hearted.

Winter sunshine and snow on the village of Atzara and surrounding countryside.

Take home some nougat (torrone in Italian), traditionally made in Tonara from walnuts, almonds, hazelnuts, eggs and fragrant Sardinian honey.

Display of finery at Nuoro's Ethnographic Museum.

belltower, you can also visit Castello Aymerich; its magnificent park (8am–4pm, June–Aug until 8pm) not only contains flowers native to Sardinia but also bay trees, horse chestnuts, pedunculate oaks, beaches and cedars from the Himalayas and the Lebanon.

Some of the most important decorated menhirs of Sardinia have been found a few kilometres away from the village and have been gathered in the **Civico Museo delle Statue Menhir** (www.menhirmuseum.it; Tue–Sun Oct–Mar 10am–1pm and 3–6pm, Apr–Sept 10am–1pm and 3.30–7pm) in Pallazzo Aymerich in the Piazza Marconi.

The route continues northwards from Laconi and reaches **Aritzo** ❸. An important mountain resort surrounded by chestnut and hazelnut woods, the town still has some historic buildings, including a 17th-century Spanish prison and an Arangino "castle", which became a private home at the beginning of the 20th century. The town's **Museo della Montagna Sarda o del Gennargentu** (tel: 0784-629 801; Tue–Sun June–Sept 10am–1pm and 4–7pm,

Oct–May 9am–1pm and 3–6pm) has displays of craft, costume and domestic and agricultural machinery.

The *Sagra delle Castagne* (Chestnut Fair) held in the town at the end of October attracts people from all Sardinia. Aritzo is also the starting point for many excursions that can be done by four-wheel drive vehicles provided by local hotel owners or on foot, with a local guide. The **Tacco Texile** (975 metres/3,199ft), an unmistakable limestone rock at the top of a conical hill, is the destination of many walkers. Not far away is the village of **Belvì**, which holds its Cherry Fair in June and has a small but interesting **Museo di Scienze Naturali** (tel: 0784-629 263; daily 9am–1pm and 3.30–7pm).

TONARA, THE HOME OF NOUGAT

The towns of Tonara and Desulo nestle in the western foothills of the Gennargentu massif, along the mountain route. These are some of the highest villages on the whole island. The town of **Tonara** ❹ is known principally for

⊘ CHANGING TIMES

The past few decades have seen some rapid changes in the customs and lifestyle not only of individuals but also of entire communities in Sardinia. This is as true of the Barbagia region as it is of other regions of the island.

Pasture land is not always in ample supply, but the grass and wild herbs available contribute to the taste – even the consistency – of the meat and the milk products of the sheep. Gone are the days when every shepherd wandered the countryside on foot with his dog. Today most shepherds use a car or a jeep for transport, be it for visiting their flock, transporting wood or food for their livestock, or delivering milk to the cheese factory – and lambs, kids or pigs to the butcher. Visitors may still occasionally see a mule or a donkey carrying goods. At high altitude, in the remotest, most inaccessible places in the mountains, they are still irreplaceable.

Modernity has arrived even in the furthest corners of the Barbagia, as the inhabitants share in the latest creature comforts. Most houses are still of the traditional variety, with ancient moss-covered tile roofs, but many have been renovated to meet modern requirements.

its production of *torrone* (nougat), which is sold throughout the island at fairs. Honey is one of the prime ingredients of *torrone*, but it is also used to make the majority of Sardinian cakes. Sardinian honey is prized for its quality and huge variety, largely determined by the diversity of wild flowers on the island, which give each honey its distinctive flavour. You can choose between perfumed citrus fruit honey, delicate asphodel or balsamic eucalyptus. The rare strawberry tree honey with its unique bitterness is highly sought after.

It is in the area surrounding the Gennargentu massif that Sardinia's traditional culture of sheep herding is most apparent. Visitors can still find a network of ancient footpaths, many of which are still in use by shepherds and their herds. These paths connected pasturelands and, in the 19th century, mountains, before they were deforested by charcoal burners. Today the paths are used by hikers to explore the Gennargentu massif. As the paths are not signposted, many people use local guides or walk the paths in groups. Hikers often come across *pinnette* (ancient round huts with thatched roofs) which are used by shepherds for shelter, especially during the lambing season when shepherds cannot leave their flocks.

DESULO AND PUNTA LA MARMORA

The village of **Desulo** ❺, at an altitude of 895 metres (2,900ft), is one of the few villages where you can still see some women wearing the traditional costume of the region. It is remarkable for its simplicity of design and use of bright colours: orange, red, blue and yellow. The Casa Montanaru houses an **ethnographic museum** (tel: 0784-619 624; by appointment).

Unscrupulous building development means the village has lost a good deal of its charm, but the main reason to visit is the splendid scenery. Many excursions start from Desulo; footpaths beaten by local shepherds lead walkers to **Bruncu Spina** (1,829 metres/6,000ft) and **Punta La Marmora**

Peregrine falcons are just one of the birds of prey to be found in the region.

A lone tree among the rocky Barbagia countryside.

◔ Fact

The Sardinian wild boar (*il cinghiale sardo*) is a smaller sub-species of the Eurasian *Sus scrofa* and typically has a length of 100–120cm (40–47ins), with a maximum weight of 70–80kg (154–76lb).

❻ (1,834 metres/6,017ft), the highest peak on the island. On the northern side of Bruncu Spina a ski lift has been in service since the 1990s. For several months of the year large quantities of snow fall on the summits and gorges of the Gennargentu, where it continues to lie for some time. Winter sports complexes and hotels are being built in the area to attract skiers. There is no suggestion that the Gennargentu can compete with the more famous ski resorts of the Alps or the Appenines, but nonetheless this area provides winter fun for Italians and visitors looking for something different.

The Italian Alpine Club (CAI) built a shelter house on Punta La Marmora (Rifugio La Marmora) which is used as a landmark and for its good spring water by hikers, even though today only ruins remain.

Between villages grapevines and fruit trees grow. Here orchards reach as far as the eye can see: cherry and almond trees, plum, fig and pomegranate trees, olives, hazelnuts, walnuts and chestnuts are all cultivated.

Procession in Fonni in honour of the Virgin Mary.

MEANA AND SORGONO

The village of **Meana Sardo** ❼ is not usually part of regional itineraries. Pleasantly placed between mountains at 600 metres (1,969ft) above sea level, it preserves the feeling and quality of life of the Sardinian mountain people. A few kilometres above the village is **Nuraghe Nolza** (Nolza archaeological area; tel: 0784-643 620; daily summer 10am–1pm and 4.30–6pm, winter 10am–1pm and 2–5.45pm). In a dominating and extremely panoramic position, it is different from most nuraghi in that it was built using clay to cement the space between stone blocks – a revolutionary idea that caused instability and many structures to collapse. The nearby village of **Atzara** has a late Gothic parish church with a Romanesque belltower and side chapels decorated with precious wooden altars.

Sorgono ❽, part of the subregion of Mandrolisai, is in a valley surrounded by woods and orchards. It is a popular place to visit during the summer months because of its pleasant

climate, which also allows for the cultivation of grapes for the famous Cannonau wine. Sights of interest in town include a 17th-century house, Casa Carta, with Aragonese windows.

Seventeen km (11 miles) outside Sorgono is the **Santuario di San Mauro**, one of the most interesting rural sanctuaries on the island. Built in the 16th century in an Aragonese-Gothic style, it has a Renaissance door with a carved Gothic rose window above it. Inside is an impressive staircase and a single vault. Surrounding the church are *cumbessias* (pilgrim shelters) that were used as lodgings during the feast day of San Mauro, held on the first day of June each year.

The festival is still popular today, and its religious ceremony is accompanied by a fair at which local handicrafts and produce are sold: iron, copper, leather and terracotta goods, walnuts, hazelnuts, dried chestnuts and honey as well as different varieties of sweetmeats. During the 19th century the fair also provided an opportunity to purchase foreign-made goods like linen, woollens and leather items, silk, majolica, china, and thoroughbred horses.

NURAGIC FINDS

Before heading for Fonni via Ovodda, first visit the small archaeological museum in **Teti ⑨**, the **Museo Archeologico Comprensoriale** (Via Roma; tel: 0784-68120; winter Tue–Sun 9am–12.30pm and 3–5.30pm, summer 9.30am–1pm and 3.30–6pm). The museum has a collection of objects found in the nearby Nuragic archaeological site of S'Urbale, and a fascinating reconstruction of a round hut from 1000 BC with some sleeping niches and domestic articles inside.

About some 15km (9 miles) to the north of Teti, in a very isolated and difficult-to-find valley, are the remains of the large Nuragic village of **Abini**. A number and variety of bronze votive figurines were found here, representing hero-warriors with four eyes or arms, which can now be seen in the Archaeological Museum in Cagliari. Daggers, votive bronze swords and other small objects are displayed in Teti's Archaeological Museum.

⊘ Tip

On Whit Monday (the first Sunday in June) and on 24 June for the festival of San Giovanni, local people wearing traditional costumes parade through the streets of Fonni on horseback in honour of the Virgin Mary.

⊘ PREHISTORIC TOMBS

One of the best-known *tombe di giganti* (giants' tombs; types of megalithic gallery graves) in the Barbagia region is the **S'Altare de Lògula**, a few kilometres west of Sarule. The *tombe di giganti* are rectangular constructions of worked stone that range from 8–28 metres (26–92ft) in length.

These graves – which, according to legend contain men of enormous stature, the mythical first inhabitants of Sardinia – are often situated remarkably close to nuraghi or on the outskirts of a Nuragic village. They are characterised by a vertical stela, whose size is proportional to that of the grave (the longest is more than 4 metres/13ft) and is placed over the entrance of the tomb. For more on giants' tombs, see page 139.

Gavoi house.

*A local woman
from Fonni.*

FONNI – THE HIGHEST VILLAGE

At 1,000 metres (3,280ft), **Fonni** ⑩ is the highest village in Sardinia. It is also one of the region's biggest centres and is popular with hikers and walkers, who use the town as a base for excursions into surrounding countryside and mountain peaks. The town's most interesting monument is the 17th-century **church of San Francesco** (daily), also called the sanctuary complex of Nostra Signora dei Martiri. The complex is surrounded by porticoes and the interior of the church is remarkable for the 1,700 religious frescoes and late Baroque altars, and a curious statue of the Virgin Mary made from fragments of ancient Roman sculptures.

The fabrics and rugs of Fonni are well known for their fine workmanship, and the locals also produce excellent traditional sweets. These are all in evidence on Whit Monday (the first Sunday in June) and on 24 June for the festival of San Giovanni, when local people wearing traditional costumes parade through the streets on horseback and visitors from the surrounding villages

*Mamuthones masks
ready for painting.*

join in pious tribute to the Virgin Mary. The festivals are well known throughout Sardinia and are described by Grazia Deledda in her novel *Canne al Vento*.

SITES AROUND FONNI

A few kilometres east of Fonni is the **Arcu Corru'e boi** (1,246 metres/4,086ft), a pass between the inner Sardinia of the Barbagie, the Nuorese and the plains of the Ogliastra on the eastern coast. Before reaching the pass you will find the well-preserved Tombe di Giganti Madau (daily), noteworthy for the good condition of their burial corridors. Peer inside the long tunnels and you get an idea of how little has changed since they were built.

West of Fonni on the road heading towards Gavoi is the **Lago di Gusana**, a large artificial lake popular with canoeists and campers; you get an excellent view from the SS 128 as it hugs the right-hand shore.

From the lake the next stop on the route is **Gavoi** ⑪, an important centre dominated by the 16th-century church of San Gavino with a Gothic rose window in

trachyte stone. Narrow alleys lead from the church square (Piazza San Gavino) lined with characterful old buildings. Gavoi is well known for its *fiore sardo pecorino*, made with sheep's milk.

From the village it is worth making a short detour to see the large sanctuary of **Madonna de Sa Itria** (daily) where, not far from the church, a 3.5-metre (5ft) high Neolithic menhir bears witness to the continuous use of the sanctuary as a place of worship throughout many millennia.

Continuing north from Gavoi through **Sarule**, **Orani** and **Oniferi** the road links up with the SS 131 from Abbasanta to Nuoro. Not far from the junction several *domus de janas* are set into the hillside. Part square and part concave, some of the individual chambers are linked to one another by means of low doorways or windows.

The pilgrimage church of **Nostra Signora di Gonari** (daily) lies between Sarule and Orani on an unmistakable wooded cone-shaped hill, from which talc is quarried. The building is unadorned and dates from the time of the *giudicati*. The festival of dedication, which is celebrated in appropriate style, falls on 8 September each year. During the Roman occupation Orani may well have been one of the most densely populated villages in the Barbagia. Many of Sardinia's artists, including the well-known contemporary painter Costantino Nivola, have hailed from Orani.

FESTIVAL IN MAMOIADA

In **Mamoiada** ⑫ (644 metres/2,060ft), a predominantly agricultural village producing vegetables, wine and fruit, one of the most original, fascinating and famous carnival processions in Sardinia takes place on Shrove Tuesday. The *Mamuthones* of Mamoiada, as frequently happens elsewhere in Sardinia, don special disguises for the carnival (in Orotelli they become *Thurpos*, in Ottana they are known as *Boes* and *Merdules*). The *Mamuthones* hide their faces behind black carved wooden masks and wear sheepskin or occasionally goatskin fleeces reaching down to their knees, with breeches of coarse velvet and the traditional shepherds' knee-high leather gaiters worn in the Barbagia until about 30 years ago. The *Mamuthones'* scary appearance is enhanced by the bunch of clanging cow bells weighing up to 50kg (110lb) hung over their shoulders and carried on their backs. They walk in procession accompanied by *Issohadores* (young escorts) in bright costumes and carrying leather lassos, which they use to capture astonished spectators or – better still – their beloveds from the crowds watching the procession.

A good place to experience the atmosphere of the festival out of season is at the **Museo delle Maschere Mediterranee** (www.museodellemaschere. it; Tue–Sun 10am–1pm and 3–6pm), which displays a collection of traditional masks and a video about the carnival.

Another major festival in the town is held in honour of Saints Cosimo and Damian. It takes place in the little

Local produce for sale at Nuoro market.

country church of the same name, which stands on a fertile upland plain near Mamoiada, directly opposite the picturesque Gennargentu massif.

NUORO, HEART OF THE BARBAGIA

Nuoro lies under the same spell of enchantment as the Barbagia itself, caught between reality and myth, a passive witness to history and to the fate of its shepherds, peasants and poets. D.H. Lawrence reckoned there was nothing to see in Nuoro, though he did admit: "I am not Baedeker." An expanding services industry and tourism have led to the town's rapid growth over the past 30 years. Today Nuoro has put on a guise of modernity, with the usual unsightly modern building developments that blight many Italian towns.

Since 1926 Nuoro has been the provincial capital again, as it was under the Sardinian monarchy. At the beginning of the 19th century approximately 3,500 people lived here. Today the population is between 35,000 and 40,000. No other town within the province can compete

on a cultural level, although the economy, work situation, tourism and trade have resulted in greater fluctuations than were the rule in the not-so-distant past, when small independent businesses flourished by making and selling only the essential requisites of life. Traces of vanished peoples in the form of remains from the Nuragic era and later epochs are to be found not only in the surrounding district but also close at hand: towards **Monte Ortobene** or in the direction of **Valverde** and **Badde Manna** (The Big Valley), from which one can see in the distance the plains and the mountain peaks of Oliena and Orgosolo. Nuoro's position as the centre and symbol of the entire Barbagia was assumed at the beginning of the 20th century; the region itself extends considerably beyond the boundaries laid down over the years, encompassing such places as **Orotelli**, **Orune**, **Bitti**, **Onanì** and **Lula** to the north.

SITES TO SEE IN NUORO

Famous sons and daughters of Nuoro, such as the poet Sebastiano Satta, the

Nuoro's flea market.

Nobel Prize-winning novelist Grazia Deledda and many others are responsible for the town's amazingly rapid rise to cultural and social prominence. Travellers can visit the final resting place of Grazia Deledda in the eastern district of town, on the way to L'Ortobene: the **Chiesa della Solitudine** (Church of Solitude; daily).

The leading citizens of the town have created a museum in the house where the famous woman of letters was born. In the **Museo della Vita e delle Tradizioni Sarde** (Via Antonio Mereu; www.isresardegna.it; Tue–Sun, Oct–mid-Mar 10am–1pm and 3–7pm, mid-Mar–Sept 10am–1pm and 3–8pm), also known as the Museo Etnografico, visitors can examine a varied and well-chosen collection of folkloric items from all over the island: traditional costumes for both men and women from various towns and villages, matching jewellery – valuable filigree work in gold or silver or of coral, and works of art by skilled goldsmiths whose families in many cases have plied the trade for generations. Apart from costumes, the museum

displays a large number of exhibits illustrating the ancient craftsmanship of the island, which even today produces magnificent rugs and wall hangings, exquisite shawls, scarves and linen and silk embroidery. Also on display are a collection of traditional musical instruments; a room devoted to festival costumes and masks and a section devoted to the sweets, cakes and breads found throughout the island. The museum complex is designed to evoke a Sardinian village.

Another museum well worth a visit in Nuoro is **MAN: Museo d'Arte di Nuoro** (www.museoman.it; Tue–Sun Oct–Mar 10am–1pm, 3–7pm, Apr–Sept 10am–8pm), housed in a 19th-century building between Corso Garibaldi and Piazza Sebastiano Satta in the Old Town. The museum displays a collection of Sardinia's best-known artists, featuring important painters such as Biasi, Ciusa and Nivola, whose brooding works document the islanders' tough rural lifestyle and modern upheavals. Look out for their contemporary art shows and archive works, which include some experimental

Nuoro elder.

Image of a boy selling spoons and oars at Nuoro's Ethnographic Museum.

⊘ VILLA PIERCY

Near Bolotana, 30km (18 miles) west of Nuoro, just off the SS129 to Oristano, is the restored home of Benjamin Percy, the British Victorian-era engineer who designed the Sardinian railway network. In 1862, fresh from his railway-building feats in Spain, France and India, the Welshman set to work on the Rete Ferroviaria Sarda, with the construction of the Cagliari–Porto Torres line, with offshoots to Sassari and Terran (Olbia). The work was completed in 1880.

Beyond the whitewashed colonial-style small turrets of Villa Piercy are the trappings of Victorian invention and good taste: mosaics, stucco-work, vibrantly painted ceilings and motifs, and an ingenious dumb-waiter system. For information about visiting the villa, contact tel: 347-6512 084, www.assopassiflora.com.

video-art that usually raises a brow. It also organises various temporary exhibitions, often dedicated to art of the late 19th and early 20th century, poetry readings and jazz evenings.

There is also a compelling **National Archaeological Museum**, close to the cathedral (tel: 0784-31688; Wed, Fri–Sat 9am–1pm, Tue and Thu 9am–1pm, 3–5.30pm), which has dinosaur fossils found at Monte Tuttavista (Orosei) and Grotta Corbeddu (Oliena), significant Neolithic finds and a huge collection of Nuragic bronze treasures unearthed at Sa Sedda 'e Sos Carros.

Further sights in the town centre include the neoclassical **Cattedrale di Nostra Signora della Neve** (Our Lady of the Snows; daily) built 1836–54 on the foundations of a considerably older, smaller place of worship. It houses a large number of valuable art treasures including a brooding painting from the studio of Luca Giordano, *Disputa di Gesù fra i Dottori*. Then there is the **San Pietro** district of town, birthplace of Grazia Deledda and Francesco Ciusa, and the **Chiesa delle Grazie** (Church

of the Graces; daily) – both the old and new buildings – which owns a boarding school run by the Brothers of the order of Giuseppini d'Asti. The monks also take care of the pilgrimage chapel, which attracts large numbers of the faithful from surrounding districts, especially during the *Novene*, held in November each year.

EXCURSIONS FROM NUORO

Two of the rural churches in the vicinity are worth an excursion: the church of **Nostra Signora di Valverde** on the wooded northern slopes of the Ortobene, from where there is a magnificent panoramic view right across to **Orune** and the lovely Valle di Marreri, and the **Cappella di Nostra Signora di Monte Ortobene,** lying about 8km (5 miles) from Nuoro at an altitude of some 1,000 metres (3,200ft) above sea level. It is accessible by car, public transport and on foot via a long and twisting road which climbs some 400 metres (1,280ft) above the town.

From the **Belvedere**, the observation platform on the Monte Ortobene, there

Mural advocating peace on Orgosolo's police station.

is a breathtaking view of the dramatic scenery in all directions. Near the summit massive karst boulders sculpted into strange shapes by weather and wind teeter on ledges below a rousing bronze statue of *The Redeemer* with a shiny, much-venerated big toe: it is the work of the sculptor Vincenzo Jerace, dated 1901. During the last few days of August (26–30) each year, the *Sagra del Redentore* is celebrated in its honour. The festival is one of the most famous and impressive on the entire island, as it demonstrates not only the colourful costumes, the traditional dances and music, but also the deep and sincere piety of the Sardinian people. Nuoro is a good base for excursions into the surrounding countryside – to the towns and villages of Orotelli, Orune, Bitti, Siniscola, Orosei, Dorgali, Irgoli, Galtellì – all of which are described elsewhere in this book.

Oliena (see page 126) and **Orgosolo** ⑭ in particular, which lie 10km (6 miles) and 16km (10 miles) respectively from Nuoro, are worthy of a more extended visit. Each of the little towns has both cultural and historic attractions as well as strong traditions of hospitality. Both lie on the Supramonte, the first limestone mountain range within the Gennargentu southeast of Nuoro. The murals in the village of **Orgosolo** are famous. Nowadays the original political message concerning the struggle against powerful landowners and government repression is played down by the villagers. The film *Bandits at Orgosolo* (1961), directed by Vittorio de Seta, dubbed the town the bandit capital of the island, a label that has been hard to shake off. The bandit Graziano Mesina, known as the Scarlet Rose for robbing the rich to give to the poor, was born in Orgosolo.

MOUNTAIN WALKS

The **Supramonte**, which contains the communities of Oliena, Dorgali, Orgosolo and Urzulei, can be approached from a number of directions – albeit in general only by foot, on horseback or in a cross-country vehicle. In each of the four villages, but in particular in Oliena and Orgosolo, walkers will find everything to meet a trekker's needs. The Supramonte

Archaeological finds from the nuraghe at Abbasanta.

⊘ TOP TREKS

Here are three spectacular walks in the limestone highlands. For the most demanding treks and technical climbs it is advisable to hire a walking guide accredited to the Associazione Italiana Guide Ambientali Escursionistiche. Sturdy boots with ankle support and other outdoor kit are essential.

Gola di Gorroppu: To explore the geological and botanical wonders of Europe's deepest (494 metres/1,620ft) and second-longest (5km/3 miles) gorge, La Gola di Gorroppu, set aside an entire day. Once inside the gorge there are dizzying views up vertical limestone walls where trees, shrubs, wild flowers and mouflon cling to the crumbling rock.

Cala Goloritzè: It takes 90 minutes of walking through centuries-old holm-oak woods to reach the transparent waters of Cala Goloritzè from the high plains of the Golgo Goloritzè. Limestone karst formations and sheer drops make it a dizzying spectacle. Climbers from all over the world come here to scale 120 metres (390ft) up the iconic spire Aguglia.

Punta La Marmora: It may not be the most demanding trek in the Sopramonte, but the classic three-hour ascent to Sardinia's highest peak (1,834 metres/6,000ft) offers panoramic rewards.

This is olive country.

is clad in unspoilt holm-oak woodland. Broom grows between giant tree trunks felled by age or lightning, but from which fresh shoots are already beginning to grow. Others have been transformed into pillars of charcoal by some long-past or more recent forest fire. In the half-shade of day or on bright moonlit nights they stand there like secret beings, monsters or devils from Dante's *Inferno*. Walkers be warned: grottoes and gullies open up without warning (across the millennia they may have swallowed up animals or even men); today speleologists are discovering their secrets.

The mountain itself is not high; its loftiest peaks scarcely reach 1,500 metres (4,921ft), with **Punta Corrasi** at 1,463 metres (4,800ft) and **Monte Ortu** at 1,340 metres (4,396ft). They lie on the northern boundary of the Supramonte, between Oliena and Orgosolo. In the southwest, within the district of Orgosolo, rise a number of ridges. They, too, are not particularly high, but, like the **Monte Novo San Giovanni**, they are steep and striking. Changing light conditions and the natural texture of

Hikers taking the easy way down Punta Corrasi.

the rock make the limestone shimmer – sometimes blue-grey or green, then silver, copper-coloured or chalky-white.

The way into the secret, enchanted world of this part of the Barbagia is via ancient footpaths or old, unmarked tracks made originally by the wild boar, mouflons, goats and pigs which even today roam through the dense undergrowth of woods and clearings in search of food. The impressions which visitors take home with them from the Supramonte are of relics from an Arcadian past: the cottages (*su pinnettu*), built of largely untreated, massive trunks of oak, yew or buckthorn, the stalls for livestock and goats, the pigsties (*s'edile*), and the few nuraghi constructed of white blocks (Nuraghe Mereu), defying decay. And then there are the innumerable underground springs and rivers, crystal-clear especially in the caves, disappearing underground only to resurface either in **Su Gologone** in the Oliena Valley, or else in the heart of the Supramonte, maybe in the **Gorroppu**, the wild gorge of the same name.

THE NUORESE

North of the Gennargentu mountains, the region of the high granite plateaux extends itself. It gets its name from the town of Nuoro. The **Nuorese** is a territory covered by vast cork and oak woods, inhabited in Nuragic times, and today sparsely populated by shepherds living in isolated villages.

Orune ⑮ is one such village, situated at 765 metres (2,510ft) above sea level on the edge of the plateau and dominating the Isalle Valley. A few kilometres out of the village at the end of a specially built road (10 minutes' walk downhill on a path) is the sacred spring of **Su Tempiesu**, the most beautiful and refined water temple in Sardinia. It is architecturally unique – a small temple with perfectly cut stones, monolithic small trachyte arches that have only a decorative function – and dates from 1200 BC.

From the positioning of the springs it seems clear that the spring did not attract large of numbers of people, as in the case of the sanctuary of Santa Vittoria di Serri. The large number of Nuragic springs and their distribution on the island demonstrate the great reverence the people had for water; so great that springs became sacred places of worship. For this reason, while the houses and even nuraghi seem to be primitive in their construction, in water temples a high level of craftsmanship in stone cutting and evocative and refined design is demonstrated.

Continuing north on the plateau, at 800 metres (2,600ft) above sea level, is the village of **Bitti** ⓰, famous for the production of *pecorino* sheep's cheese and more recently for being the home town of the *Tenores di Bitti*. It is thought that the local dialect is the closest to resembling Latin on the island.

A large Nuragic village called **Romanzesu** has recently been found on the granite plateau. The complex covers an area of 7 hectares (17 acres) and is characterised by buildings used for worship. A sacred well has been excavated, together with two *megaron* temples (rectangular temples preceded by a vestibule), a vast ceremonial space placed inside a large enclosure wall and a structure of concentric walls, of unknown function. The dating of materials confirms that the site was in use from the 13th to the 9th centuries BC. The complex is particularly evocative, lying amid a cork-tree wood (tel: 0784-414 314; summer Mon–Sat 9am–1pm, 3–7pm, Sun 9.30am–1pm and 2.30–7pm, winter Mon–Sat 8.30am–1pm and 2.30–6pm, Sun 9am–5pm). Moving towards the western border of the plateau, above the Tirso river, is **Benetutti**, a village well known for its thermal waters, one of the few thermal waters exploited in Sardinia. The most important spa is that of the Aurora or of San Saturnino on Benetutti, with sulphuric water and a temperature between 34–43°C (93–109°F).

THE BARBAGIA OF THE SOUTH

The village of **Serri** ⓱ is best-known for its position near the Giara di Serri, a basaltic plateau on which the Nuragic site of **Santuario Nuragico di Santa Vittoria** (Santa Vittoria archaeological area; tel: 0782-806 156; daily summer 9.30am–8.30pm, winter 9am–1pm and 2–6pm) is situated in a panoramic position. The archaeological complex is divided into three major sections: a temple area that includes a sacred well, a temple and a small church; a public area with a large courtyard for Nuragic festivals; and a market and living quarters that include a chief's hut. About 5km (3 miles) southeast of the town of **Orroli** is the **Nuraghe Arrubiu** ⓲ (area dell'Arrubiu; tel: 0782-847 269; daily 9.30am–dusk), one of the largest Nuragic complexes in Sardinia dating back to the Bronze Age. It is formed by a tall central tower which today measures 16 metres (50ft) high, although it is thought to have been 21 metres (67ft) high when it was originally built. The tower is surrounded by a bastion with five towers, which is surrounded by a lower wall

Peaches are cultivated on farmland around the Barbagia.

with eight towers. Nuraghe Arrubiu is situated on a high basaltic plateau (500 metres/1,600ft) near the edge of the canyon of the Flumendosa river, that here is more than 300 metres (960ft) high.

The Flumendosa is the second-longest river in Sardinia and flows to San Vito, on the eastern coast. Along its course it is interrupted by three dams that form as many lakes. The river creates a natural barrier with its deeply cut gorge between regions. The historic centre of **Sadali** was built around the 13th-century church of San Valentino, next to which a beautiful karstic spring bearing the same name erupts out of the rock as a 7-metre (23ft) waterfall. The surrounding area is bursting with water sources – not common in Sardinia – and it has created an otherworldly landscape in the limestone rocks. The **Grotte di Is Janas** (Fairy Caves; daily) are surrounded by a holm-oak wood. This section of the Barbagia is characterised by what is known as *Solitudini*, lonely, uninhabited expanses of land. The average population density in this region is fewer than 60 people per sq km (150 per sq mile) and can decrease in times of austerity.

The next village along the road is **Seui** . The town has a cluster of unusual collections under the title **Percorso Museale Sehuiense** (tel: 0782-539 002; Tue–Sun 9am–1pm and 3–5.30pm, summer 9.30am–1pm and 3–7.30pm): the civic museum's art collection covers Baroque canvases to contemporary sculpture; La Palazzina Liberty has ornate, Liberty-style interiors; and nearby Casa Farci contains artefacts of Sehuiense life and the library of Filiberto Farci, co-founder of the Partito Sardo d'Azione.

Along the SS 198 from Seui is the unmissable **Foresta Montarbu** (Montarbu Forest), reachable by a long dirt road that winds into the vast, wild area, or by getting off the Trenino Verde at the stop for San Girolamo. Footpaths in the forest are well signposted and lead to Monte Tonneri, where it is possible to see deer and mouflons. The Perda Liana, about 1,293 metres (4,242ft) high from its base, is, together with Tacco Texile of Aritzo, one of the most characteristic peaks of the island.

Pecorino comes from the Barbagia.

⊘ THE BARBAGIA DIET

Even the everyday food is natural and simple in the Barbagia: roast suckling pig, wild boar, goat, sheep and goat's-milk cheese, ham – perhaps from the local pigs which are often crossed with wild boar and fed on acorns. Since time immemorial every meal has been accompanied by one of the traditional breads such as *pane carasau* (a flat, crisp bread consisting of two wafer-thin layers); to drink there is fresh spring water from one of the many caves, or a powerful wine from Oliena, Orgosolo, Dorgali or Mamoiada. A healthy diet and traditional lifestyle have been identified as some key factors behind the fact that the Barbagia boasts the highest rate of centenarians in the world (around 22 per 100,000 inhabitants), a record it shares with Okinawa in Japan.

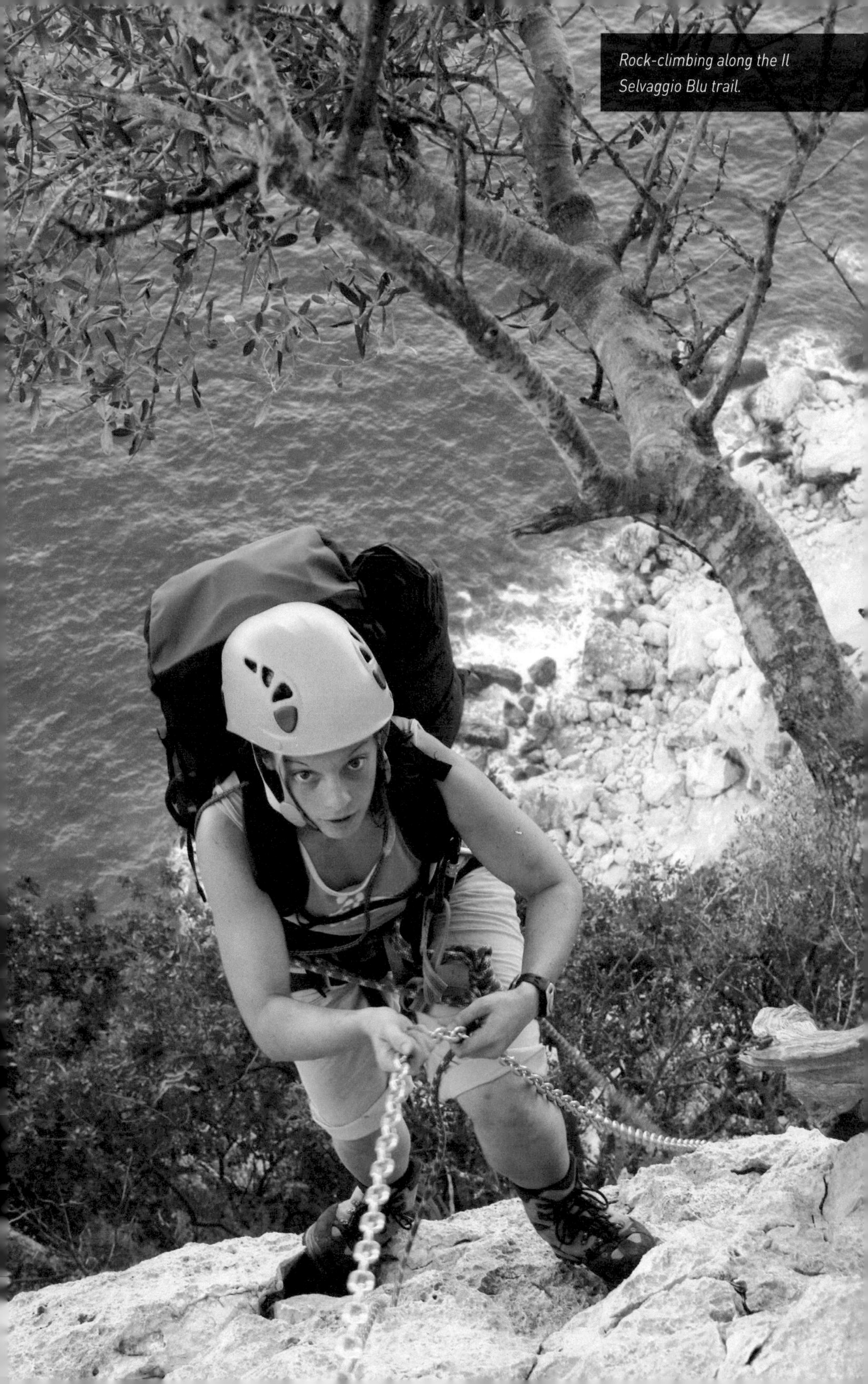

Rock-climbing along the Il Selvaggio Blu trail.

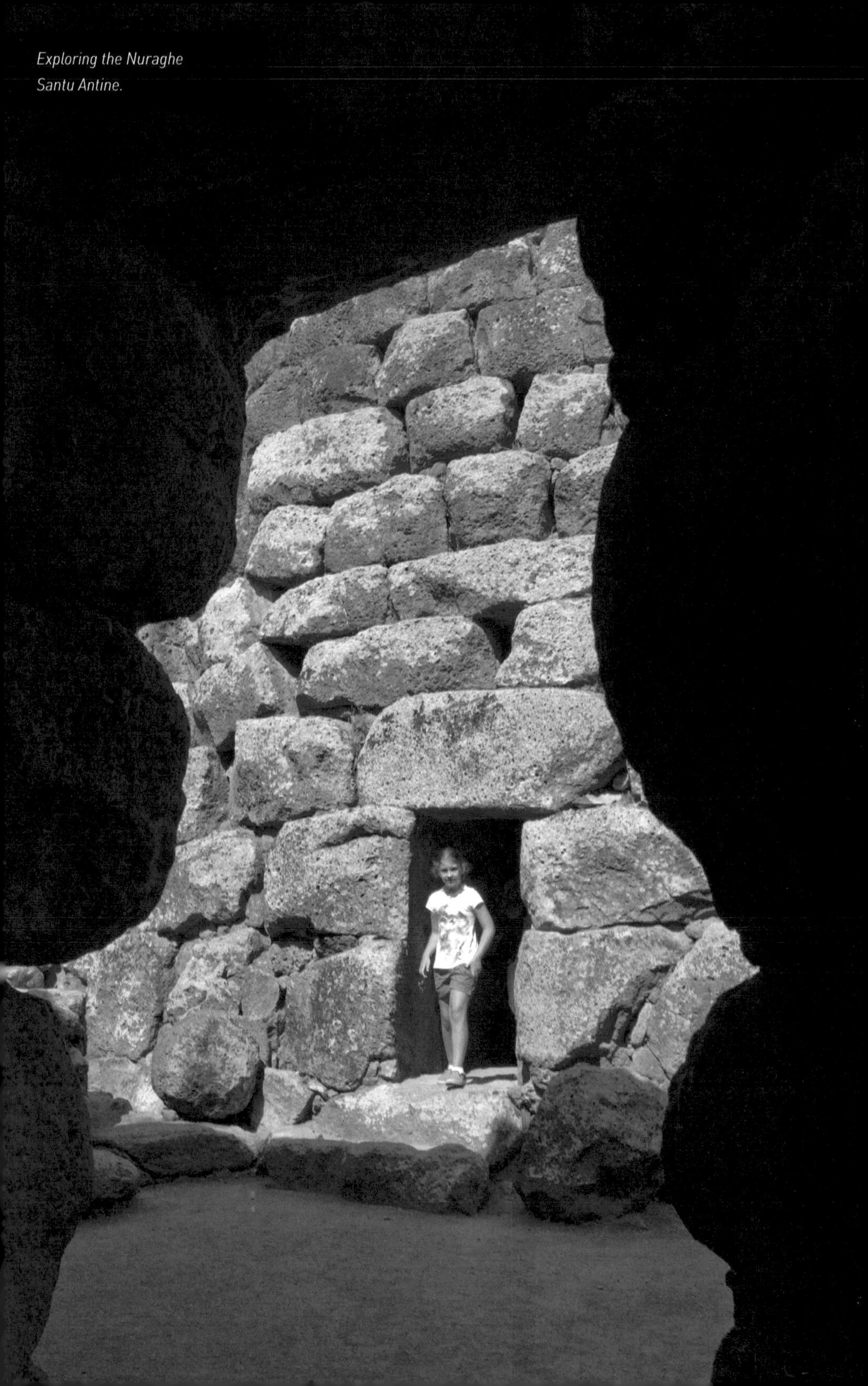

Exploring the Nuraghe Santu Antine.

SARDINIA

TRAVEL TIPS

GETTING THERE

A potential problem in visiting Sardinia in the summer months is transport: high demand and a limited number of ferries if you plan to arrive by sea mean it is essential to book well in advance.

By Air

From Europe

You also need to book your flight in advance, especially for the hectic July–August period. British Airways provides a regular and dependable London Gatwick–Cagliari and London-Heathrow–Olbia services in season. EasyJet has services to Cagliari from London Stansted, to Alghero from London Luton and to Olbia from Bristol, Manchester, London Luton and London Gatwick. Ryanair flies from London Stansted to Alghero and Cagliari.

In the past few years summer flights have increased because of greater demand. Many air companies of various countries schedule a large number of flights from/ to European towns in July and August. Alitalia and Air Italy fly to Cagliari via some mainland Italian airports from London. Alitalia

offers the best connections but sometimes not the best fares, and the route is usually via Rome (40 minutes from Cagliari) or Milan. During the summer there are many charter flights from all over Italy and some European cities to Tortolì-Arbatax Airport.

From the US

There are no direct flights to Sardinia from North America, although you can fly to Rome Fiumincino from New York and Toronto with Delta. Air Canada and Alitalia also fly direct to Milan Malpensa and Venice Marco Polo. The main European hubs with connecting flights to Sardinia are Rome, London and Paris.

The largest airport, Cagliari-Elmas, is 10 minutes' drive away from the town centre, and there is a regular bus link (see page 225). The same is also true of the other two main airports on the island, Olbia and Alghero (Fertilia).

Airport Websites

Cagliari
www.sogaer.it
Alghero
http://aeroportodialghero.it
Olbia
www.geasar.it

By Rail

The most direct route to Sardinia by rail from the UK begins by taking the Eurostar at St Pancras International in London, then involves a high-speed TGV journey from either Paris (swap stations from Gare du Nord to Gare de Lyon) or Lille, to Toulon or Marseille, where you can catch a ferry to Porto Torres. An alternative route is to take the sleeper service from Paris Gare de Bercy to Roma Termini, then another train to Civitavecchia to take the ferry to Cagliari or Arbatax.

By Sea

Advance reservation is vital for visiting Sardinia by boat in the summer season, especially if you are intending to take a car with you. Reservations cannot be accepted by navigation lines for deck seats (passaggio ponte) – the most inexpensive way of travelling to Sardinia – unless all the cabin spaces have already been sold.

The most important ferry companies, with connections to the rest of Italy, are:
Moby Lines, tel: from Italy 199-303 040, from abroad +49-611-14020, www.moby.it
Sardinia-Corsica Ferries, tel: +33-4-9532 9595, www.corsica-ferries.co.uk
Tirrenia, from abroad tel: +49-611-14020, from Italy tel: 199-330 40, www.tirrenia.it
Grandi Navi Veloci, reservations tel: +39-010-209 4591, www.gnv.it

There are daily connections between Cagliari and Civitavecchia (in Lazio, near Rome), Porto Torres and Genoa, Olbia and Civitavecchia. Other connections include: Cagliari with Naples and Palermo, Olbia with Genoa, Civitavecchia, Piombino and Livorno (Tuscany), Arbatax with Genoa and Civitavecchia; and Golfo Aranci with Livorno and Piombino. Crossing from all ports takes about 10 hours, but new high-speed ferries connect Olbia to Civitavecchia in approximately three hours.

By Coach/Bus

Obviously, there are no bus or coach services to Sardinia from Europe, only ferries or flights. There are a few private companies that can provide transport for groups from mainland Europe, including Logudotours (www.logudorotours.it) and Turmo Travel (www.gruppoturmotravel.com).

✈ Airline Numbers

Air Italy, tel: +44 2038681778 from UK, 39-0789 52682 worldwide, www.airitaly.com
Alitalia, tel: 892010 from Italy, 0333-566 5544 from UK, www.alitalia.com
British Airways, tel: 0844-493 0787, www.britishairways.com
EasyJet, tel: 0330-365 5000 from UK, 0330-365 5454 rest of the world, www.easyjet.com
Ryanair, tel: 0871-246 0000 from the UK, www.ryanair.com

By Road

From the UK the most direct road route is through France to Toulon, where there are ferry services to Porto Torres in the north of the island. The journey time is around 22 hours. Another more adventurous option for those with time on their hands is to drive through mainland Italy so as to visit other regions, before catching the ferry either at Genoa, Civitavecchia (in Lazio, near Rome), Piombino, Livorno or Naples.

GETTING AROUND

Rail travel in Italy and Sardinia is inexpensive and generally very reliable. However, Trenitalia services are generally limited to mainline stations (Oristano, Ozieri and Sassari) on the island's principal Cagliari–Porto Torres line. The whole journey from south to northwest takes a little over four hours. Two branch lines connect other parts of the island: the first heads west from Decimommanu to Iglésias (40 mins), while the other heads eastwards from Ozieri-Chilivani to Golfo Aranci (90 mins).

Sardinia's road network is very good and, unlike mainland Italy's, does not suffer from intolerable traffic congestion. Improved sections of the SS 125 road are considerably shortening journey times to and from Cagliari and the Nuoro province.

To and from the Airport

From Cagliari International

A railway line connects the airport to the city centre 6km (4 miles) away. The journey time is about 5–7 minutes. The trains run every 20 minutes between 5am and 9pm (www.trenitalia.com). A taxi takes about 10 minutes.

From Alghero International

There is an ARST bus connection from the airport to the city 12km (7.5 miles) away. Journey time is approximately 30 minutes. The company also operates bus services to Sassari and Bosa. For more information visit http://arst.sardegna.it. A taxi takes 15 minutes.

Logudoro Tours (www.logudorotours.it) run bus services to and from

Pedal power on the Bastione di San Remy, Cagliari.

Cagliari, Oristano and Macomer. There are also buses to Nuoro operated by Redentours (www.redentours.com) and seasonal connections to Stintino (www.sardabus.it) and Santa Teresa Gallura (www.digitur.it).

From Olbia for the Costa Smeralda

Bus services 2 and 10 connect the airport with Olbia, 5km (3 miles) away (www.aspo.it) and Sun Lines go to Costa Smeralda (www.sunlineseliteservice.com).

Public Transport

By Train

The main train station is in Cagliari; the main line is Cagliari–Oristano–Porto Torres. Travelling by train in Sardinia is sometimes slow, but worthwhile for the spectacular landscapes. For timetables and fares see www.trenitalia.com.

The tourist Trenino Verde, "The Little Green Train", runs from Sorgono to Isili or from Arbatax to Mandas through beautiful valleys and mountains (the locomotive is the same one that D.H. Lawrence took in 1921). There are also routes in the north – from Bosa to Macomer, and from Nulvi to Palau, through Tempio Pausania. The Trenino Verde route covers a total of 400km (248 miles). Contact: ARST tel: 070-26571;

⊙ Validating Tickets

It is important to remember to validate your bus or rail ticket before you travel. There are machines for date-stamping your rail ticket on station platforms and similar machines on buses.

www.treninoverde.com. ARST SpA also operates train as well as bus services (www.arst.sardegna.it).

By Bus

There is an extensive and efficient network of buses and coaches with services run by both public and private companies. The most reliable companies in the area are: **ARST** (Azienda Regionale Sarda Trasporti, tel: 800-865 042, from Sardinia; www.arst.sardegna.it), **Autolinee Pani** (a private company, tel: 070-913 0507; www.paniviaggieturismo.com), **Turmo Travel** (a private company, tel: 0789-21487; www.gruppoturmo travel.com).

It takes three hours to travel non-stop from one end of the island to the other (Cagliari–Sassari–Olbia).

There are a number of minibus services run by individuals and small companies. Local tourist offices have lists of these handy services.

By Boat

There are ferry services between Cagliari and Arbatax, and Olbia and Arbatax (Tirrenia, tel: 199-330 40, www.tirrenia.it). Lots of other ferry services are available to, from and between the islands. Delcomar (tel: 0781-857 123, www.delcomar.it) operates four routes: Carloforte–Calasetta, Carloforte–Porto Vesme, La Maddalena–Palau and Porto Torres–Asinara. Blue Navy (tel: 0565-269 710, https://blunavytraghetti.com) and Moby Lines (www.mobylines.com) ply the waves between Santa Teresa di Gallura and Bonifacio.

There are also lots of small operators who run ferry services and boat excursions around Sardinia's stunning coastline.

Taxis

Cagliari, tel: 070-400 101; www.cagliari
taxi.com
Sassari, tel: 079-25 39 39; www.taxi
sassari.altervista.org
Alghero, tel: 079-973 9795; www.
algherotaxi.it

Private Transport

By Car

Car insurance from most European
countries is valid in Sardinia. The biggest danger to unwary visiting drivers
is not poor roads but the haphazard
driving habits of the locals. Petrol in
Italy and Sardinia is usually not much
more expensive than in the UK.

Driver's Licences

Members of the EU who have a
national driver's licence may drive
and hire cars; non-EU drivers should
hold an International Driving Licence.

Car Hire

If you want to hire a car, there are a
number of rental companies, both
international and national, and their
offices are located not only at the
airports and ports but in towns and
seaside resorts. It is advisable, once
again, to book well in advance to
ensure you get the vehicle you prefer
(especially in August). Expect slightly
higher prices than those in Britain and
Northern Europe in general, but good
deals can be obtained through travel
agencies and flight carriers when purchasing package holidays. The following is a selection of the main car hire
outlets, but there are many more.

Cagliari

Avis, Railway Station, tel: 070-674
903, Elmas Airport, tel: 070-240 081;
www.avis.com.
Budget Rent-a-Car, Elmas Airport,
tel: 070-240 081; www.budgetinterna
tional.com.
Hertz Rent-a-Car, Elmas Airport, tel:
070-240 037; www.hertz.com.
Maggiore Rent-a-Car, Viale Monastir
116, tel: 070-273 692, Elmas Airport,
tel: 070-240 818; www.maggiore.it.
Matta Autonoleggio, Elmas Airport,
tel: 070-240 050; www.autonoleggio
matta.it.

Sassari

Avis, Via Predda Niedda 6, tel: 079-
267 5118; www.avis.com.
Maggiore Rent-a-Car, Zona Ind.
predda Niedda Strada 18 N. 38, tel:
079-260 409; www.maggiore.it.

Alghero

Avis, Fertilia Airport, tel: 079-
935 064; www.avis.com.
Budget Rent-a-Car, Fertilia Airport,
tel: 079-935 064; www.budgetinterna
tional.com.
Maggiore Rent-a-Car, Fertilia
Airport, tel: 079-935 045; www.mag
giore.it.

Olbia

Avis, Olbia Costa Smeralda Airport,
tel: 0789-69540; www.avis.com.
Budget Rent-a-Car, Costa Smeralda
Airport, tel: 0789-69540; www.budget
international.com.
Maggiore Rent-a-Car, Via Rudargia
84, tel: 0789-35840, Costa Smeralda
Airport, tel: 0789-69457; www.mag
giore.it.

Oristano

Avis, Via Liguria 17/19, tel: 0783-
310 638; www.avis.com.
Sardinya Rent-a-Car, Via Cagliari
436, tel: 0783-779 106; www.autono
leggiosardinya.it.

Main Roads

The main road connecting the
south of Sardinia with the north is
the SS 131 (Carlo Felice), built in
four lanes. It starts in Cagliari and
reaches Porto Torres, passing by
Oristano; near Abbasanta the road
divides and a branch now reaches
Olbia: the SS 131 dir. The other
main road is the SS 125 going from
Cagliari to Arzachena, following the
coast; it is a slow road which usually
takes longer than anticipated, often
because of lorries or campers (during the summer) which don't allow
overtaking. As mentioned earlier,

⊘ Driving Information

Seat belts are compulsory.
The use of headlights is
compulsory outside urban
centres.
Children should travel in the
back seat. According to EU law
child seats for smaller children
are mandatory.
Maximum speed in built-up
areas is 50kmh (30mph), in other
areas it is 90kmh (55mph) on
ordinary roads. The Carlo Felice
may seem like a motorway but it
is not; speed limits vary along it
(maximum speed is 110kmh (68
miles) on dual carriageways).
Senso Unico means One Way.

---

ongoing improvements to the SS 125
– including new tunnels and flyovers
– are shortening journey times.

Parking

Large towns like Cagliari have
adopted "blue stripes" parking places: each parking place is
marked with a blue line indicating
that you must pay. Look for a car
park attendant with a blue badge or
buy a ticket from a parking machine.
Always lock your car when parked;
never leave anything valuable in the
car or even risk hiding belongings in
the boot.

Cycling

Cycling is popular, especially outside Sardinia's main towns and cities. In recent years it has become a
particularly popular destination for
cycle touring. Specialist tour operators who organise bike tours include
http://skedaddle.co.uk, www.dolcevitabike
tours.com, www.sardiniacycling.com and
www.sardiniagrandtour.com.
   There is also an automated bike
sharing system operating in numerous Italian cities, with several renting stations in Cagliari, Carbonia and
Olbia in Sardinia. You can purchase
a card online or at authorised points
of sale. For more information visit
http://bicincitta.tobike.it.

On Foot

Many of Sardinia's towns are a joy
to walk around, as they are compact
with most of their main sights easily accessible on foot. Both Alghero
and Oristano have small historic
centres, while Sassari's medieval
quarter can be explored in a few
hours. Cagliari may sprawl up and
down hills and along beaches and
lakes, but its *centro storico* can be
explored on foot – although some
nifty legwork is needed to pack
in all the sights in one day. Some
streets around the Marina area
(Via Sardegna, Via Concezione,
Via Napoli and Via Barcellona)
are pedestrian-only, which makes
exploring the city even more enjoyable. The mountainous interior, especially around La Barbagia, Monti di
Gennarentu and Golfo di Orosei, is
wild country that attracts outdoor
enthusiasts and climbers. Don't
forget to bring sturdy walking boots
and other kit if you are planning
trekking adventures. Local walking
guides are invaluable for the more
challenging routes.

A

Accommodation

Sardinia has a wide range of accommodation available: hotels, tourist villages, holiday homes/flats for rental, camping and caravan sites, youth hostels, the rapidly expanding field of *agriturismo* (farm holidays) and, more recently, B&Bs.

Ever since the 1960s development boom on the Costa Smeralda, many Sardinian coastlines have seen luxury resorts appear. Luckily, swanky complexes and tasteless hotel buildings have not been allowed to spoil many sections of the coast and there are plenty of family-run small businesses for those after more traditional Sardinian hospitality.

It's best to decide exactly what kind of holiday you want and, if possible, make reservations well in advance – especially during the high season.

Hotel Categories

The Italian star rating system for hotels is somewhat eccentric, to put it mildly, and is not a reliable criterion for choosing where to stay. Facilities – however old – are what gives a hotel its rating, which means that some extremely tired establishments with appalling service parade

⊘ Passports at the Ready

Upon checking in at a hotel you will be asked to hand over your passport or national ID, which according to Italian law must be photocopied. This is also the case when using the internet in some cafés. Don't forget to pick up your passports before you leave for home!

Post your cards here.

themselves as stellar lodgings. In actual fact it is often the smaller hotels, B&Bs and *agriturismi* accommodation which provide the most gracious service and imaginative living spaces.

Bed and Breakfast

This is a new form of hospitality that is quickly spreading on the island, with a network of families renting out rooms in their own homes. It provides a great opportunity to be in close contact with locals and everyday island life.

Associazione Sarda Operatori Bed & Breakfast
Tel: 348-297 3461; www.bedandbreakfastsardegna.it.

Apartments and Villas

For those after flexibility, renting an apartment or villa is often the best option. There are a number of agencies which act as brokers. Here are just a few:

James Villas, tel: 0808-149 7929; www.jamesvillas.co.uk

Rent Sardinia, tel: 070-684 545; www.rent-sardinia.com
Soleya Vacanza, tel: 070-208 5095; www.soleyavacanze.it

Agriturismo

An increasing number of farms are converting to *agriturismo*, whereby visitors are offered lodging and meals in farmhouses; the advantages are a taste of excellent Sardinian food, genuine Sardinian hospitality and year-round availability. The following websites will give you an idea of what is on offer: www.agriturismo.net, www.agriturismo.it, www.agriturismo.com, www.agriturist.it and www.agriturismi.it.

The majority need booking far in advance: you can either book online or telephone the farm directly.

Camping

There are at least 200 campsites in Sardinia, with amenities ranging from basic to excellent. As well as space for tents and camper-vans, most of them have small furnished bungalows for rent and static caravans. Information can also be obtained from Faita Sardegna, www.faitasardegna.it. Another useful website is www.camping.it.

Youth Hostels

There are only a handful of youth hostels in Sardinia belonging to Hostelling International. For more detailed information visit the Italian Youth Hostel Association's website www.aighostels.it.

Admission Charges

Museum and gallery entrance fees vary between €2–12. Some sponsored exhibitions may be free. Most state-run and civic galleries offer free entrance or special rates to EU citizens under the age of 18 or over 65, or in full-time education.

B

Budgeting for Your Trip

Prices generally match those in the rest of Italy, although they really fluctuate according to where and when you visit. If you avoid July and August and the main resorts on the Costa Smeralda you can find good value. Generally, the cost of eating out and food shopping in local markets is more akin to southern Italy rather than oft-overpriced northern Italy.

A beer (*birra media*: 40cl) or a glass of house wine costs on average €3.50–4.

A typical main course in a budget restaurant will cost €4–10, while in a moderately priced eatery expect to pay €10–18.

A double room in a budget B&B in Cagliari costs around €80, while a comfortable hotel with good facilities in the city is priced at €150. Luxury hotels are concentrated in coastal resorts: in the Costa Smeralda expect to pay at least €400, while in Chia the tariff is typically €300 for a double in high season.

Taxi journey to and from Cagliari-Elmas Airport: €15–20 each way.

In Cagliari a single bus ticket is €1.30, a one-day pass €3.30 (www.ctmcagliari.it).

C

Children

Sardinians are very welcoming of children and families in general Under-18s are usually given free or

Mural on a bar in Orgosolo.

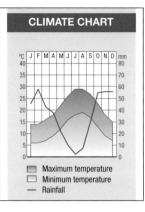

reduced admission to many state-run attractions.

Climate

Summer lasts for seven months in Sardinia, thanks to its southern location and the fact that it is an island. Average temperatures on the coast are 19°C (66°F) in autumn, 10°C (50°F) in winter, 12°C (54°F) in spring and 22°C (72°F) in summer. Sea temperatures reach 26°C (79°F) in July and August. Do remember that these are average temperatures and that in reality temperatures during the day are much higher and that during the night they often drop, even in the summer. You will be surprised to find that after a very hot day you may need a pullover in the evening if you are sitting outside.

A constant presence in Sardinia is wind, notably the *maestrale*, a strong wind from the northwest. During the summer two hot winds blow: from the southwest the moist *libeccio* and from the southeast the *scirocco*. There is no best time of

year to visit Sardinia – it depends what kind of holiday you are looking for – but in certain respects the most enjoyable period is mid-September/early October because the weather is still warm and there are relatively few tourists.

What to Bring

Bring practical clothes, and comfortable shoes or sandals. In summer, particularly at noon, the heat can be unbearable, so it is sensible to equip yourself with a sunhat and wear loose cotton clothing. If you are planning some adventures in the mountains, some sturdy hiking boots with ankle support and other kit are invaluable. Aqua shoes that protect your feet on rocks and pebbly beaches make boat trips – especially along the Golfo di Orosei – more comfortable.

Crime and Safety

There are no special problems in Sardinia as far as personal security and safety are concerned, and no specific areas where tourists are targeted. The main problem for tourists is petty crime: pickpocketing, bag-snatching and theft from cars. As when travelling anywhere, common sense should prevail: bags, cameras and other valuables should never be left unattended in cars, on beaches or anywhere else. Leave money and valuables, including airline tickets, in the hotel safe. Hitchhiking and walking are as safe as anywhere.

Customs Regulations

Goods brought in and exported within the EU incur no additional taxes or duty, provided they are for personal use or consumption.

D

Disabled Travellers

Like the rest of Italy, Sardinia remains a difficult place to get around for disabled travellers. Some trains and buses have access arrangements and places reserved for disabled passengers, but the churches and museums of Italy have been slow to offer improved access. SATH (http://sath.org) and Accessible Italy (http://accessibleitaly.com) are

good online resources. The Italian State Tourism Board (ENIT) dispenses some information for disabled travellers; www.enit.it.

E

Eating Out

What to Eat

Contrary to the assumption of many foreigners, the island's name has nothing to do with sardines. Sardinia is not traditionally a seafaring island although fish abound in the surrounding waters. Although meat is central to the island's cuisine, in many restaurants on or near the sea the menu is 80 percent fish-based. Popular seafood dishes include *anguille* (eels), *gamberi* (prawns), *calamari* (squid), *arselle* (clams) and, at the top end of the scale, aragosta (lobster), in season from March to the end of August. As fish is concerned, there is *orata* (gilthead bream), *tonno* (tuna), *sogliola* (sole), *spigola* (seabass), *cefalo* (grey mullet) and *pesce spada* (swordfish). They are either grilled, lightly fried, baked or served in a marinade or white wine sauce.

Nevertheless, typical Sard cuisine is rustic and hearty. Typical main course meats are roast pork, chicken, wild boar and lamb – the choice varies according to the season. Best known meat dish is *porchetto* (also called *porcetto* and *porceddu*) – suckling pig. A young pig is gently roasted on a spit, flavoured with myrtle, rosemary, laurel and sage, and served on cork trays with *pane carasau* (crisp flatbread) and myrtle leaves. *Capretto* (kid goat) is cooked in the same way, though it's not quite as popular. Another favourite is *agnello allo spiedo*, spit-roast lamb, best eaten in December. Vegetables come separately and are not a Sardinian strong point. Artichokes (sometimes served with peas), aubergines and asparagus are usually the best bets. Salads are invariably *verde* (green, that is, lettuce only) or *misto* (mixed, with tomato).

The island is also well-known for its cheeses. Most of Italy's *pecorino* is produced here. Made from ewes' milk it comes in various forms, most commonly the *pecorino romano* and the stronger *pecorino sardo* which is matured for three to 12 months. Sardinia manufactures light wines, and around 20 of them boast a DOC status (Denominazione di Origine Controllata, indicating a quality wine). Only one Sardinian wine – Vermentino di Gallura – is classified as DOCG (Denominazione di Origine Controllata Garantita), which guarantees an even higher quality. House wine (*vino della casa*) is usually fine and reasonably priced. Wine by the glass is almost unheard of, so diners should be prepared for a full bottle. A good meal is often concluded with a glass of liqueur or a choice of *amari* (bitters).

Where to Eat

Given the centrality of eating out to Sardinian social life and the pride taken in the preparation of meals, the standard of even moderately priced restaurants is high. Nearly all restaurants offer some local variations of typical Sardinian dishes, and few visitors will return home feeling dissatisfied. It is also worth noting that snacking in bars is much more part of daily life in Sardinia than in other European countries. As a consequence, there are numerous bars throughout the island which serve a variety of sandwiches and other snacks as well as drinks. Tourist centres and villages are usually quite small, so you will tend to find the best bars in the main square or its surroundings.

Bars serve *panini* (rolls) and *tramezzini* (small sandwiches) with alcoholic and non-alcoholic drinks. Pay first and give the receipt to the barman with the order. Most people stand at the bar, as a charge is made for sitting at a table. *Paninotecche* are sandwich bars where you can pop in for a quick meal. A *ristorante* is traditionally a formal place to eat. A *trattoria* is generally less formal than a restaurant and serves local dishes – however, in recent years the distinction between *ristoranti* and *trattorie* has blurred somewhat, so many expensive eateries now have the word trattoria in their title.

Courses are served in this order: *un antipasto*: appetiser; *un primo*: first course (risotto, pasta or soup per-haps); *un secondo*: main course, usually meat or fish served with *contorni*: side dishes of vegetables, etc; *un dolce* is a dessert; and *il conto* is the bill.

Emergencies

General emergency number, tel: 112
Police, tel: 113
Ambulance *(Ambulanza)*, tel: 118
Fire Brigade *(Vigili del Fuoco)*, tel: 115
Roadside Assistance, tel: 116
Corpo Forestale (environment), tel: 1515
Coastguard *(Soccorso del mare)*, tel: 1530
Road conditions, tel: 1518
Minor first aid (eg sunburn) can be obtained free from the *Pronto Soccorso* (Medical Standby/First Aid) in all hospitals or *Guardie Mediche*.

Electricity

230 volts – you will need an adaptor to operate British appliances, and a transformer to use 100–120-volt appliances.

Embassies and Consulates

Australia: Via Antonio Bosio 5, 00161 Rome; tel: 06-852 721; http://italy.embassy.gov.au.
Canada: Via Zara 30, 00198 Rome; tel: 06-85444; www.canadainternational.gc.ca.
Ireland: Villa Spada, Via Giacomo Medici 1, 00153 Roma; tel: 06-585 2381; www.embassyofireland.it.
New Zealand: Via Clitunno 44, 00198 Rome; tel: 06-853 7501, www.nzembassy.com.
South Africa: Via Tanaro 14, 00198 Rome; tel: 06-852 541; www.dirco.gov.za.
UK: Via XX Settembre 80a, 00187 Rome; tel: 06-4220 0001; www.gov.uk/world/organisations/british-embassy-rome.
US: Via Vittorio Veneto 121, 00187 Rome; tel: 06-46741; https://it.usembassy.gov.

Italian Embassies Abroad

Australia
12 Grey Street, Deakin, ACT 2600
Tel: 02-6273 3333
Canada
275 Slater St, Ottawa, Ontario K1P 5H9

Tel: 613-232 2401
UK
No. 14, Three Kings' Yard, London
W1K 4EH
Tel: 0207-312 2200
US
3000 Whitehaven Street,
NW Washington DC
Tel: 202-612 4400

Environmental Organisations

Lega Ambiente
Via Nuoro 43, Cagliari
Tel: 070-659 740
www.legambiente.it
World Wildlife Fund
Via dei Mille 13, Cagliari
Tel: 070-670 308
www.wwf.it
Amici della Terra
Via Cocco Ort ù 32, Cagliari
Tel: 070-490 904
www.amicidellaterra.it

Etiquette

Sardinians are generally friendly and will appreciate efforts to speak Italian or – even better – Sardinian. Any attempt to rush or pressurise them, however, will be regarded as the height of bad taste, and whatever you want will take longer.

Festivals

With over 1,000 festivals taking place in Sardinia each year, there is no shortage of opportunities to sample heady rites that hail as far back as the Bronze Age. As well as *le sagre* which celebrate the harvest, each town honours its patron saint. In recent years many cultural events exploring musical and artistic themes have been added to the rich canon of traditional events. To check the latest events, consult: www.sardegnaeventi24.it and www.giraitalia.it. Festivals range throughout the year from food and wine fairs to religious, cultural and musical festivals.

January–March

Lu Bogamarì (sea urchin festival), 1 Jan–early March; Alghero. For a month Alghero's restaurants have a sea urchin *(riccio di mare)*-based menu and there are lots of sea

urchin-orientated events, especially at weekends. You can even hire a boat and go fishing with intrepid divers who plunge the depths for the spiky echinoderms. The orange salty eggs have a life-affirming taste of the sea, and are generally served unadorned with pasta.

Festa di Sant'Antonio Abate (16 and 17 January) marks the winter solstice and recalls pagan rites with bonfires and mask-wearing.

Carnevale happens the week before Ash Wednesday, with ghoulish parades in the Barbagia and masked horsemen stomping around the medieval streets of Oristano (Sa Sartiglia) and Santú Lussugiu (Sa Carrela è Nanti). The archaic ceremonies which take place during the masked parades in Mamoiada and Ottana also present a fascinating spectacle, and there's a lively carnival in Bosa.

Easter

Sagra del Torrone (Nougat Fair), Easter weekend; Tonara.
This is the ideal time to see how the sweet Tonara version of *torrone* is made – from the intense initial mix of honey and dried fruit with *paioli in rame* (wooden paddles). Lots of music and cultural events are organised as the festival honours the town's celebrated tormented soul, the poet Peppinu Mereu (1872–1901), who loved to chew on things, both *dolce* and *amaro*.

Settimana Santa takes place in Easter week and is marked by silent processions which display Spanish and Catalan influences, including Alghero's Passion of Christ procession and the Lunissanti feast in Castelsardo. Impressive processions also take place in Sassari, Cagliari, Nuoro and Oliena.

Sa Festa Manna spans two weeks after Easter on the island of Sant'Antioco with parades and feasting to honour the Virgin Mary of Monserrato, the patron of Sulcis.

April

Sagra degli Agrumi (Citrus Fair), second Sunday before Easter; Muravera. This celebration of citrus fruit sees abundant markets full of fruits and lots of evocative folkloric dancing to the mournful sound of *launeddas*, an old wind instrument. Ox-drawn carts *(etnotraccas)* are paraded through

town by traditionally dressed locals – some in masks hailing from all over the island.

Echi Lontani
A festival of chamber music – lots of Baroque – in evocative historical places, Cagliari in late Mar–early Aug.

May–June

Sant' Efisio on 1–4 May honours Cagliari's patron saint, who drove out the pestilence in the 17th century. Trying to get a room on 1 May in Cagliari is impossible. People dressed in ethnic and historical costumes come from all corners of the country to participate in the procession, beginning in Cagliari and finishing in Nora.

Cavalcata Sarda on the penultimate Sunday of May in Sassari involves costumed processions, horseracing and stunts.

Sant'Isidoro in Orosei is a celebration of agricultural life with traditionally dressed locals festooning their carts with flowers.

Girotonno (Tuna Fair), first week of June; Carloforte.
The Isola di San Pietro's world-famous tuna fair sees the main street turned into an open-air restaurant where international chefs compete in creating the prize *tonno* dish and versions of traditional plates of *tunnina*, *curzetti* and *cassuli*. The island's wonderful Tabarkine Ligurian-Tunisian cuisine is celebrated with tastings of cashcà (couscous) and breads focaccia and *farinata* (www.girotonno.it).

Madonna dei Martiri (Monday after first Sunday of June) sees Fonni's residents carry a statue of the Virgin through the streets.

Here I Stay Festival (June). Small indie music festival in Guspina, near Piscinas, with free camping (www.hereistay.com).

Other festivals include: the **Tundimenta Seulesa** (Sheep-Shearing Festival) in Seulo; the **Cherry Fair** in Belvì; the **Honey Fair** in Montevecchio and a **wild boar fair** in Domus de Maria.

July–August

Sagra dei Culurgiones (Food Festival), early July. Tortolì.
This town in the Nuoro province offers mountains of its *culurjones* pasta pockets (hearty type of ravioli filled with potatoes, cheese and onions) served with a tomato salsa. There's lots of music and

wine-drinking all over the town's restaurants and piazzas.

Ardia (6 and 7 July) in Sedilo is a dust- and hair-raising, bare-back stampede dedicated to San Costantino.

Notte dei Poeti (Night of Poets) Concerts and plays in the Roman theatre of Nora, Pula in July and August (www.lanottedeipoeti.it).

La Sciampitta
The famous festival of folklore in Quartu S. Elena takes place every year in the first fortnight of July, with international and Sardinian folk groups (www.sciampitta.com).

Is Fassonis at the end of July–early August involves the fishermen of Sinis race on fassonis rafts in the Stagno di Santa Giusta.

Cala Gonone Jazz Festival
CGJF features international jazz artists who wig out in Doragli's Parco Ticca (July; www.intermezzonuoro.it).

Time in Jazz
Annual festival in Berchidda attracts top jazz acts each August (www.timeinjazz.it).

Musica sulle Bocche
Summer Jazz festival in various jaw-dropping Santa Teresa Gallura venues including beach, cliff-top, cloisters and piazza (www.musica sullebocche.it).

Sagra del Vermentino (Wine Fair), first Sunday of August. Monti. Up near the mountain of Limbara, this ancient vine, hailing from Portugal and Madeira, is the focus of much guzzling of the local wines accompanied by huge plates of *frittelle* (fritters) and local cheeses.

Santa Maria del Mare is a boat procession along the Temo river in Bosa followed by fireworks and feasting, on the first Sunday of August.

Li Candaleri on 14 August sees Sassari transformed by a vibrant procession of nine colossal candle towers.

Madonna Assunta on 15 August marks the cult of the "Risen Madonna" with traditionally dressed women parading a statue of the sleeping Virgin around various towns, including Cagliari and Orgoloso.

Corsa degli Scalzi is a bizarre bare-foot race of white tunic-wearing young men carrying an effigy of Cabras's saint through the streets to the sanctuary of San Salvatore.

Festival Rocce Rosse and Blues
Music festival usually in August, featuring performances by celebrated Italian songwriters like Baglioni and De Gregori as well as indie acts Subsonica and Sud Sound System (www.roccerosse.it).

Sardinia International Music Festival This Italian classical musical festival is held in Sassari in late Aug–early Sept.

September

Cabudanne de sos Poetas. Seneghe's festival of poetry at the end of August and the beginning of September comes with other cultural side dishes, including music concerts and culinary events (www.settembredeipoeti.it).

Villaggio Pescatori (Fish Festival). One week in early September. Giorgino, Cagliari.

Seafood specialities in the *marinaresca cagliaritana* tradition – *pruppu a schiscionera* (octopus with garlic), *scabbecciu* (sweet and sour fishy dish), *lissa* (roast mullets) and *fritto misto* (fried seafood medley) – sizzle and are devoured by thousands all over town. Mini football tournaments, concerts and culinary competitions add to the celebratory air.

October

Sagra delle Castagne e Nocciole (Chestnut and Hazelnut festival). Late October; Aritzo.

This humble nutty festival up in the wild Gennargentu mountains has been going strong since the early 1970s, and sees the mountain town of Aritzo swamped by foodies, who crunch the local nuts and sample lots of Barbagia's dishes and wines.

November–December

Festa del Vino Novello (all over Sardinia); November.
La vendemmia (grape harvest) is marked with festivals all over, including the Novello d'Oro (wine-tasting festival) held on the Trenino Verde, Arzana and similar events in Olbia and Milis.

Madonna dello Schiavo on 15 November involves a procession of a black Virgin through the streets of Carloforte.

Natale (Christmas) in Sardegna sees lots of presepi (Nativity scenes) created in churches and in people's homes.

Capo d'Any (New Year) Alghero, Cagiari, Sassari and Castelsardo are famed for their pyrotechnical displays to see in the New Year.

Chemists can give advice too.

Festival Sardo:Cross-Pollination

A new strain of Sardinian festival has sprouted in recent years that pays tribute to folkloric traditions while emphasising new artistic expression and cross-pollination with other cultures. Perhaps the most straightforward is La Sciampitta, a world-renowned festival of folklore, music and popular dance in Quartu S. Elena and other venues across the island in the first fortnight of July (www.sciampitta.com). As well as Sardinian folk groups, many international acts have appeared in recent years – from India, Bulgaria, Armenia, Portugal, Russia, Brazil, Senegal, Guatemala and Poland. Gavoi hosts Isola delle Storie in July, Sardinia's major literary gathering, where local and international writing talent come to read, chat and stroke chins (www.isoladellestorie.it).

Health and Medical Care

The main health issues for tourists in the summer months arise from over-exposure to the sun. Stay out of the sun during the hottest hours, and at other times cover up or use plenty of sunscreen, and wear a hat. It is also very important to drink plenty of water to avoid dehydration. If you need urgent medical treatment, call the first aid number *(Pronto Soccorso)* at one of the main hospitals, or call 112 for emergencies. Most areas have a *Guardia Medica Turistica* (emergency medical service for tourists). A list of duty pharmacists is usually published in local newspapers, and each hotel should have information about local medical care.

Insurance

EU residents are entitled to free or reduced healthcare that becomes necessary during your visit, but you will need a European Health Insurance Card (EHIC). Apply for a card online at www.ehic.org.uk (delivery in 7 days), or by calling 0845-606 2030 (delivery in 10 days); or pick up an application pack from the Post Office (delivery in 21 days). The EHIC does not cover you for repatriation in case of illness, so you should consider taking out additional travel insurance.

Illness

Vaccinations are not required, although cholera and typhoid jabs are a wise precaution if you intend to travel on to North Africa. The worst that's likely to happen to you health-wise is suffering from the extreme heat in the height of summer or getting an upset stomach – shellfish is usually to blame. Tap water is safe to drink in Sardinia, unless there is a sign saying *acqua non potabile*.

Pharmacies

Italian pharmacists are well qualified to give you advice on minor ailments. There's usually one open all night in the bigger towns. They work on a rota system, and to find the one open, check the listings posted on pharmacy doors, or in the local paper.

Discussing the news.

Dental Treatment

This is not covered by the health service, and is very expensive; your medical insurance may include dentists' fees.

Internet

Internet cafés are common in towns and tourist spots, and many hotels have Wi-Fi. Ask for *un punto internet*.

LGBTQ Travellers

Outside Cagliari and Sassari there isn't much of a gay scene. For detailed information about the latest events, check out the following: www.movimentomosessualesardo.org, www.associazionearc.eu
The Bologna-based Arcigay network (tel: 051-095 7241; www.arcigay.it) and www.gayfriendlyitaly.com provide all kinds of information for LGBTQ travellers in Italy.

Maps

Road maps may be obtained from the Sardinian Tourist Offices. For specialised maps (archaeological routes, biking or trekking itineraries), contact the local tourist

☉ Public Holidays

1 January New Year's Day
6 January Epiphany
March/April Easter Sunday and Monday
25 April Liberation Day
1 May Labour Day
15 August Assumption Day
1 November All Saints' Day
8 December Immaculate Conception
25 December Christmas Day
26 December Santo Stefano

information office, called *pro loco*, in the nearest village.

Media

Newspapers

It is possible to find foreign newspapers all year round in Cagliari and Sassari – usually a day late. In summer you can find daily international newspapers and other publications in the tourist centres. The London-based *Guardian* publishes a special European edition. There are two daily Sardinian newspapers; the best-selling is *L'Unione Sarda*, based in Cagliari, with a circulation of nearly 100,000 copies (www.unionesarda.it); *La Nuova Sardegna*, which mainly serves the northern part of Sardinia (www.lanuovasardegna.it), is the regional version of the national *La Repubblica*. Both newspapers are useful, if you know a little Italian, because they run listings sections. All the national Italian newspapers are available in Sardinia, and the major ones are printed daily in both Cagliari and Sassari.

Television

In addition to the three main national radio and television broadcasting channels run by RAI (Italian Radio and Television), there are numerous others. There are news bulletins *(Telegiornali)* almost every hour of the day, although the most popular are between 1 and 2pm and from 7 to 8.30pm. Cable television and Euro-channels are also available, as well as satellite TV.

Radio

Numerous private radio stations operate, as well as the three main national public stations (RAI Radio 1, 2, and 3). Most are broadcast on stereo FM. There are hourly traffic and weather bulletins on the RAI channels, in cooperation with ACI (Italian Automobile Association). In the summer bulletins are broadcast in English, German and French.

Money

The unit of currency in Sardinia, as in the rest of Italy, is the euro. The use of credit cards has become common in Sardinia, and the major international credit cards are accepted almost everywhere. They are particularly useful for settling bills in hotels or campsites, for purchasing expensive items in the bigger shops, or buying petrol. It is, however, advisable to travel with some money already changed into euros. A number of banks in the major cities and tourist resorts are equipped with debit/credit card outlets (ATMs), with instructions in several languages.

Tipping

As a general rule tipping is not a Sardinian custom, although tips are, of course, readily accepted. Most restaurants add a service charge to the bill (usually 10–15 percent), so choosing to leave a tip *(la mancia)* depends on your personal judgement. Your final bill will also include a small cover charge per person, irrespective of consumption.

Taxi drivers do not expect a tip, but taxis are relatively expensive. Tariffs are fixed and metered, so there is no room for haggling.

Opening Hours

Banks are open Monday to Friday 8.30am–1.30pm and (usually) 3–4.30pm.

Shops are usually open from 9am–1pm and 5–8pm, but bear in mind that opening hours do change from spring to summer and some may stay open late, or all day in the main cities.

⏱ Time Zone

Greenwich Mean Time plus 1 hour. Daylight Savings Time from the end of March to the beginning of October.

Crowned Madonna in a Sassari church.

Postal Services

Post offices are open Monday to Saturday 8am–1pm. Some main post offices are also open in the afternoon, 3–6pm.

Stamps *(francobolli)* are available from tobacconists and newsagents displaying a black-and-white T-sign which reads *Valori Bollati*.

R

Religious Services

Italy is a Catholic country. The hours of Mass *(messa)* and services vary from town to village. Mass is generally held on Saturday afternoon and Sunday: timetables are pinned inside the main door of churches. Other denominations may practise their faith here – some have their own services in both Cagliari and Sassari. Behaving appropriately when visiting churches is important: wear respectful attire (your shoulders and knees should be covered), switch off mobile phones and keep noise levels down, especially during services.

S

Shopping

Where to Shop

Shopping areas in the island are generally situated on the main road of each town, leading to the main piazza. The exception is Cagliari, where shops are concentrated along the two pedestrian streets Via Manno and Via Garibaldi; here you will find mostly clothes and shoes. Alongside the usual big-label fashion outlets you find throughout Italy, there are a few interesting clothes shops with imaginative tailoring and quirky designs including: 3C di Trogu Abbigliamento (Via Trincea Dei Razzi 71; tel: 070-288 864) and Saloon (Piazza Martiri 14; tel: 070-666 421).

Alghero is famous for its jewellery shops, which are all concentrated in the old part of town.

Castelsardo is a centre for basket-weaving; women offer their products in front of their homes. Porto Cervo is the place to look for expensive fashions – all around the Piazzetta.

Smoking

Smoking is not allowed in places that can be defined as "public", or in restaurants and bars, unless they have a separate air-conditioned area for smokers. Smoking in prohibited areas risks a fine of anything between €25 and €300.

T

Tax

Non-EU residents can claim back VAT (or IVA: *Imposta sul Valore Aggiunto*) on purchases made in Italy provided that: the goods are intended for personal or familiar use and are personally carried in the baggage; the overall value of goods exceeds €154,94 (VAT included);

Good old-fashioned phone.

and the purchase is certified by an invoice. For official details of how to claim back this tax, consult: www.agenziadoganemonopoli.gov.it.

Telephones

The local telephone code must be used in front of every dialled number.

Public phone booths, and phones in public places, are no longer common because of the spread of mobile (cell) phones. When available, they are bright orange and are operated by Telecom (the national phone company). Most are operated with a *carta telefonica* (phone card) sold most commonly in units of €5 and €10. The cards can be bought at *edicole* (newsagents), bars, tobacconists and, of course, Telecom centres, from which lengthy long-distance calls may also be made. Sardinia has good mobile phone coverage. For travellers who own an "unlocked" GSM phone, planning to make a lot of calls while in Italy, it's advisable to buy a SIM card from an Italian mobile phone shop. Local mobile network operators include Tre (www.tre.it), Vodafone (www.vodafone.it) and Wind (www.wind.it). Bring your ID or passport along as there is some bureaucracy involved.

For citizens of 31 European countries, including the UK and Ireland, roaming charges were abolished in 2017 yet under a fair-use policy some restrictions on the free use of mobile phones are still in place.

Enquiries

12 for directory enquiries
4176 for international directory enquiries
170 for operator-assisted calls
International dialling codes:
Dial **00**, then the country code
Australia **61**
Canada and US **1**
Ireland **353**
New Zealand **64**
South Africa **27**
UK **44**

Toilets

Restaurants, motorway service stations, bars and cafés provide toilet facilities, by Italian law. Some of them are not well maintained, and expect still to find quite a few squat toilets.

Tourist Information

Sardinian state-run tourist information is a bureaucratic mess with a lack of decent customer service. Often the most helpful and enthusiastic staff in the smaller tourist offices are students or volunteers. Official website of the region is www.sardegnaturismo.it.

Tourist Information for Each Province
Metropolitan City of Cagliari
Palazzo Civico, Via Roma 145, Cagliari
Tel: 070-677 7397
www.cagliariturismo.it
Nuoro
Piazza Italia 19, Nuoro
Tel: 0784-32307
www.visitnuoro.com
Oristano
Piazza Eleonora 18, Oristano
Tel: 0783-368 3210
www.gooristano.com
Sassari
Palazzo di Città, Via Sebastiano Satta 13, Sassari
Tel: 079-200 8072
www.comune.sassari.it
South Sardinia
Via Mazzini 39, Carbonia
Tel: 0781-672 61
www.provincia.carboniaiglesias.it

Tourist Offices Abroad
The Italian State Tourist Board, ENIT (www.enit.it) has offices in most major capitals or cities:
Canada
365 Bay Street, Suite 503, Toronto
Tel: 416-925 4882

UK
1 Princes Street, London W1B 2AY
Tel: 020-7408 1254
US
686 Park Avenue, New York, NY 10065
Tel: 212-245 5618
There are also offices in Chicago and Los Angeles.

Tour Operators and Travel Agents

Travel agents offer numerous holidays in Sardinia.
Specialists include:
Just Sardinia
14 Silver Business Park, Airfield Way, Christchurch, Dorset, BH23 3TA, tel: 01202-484858; www.justsardinia.co.uk
Sardinian Places
Atlantic House, 3600 Parkway, Solent Business Park, Fareham, Hampshire, PO15 7AN, tel: 01489-866959; www.sardinianplaces.co.uk

Visas and Passports

Citizens from the EU, US and Canada can enter Sardinia with a valid passport or identity card. You only need a visa if staying for more than three months. Entry regulations for citizens coming from other countries apply as for the rest of Italy, and visas can be obtained through Italian embassies. Tourists visiting Sardinia with cats or dogs must present proof at customs of their animals' inoculation against rabies. The vaccination must be given at least 20 days before arrival.

⏀ Weights and Measures

Metric–Imperial
1 centimetre = 0.4in
1 metre = 3ft 3ins
1 kilometre = 0.62 mile
1 gram = 0.04 ounce
1 kilogram = 2.2 pounds
1 litre = 1.76 UK pints
Imperial–Metric
1 inch = 2.54 centimetres
1 foot = 30 centimetres
1 ounce = 28 grams
1 pound = 0.45 kilogram
1 pint = 0.57 litre
1 UK gallon = 4.55 litres
1 US gallon = 3.78 litres

LANGUAGE

BASIC COMMUNICATION

Yes *Sì*
No *No*
Thank you *Grazie*
Many thanks *Mille grazie/Tante grazie/Molte grazie*
You're welcome *Prego*
All right/Okay/That's fine *Va bene*
Please *Per favore* or *per cortesia*
Excuse me (to get attention) *Scusi* (singular), *Scusate* (plural)
Excuse me (to get through a crowd) *Permesso*
Excuse me (to attract attention, eg of a waiter) *Senta!*
Excuse me (sorry) *Mi scusi* (singular), *Scusatemi* (plural)
Wait a minute! (informal) *Aspetta!* (formal) *Aspetti!*
Could you help me? (formal) *Potrebbe aiutarmi?*
Can I help you? (formal) *Posso aiutarLa?*
Can you help me? (formal) *Può aiutarmi, per cortesia?*
Can you show me...? (formal) *Può indicarmi...?*

☉ Emergencies

Help! *Aiuto!*
Stop! *Fermate!*
I've had an accident *Ho avuto un incidente*
Watch out! *Attenzione!*
Call a doctor *Per favore, chiami un medico*
Call an ambulance *Chiami un'ambulanza*
Call the police *Chiami la Polizia/i Carabinieri*
Call the fire brigade *Chiami I pompieri*
Where is the telephone? *Dov'è il telefono?*
Where is the nearest hospital? *Dov'è l'ospedale più vicino?*
I would like to report a theft *Voglio denunciare un furto*

I need... *Ho bisogno di...*
I'm lost *Mi sono perso*
I'm sorry *Mi dispiace*
I don't know *Non lo so*
I don't understand *Non capisco*
Do you speak English/French/German? *Parla inglese/francese/tedesco?*
Could you speak more slowly, please? *Può parlare più lentamente, per favore?*
Could you repeat that please? (formal) *Può ripetere, per piacere?*
Certainly *Ma certo*
here/there *qui/là*
What? *Cosa?*
When/Why/Where? *Quando/Perchè/Dov'è?*
Where is the lavatory? *Dov'è il bagno?*

GREETINGS

Hello (Good day) *Buon giorno*
Good afternoon/evening *Buona sera*
Good night *Buona notte*
Goodbye *Arrivederci*
Hello/Hi/Goodbye (familiar) *Ciao*
Mr/Mrs/Miss *Signor/Signora/Signorina*
Pleased to meet you (formal) *Piacere di conoscerLa*
I am English/American *Sono inglese/americano*
Irish/Scottish/Welsh *irlandese/scozzese/gallese*
Canadian/Australian *canadese/australiano*
Do you speak English? (formal) *Parla inglese?*
I'm here on holiday *Sono qui in vacanza*
Do you like it here? (formal) *Si trova bene qui?*
How are you? (formal/informal) *Come sta/Come stai?*
Fine thanks *Bene, grazie*
See you later *A più tardi*
See you soon *A presto*

Take care (formal) *Stia bene*, (informal) *Stammi bene*

TELEPHONE CALLS

the area code *il prefisso telefonico*
I'd like to make a reverse charges call *Vorrei fare una telefonata a carico del destinatario*
May I use your telephone, please? *Posso usare il telefono?*
Hello (on the telephone) *Pronto*
My name's *Mi chiamo/Sono*
Could I speak to...? *Posso parlare con...?*
Sorry, he/she isn't in *Mi dispiace, è fuori*
Can he call you back? *Può richiamarla?*
I'll try again later *Riproverò più tardi*
Can I leave a message? *Posso lasciare un messaggio?*
Please tell him I called *Gli dica, per favore, che ho telefonato*
Hold on *Un attimo, per favore*
A local call *una telefonata locale*
Can you speak up, please? (formal) *Può parlare più forte, per favore?*

IN THE HOTEL

Do you have any vacant rooms? *Avete camere libere?*
I have a reservation *Ho fatto una prenotazione*
I'd like... *Vorrei...*
a single/double room (with a double bed) *una camera singola/doppia (con letto matrimoniale)*
a room with twin beds *una camera a due letti*
a room with a bath/shower *una camera con bagno/doccia*
for one night *per una notte*
for two nights *per due notti*
We have one with a double bed *Ne abbiamo una matrimoniale*
Could you show me another room please? *Potrebbe mostrarmi un'altra camera?*

⊘ Pronunciation and Grammar Tips

Italian-speakers claim that pronunciation is straightforward: you pronounce it as it is written. This is approximately true, but there are a couple of important rules for English-speakers to bear in mind: c before e or i is pronounced "ch", eg ciao, mi dispiace, la cinghiale. Ch before i or e is pronounced as "k", eg la chiesa. Likewise, sci or sce are pronounced as in "sheep" or "shed" respectively. Gn in Italian is rather like the sound in "onion", while gl is softened to resemble the sound in "bullion".

Nouns are either masculine (il, plural i) or feminine (la, plural le). Plurals of nouns are most often formed by changing an o to an i and an a to an e, eg il panino, i panini; la chiesa, le chiese.

Words are stressed on the penultimate syllable unless an accent indicates otherwise.

Like many languages, Italian has formal and informal words for "You". In the singular, Tu is informal while Lei is more polite. Confusingly, in some parts of Italy or in some circumstances, you will also hear Voi used as a singular polite form. (In general, Voi is reserved for "You" plural, however.) For visitors, it is simplest and most respectful to use the formal form unless invited to do otherwise.

There is, of course, rather more to the language than that, but you can get a surprisingly long way towards making friends with a mastery of a few basic phrases.

How much is it? Quanto costa?
on the first floor al primo piano
Is breakfast included? É compresa la prima colazione?
Is everything included? É tutto compreso?
half/full board mezza pensione/pensione completa
It's expensive É caro
Do you have a room with a balcony/view of the sea? C'è una camera con balcone/con vista sul mare?
a room overlooking the park/the street/the back una camera con vista sul parco/che dà sulla strada/sul retro
Is it a quiet room? É una stanza tranquilla?
The room is too hot/cold/noisy/small La camera è troppo calda/fredda/rumorosa/piccola
Can I see the room? Posso vedere la camera?
What time does the hotel close? A che ora chiude l'albergo?
I'll take it La prendo
big/small grande/piccola
What time is breakfast? A che ora è la prima colazione?
Please give me a call at... Mi può chiamare alle...
Come in! Avanti!
Can I have the bill, please? Posso avere il conto, per favore?
Can you call me a taxi please? Può chiamarmi un taxi, per favore?
dining room la sala da pranzo
key la chiave
lift l'ascensore

towel l'asciugamano
toilet paper la carta igienica
pull/push tirare/spingere

EATING OUT

Bar Snacks and Drinks

I'd like... Vorrei...
coffee un caffè (espresso: small, strong and black)
un cappuccino (with hot, frothy milk)
un caffelatte (like café au lait in France)
un caffè lungo (weak)
un corretto (laced with alcohol – usually brandy or grappa. You should specify)
tea un tè
lemon tea un tè al limone
herbal tea una tisana
hot chocolate una cioccolata calda
orange/lemon juice (bottled) un succo d'arancia/di limone
fresh orange/lemon juice una spremuta di arancia/di limone
orangeade un'aranciata
water (mineral) acqua (minerale)
fizzy/still mineral water acqua minerale gasata/naturale
a glass of mineral water un bicchiere di minerale
with/without ice con/senza ghiaccio
red/white wine vino rosso/bianco
beer (draught) una birra (alla spina)
a gin and tonic un gin tonic
a bitter (Vermouth, etc.) un amaro

---

milk latte
a (half) litre un (mezzo) litro
bottle una bottiglia
ice cream un gelato
cone un cono
pastry una pasta
sandwich un tramezzino
roll un panino
Anything else? Desidera qualcos'altro?
Cheers Salute
Let me pay Offro io
That's very kind of you Grazie, molto gentile

In a Restaurant

I'd like to book a table Vorrei riservare un tavolo
Have you got a table for... Avete un tavolo per...
I have a reservation Ho fatto una prenotazione
lunch/supper il pranzo/la cena
We do not want a full meal Non desideriamo un pasto completo
Could we have another table? Potremmo spostarci?
I'm a vegetarian Sono vegetariano/a
Is there a vegetarian dish? C'è un piatto vegetariano?
May we have the menu? Ci dà il menu, per favore?
wine list la lista dei vini
What would you like? Che cosa prende?
What would you recommend? Che cosa ci raccomanda?

⊘ Days and Dates

morning/afternoon/evening la mattina/il pomeriggio/la sera
yesterday/today/tomorrow ieri/oggi/domani
the day after tomorrow dopodomani
now/early/late adesso/presto/ritardo
a minute un minuto
an hour un'ora
half an hour un mezz'ora
a day un giorno
a week una settimana
Monday lunedì
Tuesday martedì
Wednesday mercoledì
Thursday giovedì
Friday venerdì
Saturday sabato
Sunday domenica
first il primo/la prima
second il secondo/la seconda
third il terzo/la terza

home-made *fatto in casa*
What would you like as a main course/dessert? *Che cosa prende di secondo/di dolce?*
What would you like to drink? *Che cosa desidera da bere?*
a carafe of red/white wine *una caraffa di vino rosso/bianco*
fixed price menu *il menu a prezzo fisso*
the dish of the day *il piatto del giorno*
VAT (sales tax) *iva*
cover charge *il coperto/pane e coperto*
That's enough; no more, thanks *Basta (così)*
The bill, please *Il conto, per favore*
Is service included? *Il servizio è incluso?*
Where is the lavatory? *Dov'è il bagno?*
Keep the change *Va bene così*
I've enjoyed the meal *Mi è piaciuto molto*

Menu Decoder

Antipasti (Hors d'Oeuvres)

antipasto misto **mixed hors d'oeuvres** (including cold cuts, possibly cheeses and roast vegetables – ask, however)
buffet freddo **cold buffet** (often excellent)
caponata **mixed aubergine, olives and tomatoes**
insalata caprese **tomato and mozzarella salad**
insalata di mare **seafood salad**
insalata mista/verde **mixed/green salad**
melanzane alla parmigiana **fried or baked aubergine** (with parmesan cheese and tomato)
mortadella/salame **salami**
pancetta **bacon**
peperonata **vegetable stew** (made with peppers, onions, tomatoes and sometimes some aubergines)

Primi (First Courses)

Typical first courses in Sardinia include soup or numerous varieties of pasta in a wide range of delicious sauces. Risotto and gnocchi are more common in the north of Italy than here.
il brodetto **fish soup**
il brodo **consommé**
i crespolini **savoury pancakes**
gli gnocchi **potato dumplings**
la minestra **soup**
il minestrone **thick vegetable soup**
pasta e fagioli **pasta and bean soup**

il prosciutto (cotto/crudo) **ham** (cooked/cured)
i supplì **rice croquettes**
i tartufi **truffles**
la zuppa **soup**

Secondi (Main Courses)

Typical main courses are fish-, seafood- or meat-based, with accompaniments *(contorni)* that vary greatly from region to region.

La Carne (Meat)

allo spiedo **on the spit**
arrosto **roast meat**
i ferri **grilled**
al forno **baked**
al girarrosto **spit-roasted**
alla griglia **grilled**
involtini **skewered veal, ham, etc.**
stagionato **hung, well-aged**
stufato **braised, stewed**
ben cotto **well done** (steak, etc.)
al puntino **medium** (steak, etc.)
al sangue **rare** (steak, etc.)
l'agnello **lamb**
la bistecca **steak**
a bresaola **dried salted beef**
il capriolo/cervo **venison**
il carpaccio **lean beef fillet**
il cinghiale **wild boar**
il coniglio **rabbit**
il controfiletto **sirloin steak**
le cotolette **cutlets**
il fagiano **pheasant**
il fegato **liver**
il filetto **fillet**
la lepre **hare**
il maiale **pork**
il manzo **beef**
l'ossobuco **shin of veal**
il pollo **chicken**
le polpette **meatballs**
il polpettone **meat loaf**
la porchetta **roast suckling pig**
la salsiccia **sausage**
saltimbocca (alla romana) **veal escalopes with ham**
le scaloppine **escalopes**
lo stufato **stew**
il sugo **sauce**
il tacchino **turkey**
la trippa **tripe**
il vitello **veal**

Frutti di Mare (Seafood)

Beware the word *surgelati*, meaning frozen rather than fresh.
affumicato **smoked**
alle brace **charcoal grilled/barbecued**
alla griglia **grilled**
fritto **fried**
ripieno **stuffed**
al vapore **steamed**

le acciughe **anchovies**
l'anguilla **eel**
l'aragosta **lobster**
il baccalà **dried salted cod**
i bianchetti **whitebait**
il branzino **sea bass**
i calamaretti **baby squid**
i calamari **squid**
la carpa **carp**
i crostacei **shellfish**
le cozze **mussels**
il fritto misto **mixed fried fish**
i gamberetti **shrimps**
i gamberi **prawns**
il granchio **crab**
il merluzzo **cod**
le moleche **soft-shelled crabs**
le ostriche **oysters**
il pesce **fish**
il pesce spada **swordfish**
il polipo **octopus**
il risotto di mare **seafood risotto**
le sarde **sardines**
la sogliola **sole**
le seppie **cuttlefish**
la triglia **red mullet**
la trota **trout**
il tonno **tuna**
le vongole **clams**

I Legumi/La Verdura (Vegetables)

a scelta **of your choice**
i contorni **accompaniments**
ripieno **stuffed**
gli asparagi **asparagus**
i carciofini **artichoke hearts**
il carciofo **artichoke**
le carote **carrots**
il cavolo **cabbage**
la cicoria **chicory**
la cipolla **onion**
i funghi **mushrooms**
i fagioli **beans**
i fagiolini **French (green) beans**
le fave **broad beans**
il finocchio **fennel**
l'indivia **endive/chicory**
l'insalata mista **mixed salad**
l'insalata verde **green salad**
la melanzana **aubergine**
le patate **potatoes**
le patatine fritte **chips/French fries**
i peperoni **peppers**
i piselli **peas**

☺ Bar Notices

Prezzo in terrazza. Terrace price, often double what you pay standing at the bar.
Si prende lo scontrino alla cassa. Pay at the cash desk, then take the receipt to the bar to be served.

i pomodori **tomatoes**
le primizie **spring vegetables**
il radicchio **red, slightly bitter lettuce**
la rughetta **rocket**
i ravanelli **radishes**
gli spinaci **spinach**
la verdura **green vegetables**
la zucca **pumpkin/squash**
gli zucchini **courgettes**

I Dolci (Desserts)

al carrello **(desserts) from the trolley**
un semifreddo **semi-frozen dessert (many types)**
la bavarese **mousse**
la cassata **Sicilian ice cream with candied peel**
le frittelle **fritters**
un gelato (di lampone/limone) **(raspberry/lemon) ice cream**
una granita **water ice**
una macedonia di frutta **fruit salad**
il tartufo (nero) **(chocolate) ice cream dessert**
il tiramisù **cold, creamy cheese and coffee dessert**
la torta **cake/tart**
lo zabaglione **sweet dessert made with eggs and Marsala wine**
la zuppa inglese **trifle**

La Frutta (Fruit)

le albicocche **apricots**
le arance **oranges**
le banane **bananas**
le ciliegie **cherries**
il cocomero **watermelon**
i fichi **figs**
le fragole **strawberries**
i frutti di bosco **fruits of the forest**
i lamponi **raspberries**
la mela **apple**
il melone **melon**
la pesca **peach**
la pera **pear**
il pompelmo **grapefruit**
l'uva **grapes**

Basic Foods

l'aceto **vinegar**
l'aglio **garlic**
il burro **butter**
il formaggio **cheese**
la focaccia **oven-baked snack**
la frittata **omelette**
il grana **hard grating cheese, similar to parmesan**
i grissini **bread sticks**
l'olio **oil**
la marmellata **jam**
il pane **bread**
il pane integrale **wholemeal bread**
il parmigiano **parmesan cheese**

☉ Pasta Dishes

Common Pasta Shapes
cannelloni (large stuffed tubes of pasta); *farfalle* (bow- or butterfly-shaped pasta); *tagliatelle* (flat noodles, similar to *fettuccine*); *tortellini* and *ravioli* (different types of stuffed pasta packets); *penne* (quill-shaped tubes, smaller than *rigatoni*).
Typical Pasta Sauces
pomodoro (tomato); *pesto* (with basil and pine nuts); *matriciana* (bacon and tomato); *arrabbiata* (spicy tomato); *panna* (cream); *ragù* (meat sauce); *aglio e olio* (garlic and olive oil); *burro e salvia* (butter and sage).

il pepe **pepper**
il riso **rice**
il sale **salt**
la senape **mustard**
le uova **eggs**
lo yogurt **yoghurt**
lo zucchero **sugar**

SIGHTSEEING

Si può visitare? **Can one visit?**
il custode **custodian**
Suonare il campanello **ring the bell**
aperto/a **open**
chiuso/a **closed**
chiuso per la festa **closed for the festival**
chiuso per ferie **closed for the holidays**
chiuso per restauro **closed for restoration**
Is it possible to see the church? *É possibile visitare la chiesa?*
Entrata/uscita **Entrance/exit**
Where can I find the custodian/sacristan/key? *Dove posso trovare il custode/il sacrestano/la chiave?*

AT THE SHOPS

What time do you open/close? *A che ora apre/chiude?*
Closed for the holidays (typical sign) *Chiuso per ferie*
Pull/Push (sign on doors) *Tirare/Spingere*
Entrance/exit *Entrata/uscita*
Can I help you? (formal) *Posso aiutarLa?*
What would you like? *Che cosa desidera?*

I'm just looking *Sto soltanto guardando*
How much does it cost? *Quant'è, per favore?*
How much is this? *Quanto viene?*
Do you take credit cards? *Accettate carte di credito?*
I'd like... *Vorrei...*
this one/that one *questo/quello*
I'd like that one, please *Vorrei quello lì, per cortesia*
Have you got...? *Avete...?*
We haven't got (any)... *Non (ne) abbiamo...*
Can I try it on? *Posso provare?*
the size (for clothes) *la taglia*
What size do you take? *Qual'é la sua taglia?*
the size (for shoes) *il numero*
Is there/do you have...? *C'è...?*
Yes, of course *Sì, certo*
No, we don't (there isn't) *No, non c'è*
That's too expensive *É troppo caro*
Please write it down for me *Me lo scriva, per favore*
cheap *economico*
Don't you have anything cheaper? *Ha niente che costa di meno?*
It's too small/big *É troppo piccolo/grande*
brown/blue/black *marrone/blu/nero*
green/red/white/yellow *verde/rosso/bianco/giallo*
pink/grey/gold/silver *rosa/grigio/oro/argento*
No thank you, I don't like it *Grazie, ma non è di mio gusto*
I (don't) like it *(Non) mi piace*
I'll take it/I'll leave it *Lo prendo/Lo lascio*
Una ruberia
This is faulty. Can I have a replacement/refund? *C'è un difetto. Me lo potrebbe cambiare/rimborsare?*
Anything else? *Altro?*
The cash desk is over there *Si accomodi alla cassa*
Give me some of those *Mi dia alcuni di quelli lì*
a (half) kilo *un (mezzo) chilo*
100 grams *un etto*
200 grams *due etti*
more/less *più/meno*
with/without *con/senza*
a little *un pochino*
That's enough/No more *Basta così*

Types of Shops

antique dealer *l'antiquario*
bakery *pasticceria*
bank *la banca*
bookshop *la libreria*

boutique/clothes shop *il negozio di moda*
bureau de change *il cambio*
butcher *la macelleria*
chemist *la farmacia*
delicatessen *la salumeria*
department store *il grande magazzino*
dry cleaner *la tintoria*
fishmonger *la pescheria*
food shop *l'alimentari*
florist *il fioraio*
grocer *l'alimentari*
greengrocer *il fruttivendolo*
hairdresser (women) *il parrucchiere*
ice-cream parlour *la gelateria*
jeweller *il gioielliere*
leather shop *la pelletteria*
market *il mercato*
news-stand *l'edicola*
post office *l'ufficio postale*
shoe shop *il negozio di scarpe*
stationer *la cartoleria*
supermarket *il supermercato*
tobacconist *il tabaccaio* (also usually sells travel tickets, stamps, phone cards)
travel agency *l'agenzia di viaggi* (also usually books train tickets for domestic and international journeys)

TRAVELLING

Transport

airport *l'aeroporto*
arrivals/departures *arrivi/partenze*
boat *la barca*

bus *l'autobus/il pullman*
bus station *l'autostazione*
car *la macchina*
connection *la coincidenza*
ferry *il traghetto*
ferry terminal *la stazione marittima*
first/second class *la prima/seconda classe*
flight *il volo*
left luggage office *il deposito bagagli*
motorway *l'autostrada*
no smoking *vietato fumare*
platform *il binario*
porter *il facchino*
railway station *la stazione (ferroviaria)*
return ticket *un biglietto di andata e ritorno*
single ticket *un biglietto di andata sola*
sleeping car *la carrozza letti/il vagone letto*
smokers/non-smokers *fumatori/non-fumatori*
stop *la fermata*
taxi *il taxi*
ticket office *la biglietteria*
train *il treno*
WC *la toilette*

Road Signs

Accendere le luci in galleria **Lights on in tunnel**
Alt **Stop**
Autostrada **Motorway**
Attenzione **Caution**
Avanti **Go/walk**
Caduta massi **Danger of falling rocks**
Casello **Toll gate**

Dare la precedenza **Give way**
Deviazione **Diversion**
Divieto di campeggio **No camping allowed**
Divieto di sosta/Sosta vietata **No parking**
Divieto di passaggio/Senso vietato **No entry**
Dogana **Customs**
Entrata **Entrance**
Galleria **Tunnel**
Guasto **Out of order** (eg phone box)
Incrocio **Crossroads**
Limite di velocità **Speed limit**
Non toccare **Don't touch**
Passaggio a livello **Railway crossing**
Parcheggio **Parking**
Pedaggio **Toll road**
Pericolo **Danger**
Pronto Soccorso **First aid**
Rallentare **Slow down**
Rimozione forzata **Parked cars will be towed away**
Semaforo **Traffic lights**
Senso unico **One way street**
Sentiero **Footpath**
Solo uscita **No entry**
Strada interrotta **Road blocked**
Strada chiusa **Road closed**
Strada senza uscita/Vicolo cieco **Dead end**
Tangenziale **Ring road/bypass**
Traffico di transito **Through traffic**
Uscita **Exit**
Uscita (autocarri) **Exit for lorries**
Vietato il sorpasso **No overtaking**
Vietato il transito **No thoroughfare**

At the Airport

I'd like to book a flight to Venice *Vorrei prenotare un volo per Venezia*
When is the next flight to...? *Quando parte il prossimo aereo per...?*
Are there any seats available? *Ci sono ancora posti liberi?*
Have you got any hand luggage? *Ha bagagli a mano?*
My suitcase has got lost *La mia valigia è andata persa*
My suitcase has been damaged *La mia valigia è rovinata*
The flight has been delayed *Il volo è rimandato*
The flight has been cancelled *Il volo è stato cancellato*

At the Station

Can you help me please? *Mi può aiutare, per favore?*
Where can I buy tickets? *Dov'è posso fare i biglietti?*
What time does the train leave? *A che ora arriva/parte il treno?*

⊘ Numbers

0 *zero*	**18** *diciotto*
1 *uno*	**19** *diciannove*
2 *due*	**20** *venti*
3 *tre*	**30** *trenta*
4 *quattro*	**40** *quaranta*
5 *cinque*	**50** *cinquanta*
6 *sei*	**60** *sessanta*
7 *sette*	**70** *settanta*
8 *otto*	**80** *ottanta*
9 *nove*	**90** *novanta*
10 *dieci*	**100** *cento*
11 *undici*	**200** *duecento*
12 *dodici*	**500** *cinquecento*
13 *tredici*	**1,000** *mille*
14 *quattordici*	**2,000** *duemila*
15 *quindici*	**5,000** *cinquemila*
16 *sedici*	**50,000** *cinquantamila*
17 *diciassette*	**1 million** *un milione*

What time does the train arrive/depart? *A che ora il treno?*
Can I book a seat? *Posso prenotare un posto?*
Is this seat free/taken? *É libero/occupato questo posto?*
You'll have to pay a supplement *Deve pagare un supplemento*
Do I have to change? *Devo cambiare?*
Where does it stop? *Dove si ferma?*
Which platform does the train leave from? *Da quale binario parte il treno?*
The train leaves from platform one *Il treno parte dal binario uno*
How long will it take to get there? *Quanto tempo ci vuole per arrivare?*
Will we arrive on time? *Arriveremo puntuali?*
Next stop please *La prossima fermata per favore*
Is this the right stop? *É la fermata giusta?*
The train is late *Il treno è in ritardo*
Can you tell me where to get off? *Mi può dire dove devo scendere?*

Directions

right/left *a destra/a sinistra*
first left/second right *la prima a sinistra/la seconda a destra*
Turn to the right/left *Gira a destra/sinistra*
Go straight on *Va sempre diritto*
Go straight on until the traffic lights *Va sempre diritto fino al semaforo*
Is it far away/nearby? *É lontano/vicino?*
It's five minutes' walk *Cinque minuti a piedi*
It's 10 minutes by car *Dieci minuti con la macchina*
opposite/next to *di fronte/accanto a*
up/down *su/giú*
traffic lights *il semaforo*
junction *l'incrocio, il bivio*
building *il palazzo*
Where is...? *Dov'è...?*
Where are...? *Dove sono...?*
Where is the nearest bank/petrol station/bus stop/hotel/garage? *Dov'è la banca/il benzinaio/la fermata di autobus/l'albergo/l'officina più vicino/a?*
How do I get there? *Come si può andare? (or: Come faccio per arrivare a...?)*
Can you show me where I am on the map? *Può indicarmi sulla cartina dove mi trovo?*

On the Road

Where can I rent a car? *Dove posso noleggiare una macchina?*
Is comprehensive insurance included? *É completamente assicurata?*
Is it insured for another driver? *É assicurata per un altro guidatore?*
By what time must I return it? *A che ora devo consegnarla?*
underground car park *il garage sotterraneo*
driving licence *la patente (di guida)*
petrol *la benzina*
petrol station/garage *la stazione di servizio*
oil *l'olio*
Fill it up please *Faccia il pieno, per favore*
lead free/unleaded/diesel *senza piombo/benzina verde/diesel*
My car won't start *La mia macchina non s'accende*
My car has broken down *La mia macchina è guasta*
How long will it take to repair? *Quanto tempo ci vorrà per la riparazione?*
The engine is overheating *Il motore si surriscalda*
There's something wrong (with/in the)...
C'è un difetto (nel/nella/nei/nelle)...
accelerator *l'acceleratore*
brakes *i freni*
engine *il motore*
exhaust *lo scarico/scappamento*
fanbelt *la cinghia del ventilatore*
gearbox *la scatola del cambio*
headlights *le luci*
radiator *il radiatore*
spark plugs *le candele*
tyre(s) *la gomma (le gomme)*
windscreen *il parabrezza*

Tourist Signs

Most regions in Italy have handy signs indicating the key tourist sights in any given area:
Abbazia (Badia) **Abbey**
Basilica **Church**
Belvedere **Viewpoint**
Biblioteca **Library**
Castello **Castle**
Centro storico **Old town/historic centre**
Chiesa **Church**
Duomo/Cattedrale **Cathedral**
Fiume **River**
Giardino **Garden**
Lago **Lake**

◑ Coffee Italian-Style

Espresso: small, black and strong
Cappuccino: with hot, frothy milk
Caffè lungo: espresso watered down
Caffè macchiato: espresso with a drop of milk
Caffè corretto: espresso with a shot of alcohol
Caffè latte: half milk half coffee in large cup or glass

Mercato **Market**
Monastero **Monastery**
Monumenti **Monuments**
Museo **Museum**
Parco **Park**
Pinacoteca **Art gallery**
Ponte **Bridge**
Ruderi **Ruins**
Scavi **Excavations/archaeological site**
Spiaggia **Beach**
Tempio **Temple**
Torre **Tower**
Ufficio turistico **Tourist office**

HEALTH

Is there a chemist nearby? *C'è una farmacia qui vicino?*
Which chemist is open at night? *Quale farmacia fa il turno di notte?*
I don't feel well *Non mi sento bene*
I feel ill *Sto male/Mi sento male*
Where does it hurt? *Dove Le fa male?*
It hurts here *Ho dolore qui*
I suffer from... *Soffro di...*
I have a headache *Ho mal di testa*
I have a sore throat *Ho mal di gola*
I have a stomach ache *Ho mal di pancia*
Have you got something for air sickness? *Ha/Avete qualcosa contro il mal d'aria?*
Have you got something for sea sickness? *Ha/Avete qualcosa contro il mal di mare?*
antiseptic cream *la crema antisettica*
sunburn *scottatura da sole*
sunburn cream *la crema antisolare*
sticking plaster *il cerotto*
tissues *i fazzoletti di carta*
toothpaste *il dentifricio*
upset stomach pills *le pillole per mal di stomaco*
insect repellent *l'insettifugo*
mosquitoes *le zanzare*
wasps *le vespe*

GENERAL READING

The Advocate: A Sardinian Mystery by Marcello Fois. A lyrical and sometimes haunting noir novel based in Nuoro.

Bandit at the Billiard Table by Alan Ross. The late, former editor of *The London Magazine* describes his journey around Sardinia in the 1950s.The 1954 account of a summer journey is now also available as an e-book.

Death in Sardinia by Marco Vichi. Contemporary Italian crime fiction, the popular Inspector Bordelli series.

Reeds in the Wind (*Canne al Vento*) by Grazia Deledda. Originally published in 1913, the Nobel laureate's most famous work describes the decline of a noble family.

A Sardinian Cookbook by Giovanni Pilu and Roberta Muir. A passionately written introduction to the cuisine of Sardinia, full of tasty recipes.

The Sardinian Cookbook: The Cooking and Culture of a Mediterranean Island by Viktorija Todorovska. A broad spectrum of authentic regional recipes, beautifully presented with full-colour photos.

Sardinian Chronicles by Bernard Lortat-Jacob (translated by Teresa L. Fagan). Rural Sardinia is brought to life through its music, dance and family portraits. The book includes black-and-white photographs and a CD of Sardinian music.

Sea and Sardinia by D.H. Lawrence. Lawrence recalls his journey to Sardinia in 1921. His observations cover the island in all its dimensions, including the people, politics and landscape.

Sweet Myrtle and Bitter Honey: The Mediterranean Flavors of Sardinia by Efisio Farris. Sardinia's famous chef takes readers on a culinary tour. Includes recipes.

OTHER INSIGHT GUIDES

Insight Guides cover nearly 200 destinations, providing information on culture and all the top sights, as well as superb photography and detailed maps. Other Insight Guides to destinations in the region include Italy, Italian Lakes, Tuscany and Sicily.

Italian destinations in Insight's detailed and colourful **City Guides** series include Rome, Florence and Siena, and Venice.

The itinerary-based **Insight Explore Guides**, written by local hosts, come complete with a pull-out map. Titles include Naples and the Amalfi Coast, the Italian Lakes, Sicily, Venice, Florence and Rome.

⊘ Send Us Your Thoughts

We do our best to ensure the information in our books is as accurate and up-to-date as possible. The books are updated on a regular basis using local contacts, who painstakingly add, amend and correct as required. However, some details (such as telephone numbers and opening times) are liable to change, and we are ultimately reliant on our readers to put us in the picture.

We welcome your feedback, especially your experience of using the book "on the road". Maybe you came across a great bar or new attraction we missed.

We will acknowledge all contributions, and we'll offer an Insight Guide to the best letters received.

Please write to us at:
Insight Guides
PO Box 7910
London SE1 1WE
Or email us at:
hello@insightguides.com

CREDITS

PHOTO CREDITS

COVER CREDITS

INSIGHT GUIDE CREDITS

Distribution
UK, Ireland and Europe
Apa Publications (UK) Ltd;
sales@insightguides.com
United States and Canada
Ingram Publisher Services;
ips@ingramcontent.com
Australia and New Zealand
Woodslane; info@woodslane.com.au
Southeast Asia
Apa Publications (SN) Pte;
singaporeoffice@insightguides.com
Worldwide
Apa Publications (UK) Ltd;
sales@insightguides.com
Special Sales, Content Licensing and CoPublishing
Insight Guides can be purchased in bulk quantities at discounted prices. We can create special editions, personalised jackets and corporate imprints tailored to your needs.
sales@insightguides.com
www.insightguides.biz

Printed in China by CTPS

First Edition 1991
Sixth Edition 2018

Every effort has been made to provide accurate information in this publication, but changes are inevitable. The publisher cannot be responsible for any resulting loss, inconvenience or injury. We would appreciate it if readers would call our attention to any errors or outdated information. We also welcome your suggestions; please contact us at:
hello@insightguides.com

www.insightguides.com

Editor: Carine Tracanelli
Author: Nick Bruno, Magdalena Helsztyńska-Stadnik
Head of DTP and Pre-Press: Rebeka Davies
Update Production: Apa Digital
Picture Editor: Tom Smyth
Cartography: original cartography Berndtson & Berndtson, updated by Carte

CONTRIBUTORS

This new edition of Insight Guides Sardinia was commissioned by **Carine Tracanelli** and updated by **Magdalena Helsztyńska-Stadnik**.
   It builds on a previous edition updated by **Nick Bruno**, an experienced travel writer with a special fondness for all things Italian; Nick has written and contributed to numerous guidebooks on Italy, and Sardinia in particular.

ABOUT INSIGHT GUIDES

Insight Guides have more than 45 years' experience of publishing high-quality, visual travel guides. We produce 400 full-colour titles, in both print and digital form, covering more than 200 destinations across the globe, in a variety of formats to meet your different needs.
   Insight Guides are written by local authors, whose expertise is evident in the extensive historical and cultural background features. Each destination is carefully researched by regional experts to ensure our guides provide the very latest information. All the reviews in **Insight Guides** are independent; we strive to maintain an impartial view. Our reviews are carefully selected to guide you to the best places to eat, go out and shop, so you can be confident that when we say a place is special, we really mean it.

Legend

City maps

- Freeway/Highway/Motorway
- Divided Highway
- Main Roads
- Minor Roads
- Pedestrian Roads
- Steps
- Footpath
- Railway
- Funicular Railway
- Cable Car
- Tunnel
- City Wall
- Important Building
- Built Up Area
- Other Land
- Transport Hub
- Park
- Pedestrian Area
- Bus Station
- Tourist Information
- Main Post Office
- Cathedral/Church
- Mosque
- Synagogue
- Statue/Monument
- Beach
- Airport

Regional maps

- Freeway/Highway/Motorway (with junction)
- Freeway/Highway/Motorway (under construction)
- Divided Highway
- Main Road
- Secondary Road
- Minor Road
- Track
- Footpath
- International Boundary
- State/Province Boundary
- National Park/Reserve
- Marine Park
- Ferry Route
- Marshland/Swamp
- Glacier
- Salt Lake
- Airport/Airfield
- Ancient Site
- Border Control
- Cable Car
- Castle/Castle Ruins
- Cave
- Chateau/Stately Home
- Church/Church Ruins
- Crater
- Lighthouse
- Mountain Peak
- Place of Interest
- Viewpoint

INDEX

MAIN REFERENCES ARE IN BOLD TYPE

INSIGHT GUIDES

OFF THE SHELF

Since 1970, INSIGHT GUIDES has provided a unique perspective on the world's best travel destinations by using specially commissioned photography and illuminating text written by local authors.

Whether you're planning a city break, a walking tour or the journey of a lifetime, our superb range of guidebooks and phrasebooks will inspire you to discover more about your chosen destination.

INSIGHT GUIDES

offer a unique combination of stunning photos, absorbing narrative and detailed maps, providing all the inspiration and information you need.

PHRASEBOOKS & DICTIONARIES

help users to feel at home, when away. Pocket-sized with a free app to download, they go where you do.

CITY GUIDES

pack hundreds of great photos into a smaller format with detailed practical information, so you can navigate the world's top cities with confidence.

EXPLORE GUIDES

feature easy-to-follow walks and itineraries in the world's most exciting destinations, with our choice of the best places to eat and drink along the way.

POCKET GUIDES

combine concise information on where to go and what to do in a handy compact format, ideal on the ground. Includes a full-colour, fold-out map.

EXPERIENCE GUIDES

feature offbeat perspectives and secret gems for experienced travellers, with a collection of over 100 ideas for a memorable stay in a city.

www.insightguides.com

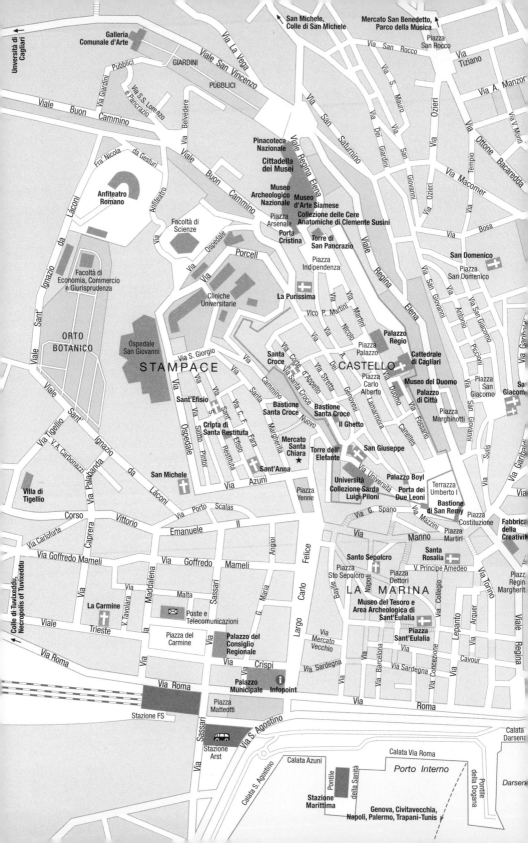